Warm Hearts, White Hopes

Warm Hearts, White Hopes

Dr. John Dubbey

Published by John Dubbey, P/Bag 0061, Gaborone, Botswana

First Published 1994

Printed by Penrose Book Printers (Pty) Ltd, Pretoria West

ISBN 99912-0-138-6

Contents

About the Author

John Dubbey was Vice-Chancellor of the University of Malawi from 1987 to 1991. Before this, he held various positions at Universities in London. Currently, he is Principal of Botswana Polytechnic.

He is the author of *Development of Modern Mathematics*, (Butterworth, 1970) and *The Mathematical Work of Charles Babbage*, (Cambridge University Press, 1978).

Acknowledgements

I wish to acknowledge with grateful thanks, the many people who have helped to make this book a possibility. Among these I would mention Jack Mapanje, whose story overlapped with mine, and whose encouragement to write has been an inspiration. I am honoured by the most generous foreword he has provided.

I would also thank Ann Price of Heinemann Boleswa, who not only made great efforts to ensure the publication, but constantly encouraged a doubtful author, editing and proof-reading the script. Brad Becker typeset the narrative and designed the splendid cover.

Veronica, my wife, was a constant source of ideas, reminder of past events and correcter of mistakes. Much to her alarm, she gets a chapter to herself, but she deserves it. My daughter, Claire was with me throughout the writing, and she did her best to keep my mind lively.

My thanks are due also to Joe Hopkins, Ken Ross, Sandy Chipangwi, David Kerr, Michael Maloney and Guy Walker who made helpful, critical comments on appropriate chapters. Any residual errors remain as my responsibility.

Lastly I would thank the people of Malawi to whom this book is dedicated. The privilege of spending four great years with these wonderful people is the ultimate inspiration for this volume.

Foreword

It is with pleasure that I offer these few words by way of foregrounding the precious moments which John Dubbey has masterfully captured on these pages. As John Dubbey was the last British Vice-Chancellor of an institution from which I graduated and where I subsequently taught for more than a decade, I thought I should exploit this invitation with one or two observations on how I saw the origins and progress of a University whose significance to national development and contribution to individual achievement was the subject of concern to many.

I consider myself qualified to provide this sketch because I went through the horrors of the despotism which, in part, caused the birth of *Warm Hearts, White Hopes*. I feel somewhat responsible for the indignity which John Dubbey and other friends and colleagues suffered at the hands of our bureaucrats. Above all, this is the time to comment on matters which are now, happily, undergoing fascinating reconstruction, after the chaos of more than three decades.

The miraculous survival of the University of Malawi in the thirty or so years of its existence under the draconian laws of Dr Hastings Banda's regime must be credited, by and large, to the courage and determination of two British Vice-Chancellors: Dr Ian Michael and Dr John Dubbey. When Ian Michael opened the gates of the University in 1965, with the declared intention of creating a radical educational institution that would boast academic excellence and national relevance, Malawi had just plunged itself in a political turmoil which has come to be known as *the cabinet crisis*. The Minister of Education, Hon. Henry Masauko Chipembere who, with Ian Michael, had skilfully laboured to turn a dream to reality, had resigned in support of the brilliant youthful ministers whom Dr Banda had expunged from his cabinet.

Ian Michael was effectively left alone. His vision of the University was naturally sidetracked by the political and other exigencies of the cabinet crisis. Soon barriers to the proper establishment of the University appeared in every direction. Those students, lecturers and professors who expressed their views on the country's political and other crises or who were sympathetic to various forms of free speech, even those who encouraged research relevant to Malawi's development, were systematically dismissed or deported.

The notorious Censorship Board was constituted to silence dissent. Radical lecturers were being encouraged into exile or denied promotion on flimsy pretexts. University courses were being severely curtailed by the repressive tentacles of government that Dr Banda and his hand-picked University Council had invented in order to create the culture of silence and fear by which the world was to identify Malawi. Even teaching materials like plays, novels, short stories and poetry collections had to be submitted to the Censorship Board for vetting before they were used in courses. The notion of "official clearance" was born. Nobody could do anything substantive without "official clearance". It began to be difficult even to attend those international academic conferences that were not being paid for by the University or the government.

Though Ian Michael stubbornly re-affirmed his original noble intention, at the time of his retirement, that admirable legacy of an institution that had been, to a large extent, resilient to government victimisation, had begun to crumble. By the mid-seventies, those lecturers who had persistently resisted exile were indiscriminately being crammed in Malawi's infamous Maximum Security Prisons that had been built to punish the "rebels". The two British Vice-Chancellors who followed Ian Michael, were ineffectual in defending the University's only birthright: academic freedom.

When John Dubbey came on the scene, the corruption that we normally associated with richer African universities was threatening to be endemic in the University of Malawi. With IMF's call for the nation's structural adjustment and insistence on the development of teacher education, the very seed of life in the University was running the risk of rotting in the soil. We all wondered whether John Dubbey had the guts to raise the University to the respectable academic status we had known.

But this is precisely what John Dubbey was determined to do. He began to restitute those University values we were forgetting. And he did this without the pomp and ceremony of his last two predecessors. In many respects, the publication of *Warm Hearts, White Hopes* demonstrates how he performed this feat. But John Dubbey had other advantages. He had never been to Africa before. Those attitudes to Africa and its people embedded in classical European anthropology that he might have been expected to bring, were difficult to detect in John Dubbey. He did not understand the weird politics of Malawi. He might even have been naive. But he loved the warmth of Malawi and its people. Often when he pleaded ignorance, for example, at meetings of University Senate or Academic Planning Committee, it was with the subtler objective of seeking to restore the University's academic conscience.

Take the University's Research and Publications Committee. John Dubbey revamped it. The committee members elected Dr David Munthali, perhaps the most dynamic Malawian entomologist and dedicated researcher available, as its full time research coordinator. The committee's small budget was inflated to encourage more staff research. In order to stop the transitory nature of the University's publications, exchange of journals and research programmes with other Universities was initiated. The University's conference vote was resurrected.

Clearly, some of the administrators with whom John Dubbey worked were outraged by the simplicity, perhaps even credulity, with which he seemed able to bring these changes. But John Dubbey was not in the least deterred by these. Indeed, slowly the isolation from which the University had been suffering began to give way. The role of the University as the leading institution in Malawi's social and intellectual development re-asserted itself.

John Dubbey was also a fervent Christian; and he did not apologise about the issue. He was humble; in certain cases, he might even have been too willing to learn from anybody. Above all, being a well known mathematician who had taught at London's South Bank Polytechnic, John Dubbey dealt with

University matters with the precision of that tradition. All these qualities paid immense dividends.

When he started looking at the Finance Office's records then, it was not with the sinister intention of wanting to catch corrupt administrators. Rather, it was with the objective of seriously looking for ways of cutting down unnecessary expenditure when IMF's structural adjustment directives were choking government departments. When the IMF measures to get the University to impose fees on all students was having its effect on the poor (usually more intelligent) students, John Dubbey was agitated. The implementation of these policies would adversely affect the University's academic excellence. He therefore sought tougher measures in order to streamline the budget. He was beginning to redress this situation when the first bombshell fell.

I was suddenly arrested and imprisoned without charge or explanation. John Dubbey was stunned. Then, Blaise Machila, a colleague from the Department of English, was also detained for seeking clarification about my detention from the police and the State House. Apparently, as in my case, some powerful Malawians in John Dubbey's administration directed the police to shut up Blaise Machila with imprisonment.

Much against the spirit of Malawi as "the warm heart of Africa", nobody warned, advised or informed John Dubbey about how he might proceed on this slippery political platform. He was settling into this isolation when another problem came. Students at Chancellor College, the biggest constituent college of the University, produced a students' newsletter which was obliquely critical of the administration of the Principal, Dr Zimani Kadzamira, (who is brother to Dr Banda's powerful first lady and nephew to the ubiquitous Mr John Tembo, the Chairman, almost for life, of the University Council!). The students who had contributed to the newsletter were sacked on instructions from Mr Tembo. Then what Dr Banda had publicly sworn he would never live to see happened. More than two hundred students at Chancellor College peacefully marched to John Dubbey's office in protest about the dismissals. Chanting songs of freedom, they marched past the Eastern Division Police Headquarters! The police merely watched the marchers.

Thus the revolution which was to have far reaching results

had started. It ended with the Principal's unceremonious transfer to Bunda College of Agriculture. The stage had been effectively set for the origin of that spate of open letters to Dr Banda, Mr Tembo and officials of the ruling Malawi Congress Party, which were to create the liberating tradition future generations will remember. These were crowned by the now famous Catholic Bishops Pastoral Letter of March 1992, which may have conclusively won Malawi the multiparty politics we are about to see.

By the time these open letters were transformed into the largely opposition's multiple weekly papers which we read in Malawi today, John Dubbey had already left the scene for the greener pastures of Botswana! He had left behind an admirable legacy of the nature of independence a Vice-Chancellor ought to have. For example, he had taken a tough stand over the detention of Blaise Machila. He had single-handedly decided that my wife and children would be allowed to stay for one year in the University house we had occupied, Malawi's detention tradition notwithstanding. My salary was to be paid to my family in that time. John Dubbey's colleagues in administration were obviously enraged by these arrangements. They had got used to throwing out lecturers' wives from University accommodation and with-holding their salaries from the second day or week of their husbands' detention!

It is these and other perceptions of the events that led to his effective resignation which make *Warm Hearts, White Hopes* an engaging read. Most students and academic staff were baffled by John Dubbey's unflinching firmness in his endeavour to re-establish the University of Malawi's credibility both nationally and internationally through the research and academic excellence which he insisted upon. Some still wonder how he escaped deportation. *Warm Hearts, White Hopes* offers the much needed answer.

There is another story absent in these pages. Perhaps John Dubbey is too humble to admit its relevance. When I was released from Mikuyu Prison in May 1991, the inmates I left behind continuously joked and asked about "that daft slim Englishman in golden glasses who dared to enter the prohibited walls of Mikuyu Prison in order to visit his member of staff, (Blaise Machila). How did he get the permit to come here, where not even priests are allowed?" There is a Malawian saying which goes: *It is the stranger who brings the sharper blade.* John Dubbey is one such stranger. But for me, *Warm Hearts, White Hopes* charts that singular struggle of a man to survive in an environment which should not have been academically or politically hostile. I see *Warm Hearts, White Hopes* almost like a religious experience and a celebration of John Dubbey's own warmth and unstinting generosity towards Malawi and its people.

Jack Mapanje
January 1994
University of Leeds, England

Chapter One
Warm Hearts, White Hopes

Malawi is the warm heart of Africa. This phrase, which began as the bright idea of a tourist promoter, has grown into a national slogan. And the reason why this change of status has endured is very simply that everyone believes it. By everyone, I mean the visitor to Malawi who without exception rhapsodises about the grandeur of the land, the variety of the colours and the almost legendary friendliness of the people; but also this includes the Malawians themselves. They believe it is their calling to be this warm heart, to display this most positive, amicable approach, often in the most difficult of conditions. Life may be hard, painful and all too often, short, but the display of warmth and goodwill is never forgotten. While we will be exploring below this surface and sometimes finding examples of less desirable characteristics, there can be no doubt that the surface itself remains sunny, attractive, even inspirational.

Many white people from David Livingstone onwards have travelled to Malawi, and for a variety of reasons. Sometimes to convert, to exploit, to farm, to colonise, to educate, to make money, to serve, to help, but always with hope. Whatever the intention, good or evil, whether or not the essential partners of faith and love are present, there is always the hope that something will be achieved, and this is what makes white people in places like Malawi different from white people back in their own countries. Certainly our own time in Malawi was a transforming experience. What we hoped for and what we achieved, is the subject of the book.

It is not my intention to restrict the idea of the white hope only to those of a particular coloration. The use of the term is taken to refer rather to youthfulness, vigour and idealism and at whatever age and whatever race. Our work was with the University of Malawi, and it is in this type of institution that one expects, and we certainly found, the enthusiasm, the commitment, the expectation of what we would describe as the young white hope. This is our story of warm hearts and white hopes.

We begin the narrative sometime in the middle of 1986, and at our residence in Sidcup, Kent, a suburb of London.

The phone rang very early. Veronica came running upstairs to wake me up. 'I think it's from Malawi. You'd better hurry,' and the voice from Malawi said: 'Hullo John, this is Robert Mbaya, the Registrar. Congratulations, you have been selected as the next Vice-Chancellor of the University of Malawi.'

This was the news I had been expecting since the interview two weeks previously. It has been my lot to appear before many interviewing panels, not always with success, but this one I knew intuitively was going to be different. Later on I learnt about the machinations and rows behind the scenes which had made it possible, but this time I had no doubt about the outcome. As I set foot in Africa for the first time, as I entered Malawi after a memorable half day in Harare, and took my seat in the University board-room for the one and a half hour interview, I sensed that no matter who the other candidates were, this is where I was meant to be.

After the interview in Zomba, the former colonial capital of the then Nyasaland, I was whisked off to Blantyre prior to returning home to England the next day, and it was in the bar of the hotel that I got talking to an elderly Malawian named Duncan McFarlane, the name he had adopted from the Scottish missionary who had brought him up. When I explained to him my business in

2

the country, he replied without any hesitation, 'I believe God has sent you here to be the next Vice-Chancellor.' I said this was my view too but if he could put in a word with the President for me it might help things along. Duncan, like most people, had no hot line to the Chancellor of the University, but meeting him in this way was an encouragement I never forgot. President Banda certainly did influence the choice of Vice-Chancellor, but this was not good for me to know at that time.

This all amounted to quite a change of life for me. I had never worked outside London before, and one very treasured possession we took to Malawi was a most elegant canteen of cutlery, my reward for years of loyal service to that wonderful employer, before it began to show signs of dementia and was put out of its misery by Mrs. Thatcher's government, the Inner London Education Authority. Not only was Africa new but also I had never worked full-time in a University before, so to come in at Vice-Chancellor level was somewhat unusual. To add to the overall unsuitability on these two important grounds, we had the additional handicap that we had lived in Sidcup for a solid twenty-four years.

The day we moved to Sidcup, immediately after our wedding, the London *Evening Standard* printed a feature about what young people thought about various places in the Capital. Those interviewed indicated that Richmond, for example, was elegant but square. Chelsea was trendy but square. Greenwich was historical but square. Sidcup, however, was just plain square.

Some years later, coming back from an Italian holiday, we spent a brief week-end in Switzerland, at L'Abri, the home of a group of evangelical Christian intellectuals, followers of the late Francis Schaeffer. Sitting round the lunch table with about twenty others, the host announced that we would each, in turn, introduce ourselves. When we said we came from Sidcup, the host whooped in delight and a ripple of excitement went round the table. 'My friends,' he said, 'here we are privileged to meet some people who actually live in Sidcup!' The cause of the unexpected excitement was that a few days previously, the group had made a study of Becket's 'Waiting for Godot' and had encountered one of the major characters, the tramp whose aim and whose catch-phrase was that he must get to Sidcup, where all presumably will be put right.

It would probably be correct to say that apart from a standard reader for French students learning English, which takes our suburban town as its model for all that is typical of unspectacular life in Britain, this is the only literary allusion to Sidcup which exists, although Trog in the *Daily Mail* once referred to his fictitious new work to be entitled 'Sidcup Revisited'.

We were always glad to address ourselves as Sidcup, Kent, to demonstrate that we were after all, county people, and Kent is of course, a most respectable county. However, it has to be admitted that this is a border town, and essentially no longer rural Kent, but in reality South-East London. This is, in a number of ways, one of the most neglected and down-trodden parts of London. Tube trains network the rest of the Capital, but stop at New Cross, the gateway to the South-East. There are few theatres or galleries of significance in this part of London. Even the epitome of South-East London style, the connoisseurs' team of the fifties and sixties, Charlton Athletic, has been moved from the beloved Valley to places like Selhurst Park and Upton Park, and after years of exile and much campaigning, justice has at last been done for the South-East with the return in 1992 to a shrunken but still recognisable Valley.

But talent abounds. This is the area which gave the world Bob Hope, Frankie Howerd, Kate Bush, Boy George, Marty Wilde, several of the Rolling Stones and Pretty Things, along with others too numerous to mention, so it can't be all bad. It would be pleasant in addition to name a few South-East London intellectuals if only one could think of any.

However, this is the world in which we spent our formative years, and we are ever grateful for our Sedcopian background. This is where we developed our marital relationship, where our Martin, Ruth, Rachel and Claire were born and grew up; this is where, with Veronica's enabling, I completed my two research degrees while commuting to work, first at Thames Polytechnic in Woolwich and then at South Bank Polytechnic in Southwark.

What was the cause of this transition from the safe tenured position, to the unknown, and possibly hazardous life of Central Africa? The move meant a change from a reliable salary to a contract position, from the predictables of Sidcup to the volatile uncertainties of the third world, from a life with few responsibili-

4

ties to a position requiring major initiative and direct accountability to a Head of State.

Several surface replies could be given. The children were now aged 23, 21, 19 and 9, so it meant that the older three had virtually left home, while Claire, the youngest could come with us, and nobody's education would be disrupted, a factor which would have deterred us in previous years. Secondly we had, like many others, a desire to do what we could to help those living in the third world, and eventually came to the view that to actually go and work there would be much more appropriate than just giving donations. Then there was the aspect, best described by an Australian of my age who came to Malawi to run its first Medical School, of making his 'last hurrah'. To try to do something really significant before the spectre of retirement loomed.

All these were true for us, but none gave the real reason, and this was consistent with what we had sought to do all our married lives and even before. That was to seek God's purpose for us, to operate within His perfect will, and that we found in what we believe was a real calling to serve in this way in Malawi. Having said this, we have arrived at the main purpose of this book. To demonstrate, through our experience, the amazing grace of God towards us, and to encourage others to take a similar risk of faith. We do not pretend there is anything particularly special about us. A few minutes acquaintance would soon dispel such an idea! But we did undergo a most remarkable experience which we believe is available to other unremarkable people like ourselves, and this is the motivation to write.

In this spirit I put in a speculative application for the Vice-Chancellorship, and was rather surprised when actually invited to come to Zomba for an interview in May 1986. My first reaction after the immediate surprise and pleasure, was to learn quickly about this unknown land and its University, and what might be the basic problems of education at this level. Through phoning around various agencies I was very fortunately put in touch with a man who had recently returned after seventeen years working as an education officer in Malawi. He told me about the beauty of the land and the amiability of the people, and something about the Government in relation to the University. He told me that the Life President, Dr. Banda, who had founded the University and remained as its Chancellor, had a preference for British Vice-Chancellors, and all three previous holders of the post were from Britain. However he was sure this policy was about to change to the extent that advertising in Britain was only an afterthought. I would enjoy my two days in the country but the real contest for the job was between two strong Malawian candidates. I thanked him for this information and later spent a much longer session with him but even at this stage I did not feel in any way dismayed by his prediction. In the event, neither of the two he had mentioned even applied for the position, and the Chancellor insisted once again that the post would remain British.

I also had a brief time to read educational literature that might be relevant, and immediately came across what I considered to be the fundamental problem, and it was surprising how quickly into the job I found myself grappling in an international context with this very issue. The question was that, given the very limited resources available for education in a developing country, how should it be shared between the three sectors, primary, secondary, and tertiary? On the one hand it is desirable on both social and economic grounds that primary education should be available to all, but several countries, and this included Malawi, simply could not afford this. What then was the justification for a necessarily expensive activity like higher education, when even basic education was not available to all the population? In particular, it could be shown that the cost of one place at the University was about 250 times that of a place in primary education. Would it not be better to close the University and use the savings to launch new schools at the rate of about one for each undergraduate student so displaced? Right from the start a basic part of my work was to justify the very existence of the University and, as I will show, this involved an immediate personal dispute with the World Bank, no less, and a continual need to explain to a number of audiences the value of the University.

My first acquaintance with the continent of Africa was a twelve hour stopover in Harare and this proved to be a very positive experience. I strolled round the city centre, the park, the Art Gallery and the Cathedral, and was struck by the peace and calm which seemed to prevail there after the recent war for independence. The Cathedral was holding a mid-day healing service, and people from all races were attending to receive ministry. As I sat there, a young man came over to me and asked for counsel. I asked him his problem and he told me that basically his troubles arose because he came from Malawi. At once my whole attention was aroused! I felt deep down that I was on the right track in making this journey, but always it is good to have confirmation. Was I about to receive an experience like Paul's man from Macedonia? Unfortunately not. His next words were not 'come over and help us' but something like 'I can't get a work permit and I'm broke'. The conversation did not turn out as it might have done, but at any rate I was able to meet and give help to my first Malawian.

The first impression on arriving in Malawi, at six in the evening, is how quickly it becomes dark. There is sunshine almost every day from six to six, but after that darkness quite literally descends, and that is the end of outdoor activity for the day. On the first night I was still able to gain impressions of the beautifully laid out road from the airport to the capital city of Lilongwe, the amazing cleanliness of the city, and the delight of staying at the Capital Hotel.

The next day I made the magical journey from Lilongwe to Zomba. Here for the first time I experienced the real heart of Africa, the villages, the markets, the ox-carts, the mountains, the greenery, the men, women and children. Whatever the outcome of the interview, I was never to forget these two days.

Back in England, I waited two weeks for the phone call, another two months for the contract, and it was certainly worth waiting for. I visited places like the British Council and the Overseas Development Administration (ODA) in order to learn more about Malawi. Not all of the officials I met seemed wholly delighted at the news I brought them. 'We have told the Malawians they should appoint one of their own people. This post is no longer supplemented', was one of the points put to me. I responded that Malawi as a sovereign country was entitled to choose anyone it liked to be Vice-Chancellor, and that in any case the lack of a British supplementation to my salary was not an issue I intended to lose any sleep over. This was my first indicator that overseas aid was by no means free of the patronising colonialism which believes it knows best what the aided country needs as opposed to what the country itself might wish.

In contrast, the Malawians made a most generous gesture in the contract they sent me. Realising that unlike the previous holders of this post, I would be denied the substantial British contribution to the salary, they actually worked out what this contribution would be, converted it to its value in kwachas, and made this their own supplement to me. With this act of consideration, I had absolutely no hesitation in writing an immediate letter of acceptance. True, there were currency devaluations, which over my term of office left the kwacha at half the value when I started, and the very high rate of income tax meant that my pay was considerably less than what I had been receiving in England, but I experienced that most happy state when the value and satisfaction in the work far outweighs the loss of remuneration. I found too that in contrast to experiences elsewhere, the Malawi Government was always scrupulously honest and humane in its financial dealings. Right from the start I had the conviction that here was a country and a people who were worth making every effort for.

The interview took place in May 1986, and it was agreed that I would start in the new year. This afforded a few months to wind up my exciting fourteen years at South Bank, and to prepare for the work in Malawi. I discovered a number of connections with British Institutions. The Agricultural College at Bunda had a long association with the Aberystwyth College of the University of Wales, and when I paid a visit there, at least twenty of the staff who I met at a dinner had spent some time at Bunda. Rather to my dismay, after an excellent and entertaining meal, the chairman announced that I would speak and answer questions. Making unexpected and unprepared speeches I soon discovered is an occupational hazard of a Vice-Chancellor, but with a little experience it is alarming how easy this can be, and what an expression of evasion, exaggeration and hypocrisy can follow. However, questions are a different matter, and on this occasion I had to take quite a barrage of complaints about how badly the University treated its College of Agriculture. I could only plead personal innocence, and promise to do something about these matters when I could.

Then I visited Huddersfield Polytechnic which has had a link mainly, but not entirely, with Engineering since 1970. These links, funded through the Higher Education Division of the British Council, have proved to be of great value to a developing

University and are much appreciated. A relationship between people is formed which is able to adapt over the years to the increasing maturity of the younger institution.

In November 1986, I paid a second visit to Malawi, this time to make an intensive preparatory week's exploration. The first task was to visit all the Colleges, and this gives the opportunity now to introduce each one. The University itself was founded by the President at Independence in 1964, Professor Ian Michael was appointed Vice-Chancellor, and the first students were admitted in 1965. The decision was made at the outset that the University would include all higher education in the country, a remarkably farsighted proposal. It meant that the University would be scattered over the country, but I gradually discovered that the advantages of this arrangement overcame the consequent practical inconvenience.

I have already referred to the Bunda College of Agriculture. This College existed a few years before Independence but was then upgraded to offer diplomas and then degrees of the University. The College is situated under Bunda Mountain and is about fifteen miles from the capital city of Lilongwe, approached for the last seven miles by an unmade road. This famous Bunda Road, the cause of so much debate and despair, had been forcefully introduced to me by the staff of Aberystwyth, and with its dust clouds in the dry season and clogging muddiness of the wet season, served as a basic challenge to the Vice-Chancellor's performance. What would he do about this road? That was the examination question which could not be avoided. I had to remind myself constantly that there were other issues at Bunda besides the Road.

The College had just over four hundred students, all in residence, mostly studying for diplomas with a more fortunate minority taking degree programmes. There was much space available, and the campus included a small lake and a farm of over two thousand acres.

Nearby in Lilongwe itself was the Kamuzu College of Nursing, the newest of the Colleges, having been founded by the President in 1979 to improve the standard of nursing in the country. This College had about one hundred and thirty students, working for both the University diploma and State Registered Nursing status. The Blantyre School of Nursing also joined the University in 1987, adding a further hundred students.

9

About 180 miles away was Zomba, the capital city in the colonial regime, but appointed the University city by the President when he moved the capital more into the centre of the country, in Lilongwe. Zomba is the University city in the sense that the University Office is situated there, as well as the largest of the sites, Chancellor College, with just over one thousand students. These undergraduates are spread over the five Faculties of Humanities, Science, Social Science, Law and Education, and within these faculties, over twenty different departments.

Zomba was renowned as the most beautiful capital of the Commonwealth, in its idyllic situation at the foot of Zomba Mountain. Little had changed in the physical appearance except for the enhancement of the resplendent new buildings of Chancellor College, culminating in the magnificent Great Hall, built by the President in 1982 as a national cultural centre and the largest indoor building in Malawi.

Then there is the Polytechnic at Blantyre, the largest city in Malawi. The Polytechnic houses the Faculties of Engineering, Commerce and Applied Science. It also includes some Technician and Secretarial courses so that the total student population is almost one thousand. The original decision that all Colleges should be considered an equal part of the University is justified in the sense that students will choose the subject they want to do without having to worry about the status of the College they select. As a consequence, the best students in the country are opting for Engineering and Business Studies, knowing that an award from the Polytechnic counts exactly the same as from any other College of the University. This is in contrast to other countries which tend to downgrade the Polytechnics, so that the better students and staff do not wish to go there. The system in Malawi, however, ensures that the country obtains the good quality Engineers and Business people which it needs.

There is almost, but not quite, a fifth College, the Institute of Education. This College is charged with providing curriculum development and in-service training for the Primary Education sector. It is jointly the responsibility of the Ministry of Education and the University, with the Vice-Chancellor as Vice-Chairman of the Council. I always felt very much at home in this College and did my best to bring it fully into the University. I argued that as the

University was responsible for all secondary teacher training at Chancellor College, it ought also to take a strong interest in the much larger primary sector. However, not all sensible arguments prove to be successful.

This completes an introduction to the four plus Colleges of the University. The immediate impression was of the distances between them, and the huge amount of travelling it would take to maintain a fairly regular presence at all of them, but my initial welcome at each place was beyond expectation. I felt slightly heroic about all this because on my first day I had succumbed to a nasty stomach upset, yet I still survived the travel from one College to another, and staggered through the many banquets provided, in order not to offend my very generous hosts. On the last two days I met my predecessor, Dr. David Kimble whose experience and knowledge of Africa was immense, and he gave me an extended briefing at the resplendent house which was to be our residence for the next four years. I also attended the University Congregation. This was held in the Great Hall with over two thousand present. Dr. Kimble gave his address which, by tradition, had to be 45 minutes at least, and he succeeded in keeping his audience rolling in the aisles throughout this time, while I wondered however one was supposed to follow such an act a year later. The most memorable thing for me was the way in which the parents in the gallery reacted to their sons and daughters receiving their awards. In a British University on a similar occasion there would be mostly polite applause with a little noise here and there, but in Malawi the delight of the parents was unstoppable. They shouted, sang, danced, gave little speeches, ululated, and in every way made this what it should be, a most joyful occasion for everyone.

On this note of joy, it would seem proper to finish this first chapter. I had plenty to tell the family about.

Chapter Two
Into Africa

After South Bank we had a good two weeks to celebrate Christmas while packing up the house, making our farewells to friends and relatives, and preparing what we could for the great unknown on December 29. Five of the family were going to make this first journey into Africa. In addition to Veronica, Claire and myself, Rachel came for her University vacation, and Ruth who had just finished working on a kibbutz after qualifying as a Physiotherapist, wanted her first job to be in a Malawian hospital. Martin and his wife Janet came to Heathrow with us and Richard Wells also helped to drive us there.

We proved to be extremely naive travellers. My recollection of the earlier part of the day was seeing yet another case filled to capacity, then rushing off to Sidcup High Street to buy one more, and then repeating the sequence all over again. When we came to the check-in, despite having five baggage allowances to aggregate, we were more than a hundred kilos overweight. At this point of near disaster as we began to do the simple calculation based on about £10 per kilo, we had our first blessing and very great encouragement to the journey. The lady who had weighed us in, simply said: 'Happy new year from Air Zambia!'

The first introduction to Africa for my family was a seven hour transit at Lusaka, before we arrived at Kamuzu International Airport, Lilongwe, about mid-day. At once we all felt assured that we had come to the right place. We were made most welcome in the lounge, Malawi Radio was there for an interview, and after no little form-filling we managed to find our freight sent the previous week and despatch it on its way.

Unlike many other international airports, Lilongwe goes out of its way to make a good first impression. The buildings are clean and shining, the grass is green and short, the grounds are carefully landscaped, and there is an air of calm efficiency. The journey by road to the capital city of Lilongwe is a delight, and on arrival one finds no metropolis but a place of woods, streams, parks, open spaces with the occasional splendidly designed modern building to indicate a place large enough to hide over 100,000 inhabitants.

I must have visited Lilongwe on average once a week during my time in Malawi, and the pleasure felt initially does not diminish. However, it does become more conditioned by the increasing realisation that the majority of these hundred thousand live in the most miserable conditions, that expatriates, mainly the diplomatic community do not enjoy living in this somewhat sanitised city and would much rather be in Zomba or even Blantyre. Further, Lilongwe was largely built through South African funding at the time of grand apartheid with the desperate need to find friends somewhere in Africa. But these were not our thoughts on first arrival, and together we spent a leisurely day at the Capital Hotel before the magnificent drive to Zomba.

On the way to Zomba we stopped only once and that was to greet a car travelling in the opposite direction. This was taking Stanley Nyirenda to the airport to fly to America in order to begin his PhD studies. I did not meet Stanley again for three years, until he came back to do field research on the fascinating subject of Implementation – a proper study of why the best laid schemes, especially in that part of the world, so maddeningly seem to 'gang aft aglay'. From my earlier encounter with him at the interview and longer conversations over his research, I often speculated on what a partnership we might have made had the opportunity been there.

Eventually we arrived in glorious Zomba, to our resplendent

but empty house. The freight had already arrived, a huge crate weighing nearly half a ton, but without, it seemed, any means of opening it. At this point we had our introduction to Emmanuel, officially the cook, and according to Dr. Kimble the best he had encountered in over thirty years in Africa, but in practice the Admirable Crichton of our family, the man capable of repairing anything, of improvising anything. Immediately he set to work, armed only with a small screwdriver to open our elaborately constructed container, work his way bodily inside it, and fish out the multitude of tea-chests and cardboard boxes crammed into it. Our daughters distributed the contents into suitable places around the many large rooms available, while Veronica and I set out to find some food.

There are two main places to buy food in Zomba; there are the two very respectable western style supermarkets and there is the traditional Zomba market. We made possibly the mistake of going for the latter, for while it is a real African experience and the best market in the country, it can for the uninitiated be something of a cultural shock. Our mistake was to invite our chauffeur, still in his uniform, to show us round. His striking presence accompanied by our own newness, quickly made us the unwanted centre of attention, and soon we were surrounded by tradesmen and beggars, real or otherwise, and we could hardly move. I never wanted to go again, but Veronica enjoyed every minute and was back the next day with Rachel, and bargaining on her own terms.

So we move on to our first supper in Malawi. I dwell on this otherwise mundane and not too generally interesting experience to indicate a radical change in our philosophy. We had never before had a household staff, and wondered what we would make of it. We are egalitarians by nature, and Veronica, Ruth and Rachel are all excellent cooks, so what were we doing sitting down to receive from Emmanuel? I have to confess that it took us no more than about thirty seconds to get used to this idea and to like it! We further rationalised that in submitting ourselves to this kind of service, we were providing sustenance for a family who in times of high unemployment would otherwise have very little to live on. We therefore feel no sense of shame at all that we employed a cook, a houselady, a chauffeur, two gardeners and a night guard, the latter four paid by the University. Provided that a fair wage is

14

being given, that staff are not being exploited, and that we form good relations with them and their families, we are blessed ourselves and in turn provide a livelihood for others.

Now work had to begin. As we saw the new year in, I meditated on the fact that I had now become the head of a whole University and in a country about which I was very ignorant. It seemed a daunting responsibility but I had any number of ideas and looked forward to putting these into practice. The actual start was extremely quiet. New Year's Day was a public holiday, and the next day being a Friday was in effect a vacation as well. We were able to concentrate on settling in, dealing with car insurance, school uniform for Claire, and meeting our neighbours. The following Monday I went to the University Office and put my feet under the table for the first time – except that the chair caved in when I attempted to do so and had to be removed for repair, and I started work in tropical heat with the aid of a fan in close proximity.

On Tuesday a man came into my office and said he wished to give K100,000 to the University. He was the General Manager of Mobil Oil, and his company wanted the money to be used as a trust fund to provide encouragement to students in Mechanical Engineering. This I thought must be what being a Vice-Chancellor is all about! To be able to just sit in the office, and gratefully receive donations from industrialists who clearly all recognise the value of the University and desire to help in any way they can. It did not take long to discover that this is not the reality, and despite many efforts to raise external funding which I regarded as a major personal priority, I did not have another such visit for at least three more years. The beginners' luck which I had experienced with the Mobil Oil visit, was in fact the culmination of years of patiently establishing a relationship with the company by the then Principal of the Polytechnic, the late Arthur Kambalamatore. It still was a most pleasant way to begin a new task.

My initial aim was to tour all the Colleges and talk to as many people as possible, but before this could be done there was an immediate job which needed attention. The University was due to receive its three yearly visit from the British ODA organisation to discuss progress over the last triennium, and explore the nature of further aid to be provided. It was British policy to support what they considered to be areas of national development, mainly by the provision of salary supplemented staff, until such a time when local staff could take full responsibility for these disciplines. The areas decided for support were Engineering, Accountancy, Management, Mathematics and Science Education, and altogether about thirty British staff were provided. I had been given a briefing in London just before coming out, and various concerns were expressed, most particularly with the Science Education scheme which in the opinion of the donors was going so badly that it might not receive further support.

It was therefore necessary for me to prepare thoroughly for this visit, with over half a million pounds of external funding at stake, to quickly grasp the major movements in the University, to gather together the propositions for discussion with the visiting party, and in particular to assemble the case for the continuation of the Science Education project. This involved the instant need to confer with each of the College Principals and as many of the ten Deans of Faculties as could be found.

It became possible to discern a movement in all parts of the University towards an increasing specialisation with a shift in thought if not yet in action towards degree and postgraduate rather than diploma work. When the University had opened in 1965, the great need was for an educated Civil Service to replace the colonial administration, and initially the emphasis was on general courses at diploma level since in this way graduates could be turned out more rapidly. Some of the better students had been given the chance to go on for degrees, but in the absence of policy directives, this state of affairs had drifted on to the detriment in my opinion of the potential value of the University. It is not my intention to support the idea of 'academic drift' for its own sake, but rather to observe that a diploma which only took students three years beyond 'O' level, did not fulfil individual potential and did not provide the professional preparation needed by the many sections of society which our programmes supported.

I discovered almost by accident a major answer to the problem of Science Education. In talking to the Dean of Education, we came across some figures which indicated that in the degree/diploma programme in Education at Chancellor College, which had a fairly steady intake of about a hundred students per year, up to 1986 the numbers opting for Science and Mathematics remained at twenty or

16

less, and then jumped to seventy for that year. How had such a transformation taken place? The answer was not strictly educational. Someone had the bright idea that if students taking this route were guaranteed, provided all years were passed, that they could do the five year degree rather than the three year diploma, there would be much greater demand, and the success of this theory was borne out by the figures. Whatever the motivation, the policy was a sound one. How could Science of Mathematics be effectively taught in Secondary Schools if the teacher's own education came to an abrupt end so soon, and with the low prestige and salary in an already underpaid profession of the diploma qualification, who would want to work at this level? Not only was this an excellent argument to put to the visiting party but it gave me a resolve to make Education an all degree qualification, and to look questioningly at all areas in which diplomas still dominated with a view to asking the fundamental question, 'what use is this diploma either to the student, or the profession he/she will work in'? As in many cases the norm was three years to a diploma followed by another two to a degree, with only the top third of the class being permitted to do the final years, this would not be easy, but I think that considerable progress was made during my term of office.

On the last day of my first month we learnt at a round up meeting that the ODA visit had been successful. They had come with the intention of reducing the total funding available, but instead decided to give a moderate increase, and in particular to continue their support of the Science Education project. Several contracts were not to be renewed but the posts were to remain, and this gave the opportunity to look for some new staff from Britain.

Another set of visitors at this time whose presence coincidentally helped in arguing the case with ODA were two representatives from the Free University of Amsterdam. This University has, through the Dutch aid organisation NUFFIC, supported Science Education in Southern Africa for many years and in 1986, the Ministry of Education had suggested they visit Malawi. The two literally arrived on the doorstep, for there had been no notification of their coming, and to make matters worse they were expecting that the University had already worked out a basic plan as to what they could do. Everything had to start from first principles. We hurriedly convened a meeting of all those who might be interested, and together formulated our plan. It would not be possible to offer a pre-entry Science course as they had been doing for many years in Botswana since we did not think an additional year would be an attractive proposition to students wanting to do Science. Rather we took it as a challenge to make up for any deficiencies they might have suffered at school through lack of equipment and poor teaching, and we did achieve some very good results especially in Mathematics.

It was not possible either to set up a programme for new Science teachers since our new policy to offer degrees to all had the implication that there would be a delay before any new ones came on the scene. Instead we felt the best intervention to be made would be with respect to the Mathematics and Science teachers already doing the job by providing intensive courses in the long vacation with visits to the schools by experts in the fields in term time. In the course of an eight year cycle, every teacher of Mathematics and Science would attend two of these six weeks updating courses. This was the start of numerous meetings to work out the proposal and put it in a form satisfying to the two Universities and the two Governments concerned. It was good to be able to inform ODA about this potential reinforcement to Science Education but it has to be admitted that the path to implementation was far from smooth, and the project, eventually well supported financially by the Dutch, did not actually commence until 1990.

I was able to complete my first round of visits to all the Colleges by the middle of January, and discover some of the other jobs which I had. I made my first visit to Kamuzu Academy, the public school founded by the President, and featured in a BBC documentary as the 'Eton of Africa'. There I had my first meeting with the Headmaster, Michael Maloney, who became a good friend despite our three hundred miles distance, and he informed me that the Vice-Chancellor was a member of the Board of Governors.

I revisited the Institute of Education in Domasi quite near Zomba, where under the compromise arrangement, the Principal Secretary for Education is the Chairman of Governors and the Vice-Chancellor is the Vice-Chairman. On this occasion, the Principal embarrassed me in front of his staff by asking which of them had particularly impressed on my previous visit. Fortunately

18

I remembered the occasion when Bobby Robson as England manager was visiting Mexico in preparation for the World Cup, and he was asked which of the Mexican team had most impressed him. His brilliant reply was that they had all moved so fast he could not read the numbers on their backs, so I was able to give a similar reply in Domasi. As earlier stated I always valued the many visits I made to the Institute, and tried without success to have it properly integrated into the University.

The other additional function, always carried out by the Vice-Chancellor, was the quite demanding position as Chairman of the Malawi National Examinations Board (MANEB). This Board became responsible for all public examinations in the country, and these included the Malawi Certificate of Education, equivalent by cross-reference to the Associated Examination Board of UK to 'O' level, the Junior Certificate of Education taken two years earlier, the Primary School Leaving Certificate, the Primary Teacher Training Certificate, and eventually the Kamuzu Academy entrance examination. The work done by the MANEB staff was most admirable in that despite numerous pleas to Government, the institution remained grossly understaffed as more and more work was pushed its way. Yet despite massive problems of organisation and security, it gained a reputation for accuracy of work, detection of malpractices, and completion of its tasks often ahead of schedule.

It would be useful at this stage to give a rapid survey of Education in Malawi, and the enormous problems not untypical of a country in this region, which it faces.

For a start, Primary Education is not yet universal and this is unlikely to happen for some decades. The total recurrent budget for Education, just over 10% of the national expenditure, is of the order of one hundred million kwachas, equivalent to about £25M of which about one third goes to Primary Education. The 15,000 teachers cannot be paid much out of this budget and school fees are necessary for all ages. Only just over half the age group receive any education at all, and as the size of this group is increasing by over 4% per annum, the Government plan to provide Primary Education for 85% by the end of the century looks unlikely to succeed. The million children who do receive at this level provide a student to teacher ratio of 70 to 1, and this is even worse at the initial stages of schooling where classes of over a hundred are the rule rather than the exception. The classrooms are bare, with little sign of furniture or books, and from an early stage, the children have to learn English as the medium of text-books and examinations. To provide proper learning conditions for all children in reasonably sized classes with adequately paid teachers would require at least ten times as much to be spent on Primary Education.

For those who survive the Primary School system, and no more than half those who started complete the eight standards, there is a place at a Secondary School for only about one in ten. There are just eighty Secondary Schools offering the four year course through Junior Certificate to Malawi Certificate to about thirty thousand pupils.How the more fortunate ones are selected, I was never able to find out, but with quite heavy fees and a notable absence of bursaries, it is extremely difficult for a child of the poor majority to progress further. There is in addition the Malawi College of Distance Education which provides correspondence courses to Junior and Malawi Certificate level at over a hundred centres around the country, and despite the difficulties of this type of learning up to 40,000 register for this alternative to secondary education as it has become, and an increasing few pass 'O' level very well.

From the 5% of the age cohort who receive Secondary Education, there are places at the University for about one in seven who pass the 'O' level, and we can therefore afford to be highly selective in recruitment and expect a high standard of work and commitment from those who have fought their way through this highly competitive system.

It is necessary to quote these melancholy facts to give perspective to the task of the University, and to indicate what still needs to be done. Education is rightly highly valued in countries like Malawi. There are virtually no discipline problems of the order to be found in western countries. A Malawian student given half a chance will take the fullest advantage, and the standards achieved are comparatively good but great help from the more fortunate countries is still needed in this sector.

At our Malawian home we settled very gladly into this new way of life and had no immediate desire to return to England. One of the greatest advantages to improving the quality of life was the absence of television. Having lived with the medium for so many unproductive years, we were most happy to make the supreme switch-off. It meant that in the long evenings, and it is always dark in Malawi at six, we had to do creative things, play games, read books, entertain friends, or even talk to each other! For this reason alone I would recommend a long holiday in Malawi for those who have suffered for years from television.

Our only problem at home in the first month concerned Ruth, and through this I learnt much about the unacceptable side of the operation of the country. We had written directly to the Ministry of Health while still in England, and to our delight they had responded immediately, offering Ruth a job as a Physiotherapist at the Zomba General Hospital. I suggested to her that she take a few days to settle and then report to the Hospital with her job offer. When she did this, she was told that before she could begin she must have Government clearance. This clearance procedure which should have been very simple turned out something of a nightmare. As the days passed and Ruth became naturally more frustrated, I would spend a considerable amount of my time phoning around quite senior civil servants, seeking, pleading, almost threatening that the clearance might come through quickly. After all Ruth was only intending to stay for six months at most. Eventually after six weeks, the request was granted, and Ruth was able to start work; only the patients she might have treated over these weeks were the sufferers. Friends informed me that six weeks was very good; twice as long is the norm, but this provided no comfort for an absurdity in the name of security which the country really must put right. There were many other examples of the obsession with security. For a member of University staff to go abroad for any reason, private or professional, it was necessary to ask for clearance from the Government preferably eight weeks in advance, and the same rule applied for visitors coming into the country. This was a cause of much annoyance as clearances would arrive very late, in some cases after the time of flight.

In April I was invited to attend a conference in Harare, Zimbabwe. This was my first journey outside Malawi, and I learned the hard way a number of home truths about travelling. First despite the Registrar's assurances that unlike other staff who required clearance letters to travel, I did not need one, I discovered that I did, and had an unmemorable discussion with immigration officials on this matter. Then, as pocket money since the conference was fully funded, I put a handful of kwacha notes in my wallet expecting to exchange them on the way. This proved to be quite impossible, and so I spent a whole week with in effect, no money at all. I paid a second visit to Harare Cathedral, and just like old times, was approached by a man who asked for money. This time I had the foolproof answer that I had no Zimbabwean currency, but he responded by saying that Malawian money would suit him just as well! Given donor funding, it is perfectly possible as I discovered to live abroad on nothing, that is until the last day when it was pointed out that I needed ten Zimbabwe dollars as airport fee to leave the country.

We were very well serviced at this conference by students of the University who the organisers had drafted in. I explained my predicament to one of them, and she said she would consult an organiser about what could be done. When I next saw her she said that sadly, the organisers could not see a way out, but she added, please have ten dollars of my own money to help you get home! I think I gave her some kwachas in the hope they might be useful.

The conference itself was in two parts. It was first a meeting of AESAU, the Association of Eastern and Southern African Universities, in effect a gathering of Vice Chancellors from this part of the world, and like Aesau himself, it was an hairy experience. Also in Harare was the executive committee of the International Association of Universities, and the two groups were scheduled to have a joint session. The link between the two was Walter Kamba, Vice-Chancellor of the University of Zimbabwe, and at that time both Chairman of AESAU and one of the Vice-Presidents of the IAU.

The AESAU meeting, apart from providing the opportunity to meet colleagues from neighbouring countries, was a wash-out. It seemed clear to me that despite the potential of such an organisation which had gone to the length of publishing a book about itself, there was no real drive to make the organisation work. Professor Kamba started by announcing his resignation from the chair. We elected the Vice-Chancellor of Zambia in his place, but unfortunately there was a re-organisation of higher education in that country only a month or so later, the University was split in two, new Vice-Chancellors were appointed, and our man was out of his post and therefore no longer eligible to lead AESAU. Despite the efforts of some of us to organise another election, this has not happened, and to the best of my knowledge, AESAU has never met since this time in 1987.

The joint meeting with IAU was something else. The subject for discussion was a 1986 paper from the World Bank, 'Financing Education in Developing Countries' and the author, George Psacharopoulos was at the conference to present his thesis. The document had already been the subject of much academic criticism and was due in any case for a rough response from the delegates. What was less expected was that when President Robert Mugabe came to open the conference, he proceeded to spend most of his forty-five minute address in a vociferous attack on the World Bank document.

After this surprising opening by the Head of State, George Psacharopoulos spoke to his paper. I had several of my own criticisms of the document but felt that in the company of so many senior academics from all over the world, it would be better to learn from what they had to say. That was until near the end of the speech when he turned to the subject of cost recovery and the importance of student loan schemes. Then he added by way of illustration that the Bank was insisting on such a scheme for the University of Malawi.

I sat there amazed. This was the first I had heard of any such proposal. The whole concept of student loans seemed so unwanted and inappropriate for Malawi, and to learn of it in this fashion demanded a response. I asked the chairman if I could speak the next day, then phoned the University to learn that it was all true. A Government delegation without including or consulting anyone form the University had made a package of agreements with World Bank in Washington including this one. Later I spoke personally to Mr. Psacharopoulos to ask him why Malawi had been singled out for this treatment when only two years previously the country had submitted to a World Bank demand to impose a student contribution of two hundred kwachas per annum. His reply was that Malawi had been selected the second time because of its helpfulness over the first. In other words if a small country can be bullied once it can be bullied again. One also learns that the people who make this type of decision are seldom the ones who have to stand before the students and tell them.

I went straight back to the hotel room and worked into the night preparing my paper for the next day. The main issue of the World Bank paper which had so angered the President of Zimbabwe and most of the academics present was that in attempting a rate of return analysis of benefits from education, it was alleged that the return from Primary Education was greater than that from Secondary Education which in turn was greater than that from Tertiary Education. Therefore a developing country should invest mainly in Primary Education and if it wanted the luxury of Universities, then it should ensure that the students who gained such great personal benefits should not be subsidised but should make a substantial contribution themselves. This was an attack on the whole basis of University Education, and all the more dangerous coming from such a powerful source. It was necessary not only to expose the fallacies in the World Bank reasoning, but also to defend the very purpose of a University in a developing country. By taking Malawi as a case study I thought that I could refute the basis of the World Bank document, and this I proceeded to do the next day.

The speech I gave went down extremely well, drew much applause from this distinguished audience, and many requests for copies were made. The journal, *Higher Education Policy*, issued for the first time by the IAU, published the speech almost verbatim. When I next attended an international conference, in Berlin, December 1987, it was remarked that my contribution had been influential in changing World Bank policy towards Higher Education as indicated in their next, more moderate document. I quote some extracts from the speech:

'As the new Vice-Chancellor of the University of Malawi, I was intrigued to learn last night that the University is to receive this loan treatment, or so it will read in the papers in a few days time.I understand that the decision was made about a month ago in Washington between, as you had suspected, officials of the World Bank and officials of the Government of Malawi, who included no members of the University. When the experts of the World Bank, before my time, discussed the question with the University, they met with a total rejection of the loans concept from the students, from the Senate, and from the Council of the University. And so I take this opportunity to say what I might have said if I had had the chance to speak to the World Bank, to give a brief case study of a nation like Malawi, and of the way in which these proposals might affect it.

'Basically, we reject the concept of loans and the proposals outlined in the document because they will certainly cause great damage to students and University morale.They will grossly favour the wealthier students.And, what is more, they are totally irrelevant to the educational need of Malawi.

'Let me first introduce the University of Malawi. The University has two thousand students and the annual expenditure is now running at 12 million kwacha, a unit cost of 6,000 kwacha per student. The kwacha, after recent devaluations, exchanges at roughly 2.6 to the US dollar, so that the unit cost, which I do not pretend is not high, and I will explain why it is in a moment, is of the order of US$2,300. For convenience I will now express all money sums in terms of US dollars.

'The University has for a number of years given students a personal annual allowance of 144 kwacha, or US$55, and we are under much pressure from students to increase this amount, which has ignored inflation for a considerable time.University education in Malawi used to be free, but under great pressure from the World Bank we imposed an annual charge of US$77 from 1985, so in effect we are now giving students a negative allowance of US$22. This imposition of a fee of US$77 has caused considerable hardship for at least a quarter of our student population, and the University has had to set up a hardship fund with contributions from companies and embassies to meet this need.

'I would make the point then that Malawi is by no means lavish with its allowances. Both the fee charged and the allowance given, are negligible, of the order of three per cent of the actual unit cost. Further we can state with confidence that the Malawian student is paid modestly, but works hard, seldom repeats a year and has a very low wastage rate. Why is it then that unit costs for the University seem to be high, and hence the rate of return from tertiary education appears to be low?

'There are fundamental reasons why one should expect unit costs to be high in a university like Malawi. The University, like many others in Africa, was founded quite recently and therefore remains necessarily small. Any institution whether large or small, requires a comparable basic structure and from this it follows that the unit costs of a small University are going to be greater than those of a larger one. Further, the single national university has to provide for a wide range of subject areas since there are no alternative institutions, and consequently incurs the additional costs of having a large number of small departments.

'It is also necessary for the University to be near to 100% residential. Our students are selected on merit and they come from all parts of the country. We have to provide residential accommodation at the University itself, and that again pushes up the unit cost.

'The real answer, I believe, lies in expansion. We have already at the University the staff, the supporting staff, the infrastructure to take on a much larger student population than we have. What we basically lack is the capital in order to provide sufficient residential accommodation for the extra students we could accept. If the World Bank would support us more in this way, then the unit cost could be much reduced, and therefore the rate of return much increased.

'I understand that the figure which the World Bank had in mind to support the unwanted loan scheme was of the order of one million dollars.If instead this same amount were devoted to providing capital and revenue support, we could increase the student population by about four hundred. This increase would then reduce the unit cost from 6,000 to 5,000 kwachas, raise the rate of return, and make agencies like the World Bank think we were not so inefficient as they first thought.

'I would like to end this financially based argument briefly by turning from costs to values, and attempting to justify the existence and continuation of the University of Malawi as an entity. I would justify it on the grounds that the University is the only provider of high level manpower in all aspects of the national economy for the nation; that the University is the main co-ordinator of research across the board in the country; that the University is the centre for the development of the arts, literature and music, in the nation of Malawi; and most important of all on my agenda, the University is there to provide confidence to the nation, confidence that the people of Malawi can provide as good engineers, poets, philosophers, teachers, sociologists as their counterparts anywhere in the world.'

There was one other way in which I might have helped my new country that week in Harare. We were entertained exceptionally well, and one of the major highlights was the privilege of being present at the official opening of the superb new Harare Stadium. There were speeches by the President, an athletics meeting and traditional dances. But what I was waiting for was the football match between Zimbabwe 'B' and Zambia. Zimbabwe could not field their first team as they had to play Mozambique the next day in an Africa Cup match. The previous week, Zambia had beaten Malawi 3-1 in the first leg of the same competition and were due to play the second match in Blantyre, the next Sunday.

Now the Zambian squad was there to play against Zimbabwe's second team, and in this carnival atmosphere we looked forward to open football and plenty of goals. In the event we had one of the dullest matches imaginable, ending in a 0-0 draw with most spectators having gone home by half-time. I put this down to the defensive play of Zambia who even used a sweeper on an occasion of this nature. The only possible justification could be that they were rehearsing for the return with Malawi, with the intention of preventing the home side from scoring. It also occurred to me that I was probably the only person from Malawi at the match, so I reported what I had seen to the Malawi national team whose manager was Reuben Malola, seconded from the University.

Whether my advice was taken seriously or not I cannot tell, but it was still a great pleasure to watch Malawi win 2-0 the next week and qualify for the final rounds having scored an away goal. Due to losing a match on a penalty shoot-out, Malawi came third in the competition, but in the course of these final rounds they did beat both Egypt and Cameroon, who a couple of years later were prominent in the World Cup.

When I returned to Zomba I had a message asking me to contact the Registrar most urgently. It was indeed an urgent occasion. The President had dissolved Parliament and called for a new General Election. It was his requirement that as English is the official language of Parliament, no one can stand for election who has not passed a test of proficiency in English. Where I came into the picture is that traditionally, the Vice-Chancellor is Chief Examiner for this test. I was told further that this examination would take place in just five days time. However while I had been away, the English department had drafted a test for me to look over that evening. Through working solidly over the Easter week-end, we managed to design, administer and despatch the test all over the country. There were no complaints from any source, so we assume that the University had done its job satisfactorily. This was a most pleasing outcome to a novel, rushed and quite unexpected task, but apart from this the important thing for me was that the week-end's work had brought me into close contact with the Head of the English department, Dr. Jack Mapanje. And that is a story for another chapter.

Chapter Three
Malawi

A few days before flying out to Malawi, I was invited to attend a seminar at South Bank. This was related to the course run at the Polytechnic for Overseas Hospital Administrators, and it was the routine for each student in turn to make a presentation about their own country and its health service. This time I was invited because it was the turn of the only Malawian on the course, a hospital administrator named Archangel.

He began by drawing a map of Africa and then circling in a small area. 'This' he said, 'is Malawi, the warm heart of Africa'. In the short silence which followed to take in this interesting information, a participant from a different part of the world muttered, 'from the location, it looks more like the right kidney'.

Not many people are in fact able to locate Malawi with much accuracy. Whether it should be described as East, Southern or Central Africa caused much confusion among our correspondents, since all these descriptions are partially correct without any hitting the mark exactly. To demonstrate that it does lie in this part of the world, I witnessed in 1989 Malawi taking part in and winning convincingly what was described as the Eastern and Southern African

Football Competition. This was against countries as far afield as Kenya, Ethiopia and Zimbabwe.

In fact Malawi is a landlocked country with a population of about nine million, swollen by nearly a million refugees fleeing from the conflict in Mozambique. It is long and thin and about one third of the area is occupied by the glorious Lake Malawi, the third largest lake in Africa, and the thirteenth largest in the world. The country is bordered by Mozambique to the south and east, Zambia to the west, and Tanzania to the immediate north.

David Livingstone reached the lake in 1859. His efforts in Africa inspired the setting up of the Livingstonia mission on the west side of the lake, and after two costly attempts at Cape Maclear and Bandawe in which many young missionaries and their families lost their lives through malaria, it was finally established in the north of the country by another Scottish missionary doctor, Robert Laws. The town named Livingstonia as founded by Laws in 1875 is a remarkable memorial to this great man of vision who remained there until 1925. At three thousand feet above sea level, the town is approached by a road cut out of the hillside which has twenty-two hairpin bends, and at the top there remain the church, hospital, secondary and primary schools and technical college which he built. He established water, postal and electricity supplies, the latter of which is alleged to be superior to the present day facility. Under the fifty year influence of Dr. Laws, Livingstonia became a powerful centre for evangelistic and educational outreach, and its effects were felt throughout Central and Southern Africa. The standard of education in this part of Malawi was considered to be much higher than elsewhere, and it was even suggested in the days before Independence that when the new University of Malawi would be instituted, it should be located at Livingstonia.

Other missions and trade centres were being set up, and there are quite a few books written by these earlier explorers such as Edward Young's account of bringing the first steamboat on to the lake, and the remarkable story of L. Monteith Fotheringham's battle against the Arab slave traders who infested the area at this time. Against this potent threat, Britain established a protectorate in 1891 which was named Nyasaland in 1907.

It would appear that the country was greatly blessed by the

quality of the early missionaries many of whom are still revered, and through whose example the land accepted the Gospel so readily. In the early twentieth century, however, the planters who followed were better known for their cruelty and exploitation. An uprising against the landowners in 1915 led by the Rev. John Chilembwe, was put down harshly, and the darkness which prevailed for the next fifty years is accompanied by a total lack of literature about this period. The country became neglected and backward.

In 1953, the country was joined by the British with Northern and Southern Rhodesia to form the Federation of Rhodesias and Nyasaland.This act aroused great opposition in Nyasaland where the Federation was perceived as a parallel to South Africa which had formally adopted the policy of apartheid in 1948. It was feared that the white settlers would control the copperbelt of Northern Rhodesia and the abundant farmland of Southern Rhodesia, leaving Nyasaland simply to provide the cheap labour. The Nyasaland Congress Party was established to organise opposition to the concept of Federation.

The movement for independence in Africa in the 1950s was particularly strong in London where many of the future leaders were living. Among these were Kwame Nkrumah, the first leader of an independent African state when Ghana achieved this status in 1957 and Dr. Hastings Kamuzu Banda from Nyasaland. Dr. Banda was naturally drawn into his own countrymen's movement.

According to his biographer, Philip Short, Banda was born in February 1898. The official record as given in Who's Who for this event is 1906. As the President's age is maintained as a state secret, and as Short's book is banned in Malawi, then it is probable that his carefully researched conclusion is the correct one. Banda was educated by Scottish missionaries, and in search of more learning left home in 1917, and did not return to his country for another forty years. His travels took him first to South Africa, then to the U.S.A. where he began to study Medicine, and then to Scotland where he completed his medical studies at Edinburgh University. He then moved to England to practice medicine, and he had surgeries in Liverpool and Newcastle before settling in Harlesden, West London.

It was while in the London practice that his political activities began. He helped to finance movements in Africa, especially in

Nyasaland, housed visitors from his country and worked for the independence from foreign rule of the African countries. He vehemently opposed the idea of the Federation but continued his resistance from abroad. In 1953 he joined his friend Kwame Nkrumah in Ghana where he stayed until 1958. It was then that his countrymen recognised him as their potential leader in the struggle against Federation, and on July 6 he returned after his long exile.

Immediately he took over the leadership of the Party, and travelled around the country speaking to large crowds against Federation and for Independence. The support he received made the country increasingly difficult to govern, and as a desperate measure, he was arrested on 3 March 1959 and sent to prison in Gweru, Southern Rhodesia. On the same day a number of Malawians were killed during a demonstration in Nkhata Bay in the north of the country, and this day is annually commemorated most solemnly as Martyrs' Day.

Banda's imprisonment did not pacify the people of Nyasaland, and the breakdown of normal order became worse. Then fortuitously there was a change of attitude in Britain. Harold MacMillan made his 'Wind of Change' speech, the Federation policy was reviewed, and the decision conveyed by Iain McLeod, then Commonwealth Secretary, to release Banda from prison after just over a year.

Elections were organised which five parties contested, and Banda as leader of the Party that won almost all the seats became Prime-Minister, and leader of the delegation to London for talks about Independence and the dismantling of the unsuccessful Federation. He had thus followed the path of many African leaders at this time. The typical leader was first vilified as a rebel, a trouble-maker, even a terrorist, and thrown into prison, then after a convenient lapse of time, recognised as a leader, a visionary and a peacemaker, released, and made Head of State.

Banda's two main aims very soon materialised. The Federation was duly destroyed and forgotten, and for which the new states of first Zambia and then Zimbabwe were most thankful, and Malawi achieved its Independence on appropriately 6 July, 1964. Dr. Banda became unopposed, the first President of the Republic of Malawi.

The new country was founded on and nurtured by this one

man's policies from which there has been virtually no deviation. While in Gweru Prison, he formulated three basic infrastructural ideas. These were that the capital should be moved from Zomba to Lilongwe, more in the centre of the country, that there should be a University of Malawi, and that there should be a coastal road along the western side of the Lake.

The new capital proved to be an expensive ambition, all the more as Malawi was over 90% dependent on British Aid at the time of Independence, and any further funding from this source was refused. In Banda's own words, he turned to the devil for help, and in the 60s and 70s, South Africa, increasingly being isolated from the rest of the world, built the new city of Lilongwe. A consequence was that Malawi became for many years the only African country with diplomatic links to South Africa, and in so doing cut itself off from good relations with neighbouring countries, and disqualified itself from receiving aid from many donors, especially the generous Scandinavian countries.

The University was immediately established at Independence, Ian Michael was recruited as the Vice-Chancellor, and students admitted in October 1965. Initially the University was housed at a vacant school site in Blantyre, but the President wished the old colonial capital, Zomba to be the new University town, and the very fine setting for Chancellor College was selected and opened with some handsome but unfortunately flat roofed buildings in 1974. Meanwhile, Bunda College of Agriculture just outside Lilongwe had been designated part of the university, as had the Polytechnic in Blantyre. The College of Nursing was added in 1979, and the School of Medicine in 1991. However, the President and Chancellor had asserted that Zomba was the University town, and even in 1991 it was still hard to convince that many people that most of the University was actually outside Zomba.

The coastal road was a laudable idea, but thirty years after Gweru it is still not finished. Instead the main road which before Independence only joined Blantyre to Zomba, now bisects the country from Nsanje in the south to Karonga in the north, a distance of about eight hundred kilometres, but without touching the Lake.

The keystone of Banda's economic policy was Agriculture. The first essential of an independent, developing nation was the ability to feed itself, and if possible to have something in addition for export.He took on the portfolio of Agriculture and has retained this Ministry every since. His aim has been to encourage the people to work the land, to grow maize in particular as the staple diet, and attain this food independence from which the other human dignities of clothing and housing will follow. Every year he travels the country at the height of the rainy season on his crop inspection tours to give support to his ideas at first hand. The policy is successful in that while tobacco, tea and coffee are grown on huge estates as the major exports and foreign currency earners, the population which has almost quadrupled since Independence, is virtually self-sufficient in staple foods with sometimes the excess to export to the neighbouring countries. Also the population unlike in other developing countries has not spilled over into the cities, and according to World Bank figures, 88% still live in the villages, the seventh highest of any country in the world.

The great emphasis on Agriculture while achieving some impressive results as indicated, is dangerously dependent on the weather which as we discovered in a relatively short time, is just as unpredictable as that in England. If sufficiently heavy rain falls consistently at the right time, then all is well, since the basic farming techniques constantly repeated by the President are there to capitalise on the good conditions. If the rainfall is less than a certain minimum, or does not come early enough, as in the present drought affecting most of Southern Africa, then the country can be in serious trouble. The problem is aggravated by reluctance to seek help from the Minister of Agriculture lest this be interpreted as criticism of the President which is often taken as a criminal offence. It is one of the tragedies of Malawi that people can be starving, and the country has one of the worst records in the world for malnutrition and infant mortality, without the President being informed.

The President's foreign policies, a few of which are hinted at here, are covered more in Chapter Six. The other main thrust of his leadership is the insistence on what he describes as the four cornerstones of the party and the nation, those of Unity, Loyalty, Obedience, Discipline.

The policy on Unity is successful in that there are on the surface at any rate, no inter-tribal conflicts, with the continuous exhortation to the people to consider themselves as one nation.

34

This is quite an achievement since Malawi like other African countries had no say in determining its own boundaries. These were mostly decided at the 1875 Berlin Conference, the culmination of the so-called 'scramble for Africa' among the European nations. These boundaries were determined with little thought for the wishes of those concerned, and in particular, lines were drawn through tribal territories, so that most African countries received an arbitrary collection of tribes and languages. In many cases it is long standing ethnic rivalries which have made unity and development exceptionally difficult for many of the new African nations.

It is to the credit of the President that these have not marred the progress of Malawi. This is not necessarily to applaud the means by which this has been achieved, but simply to assert that it has been done, and this is a great asset which the country must struggle to hold on to. There is, however one manifestation of non-unity which to an outsider was most difficult to understand, and that in Malawi is the phenomenon of Regionalism.

The country was divided by the British for administrative purposes into three Regions, the North, Centre and South. Only 10% of the people come from the North, the rest being shared between the other two Regions. I emphasise the expression 'come from' because in Malawi, your home is not where you happen to live now, but rather where you, or better your ancestors, have come from. You and your parents may have lived in Blantyre for many years, and you might even have been born there, but if your great grandfather and his forebears lived in a village in the North, that is where you 'come from'. When for example, secondary school and University places are awarded on a District quota basis, it is your District of Origin, and not your place of residence which determines who you have to compete with.

We always enjoyed our visits to the North, and only the distance of nearly five hundred miles prevented us from going there more frequently. The Viphya Forest, the Nyika Plateau, and our friends at the Ekwendeni Mission and Hospital were great attractions. There was also Livingstonia to visit, the former Bandawe Mission, and our favourite beach on the Lake at Chinteche. Far from being the 'dead north' as described in the Colonial days, we always found this Region to be a most stimulating place of enterprise and activity.

The educational influence of Livingstonia was one but by no means the only reason why those from the North seemed to do better in examinations (we discovered that despite the low share of the population, northerners had secured over 35% of awards from the University) and generally to be better represented in the business and professional world than those from elsewhere. The quota system for educational advancement seemed to be deliberately devised to equalise the advance of the northern people. The system for the University whose manifest unfairness I constantly tried to point out, meant that although pupils from the North if considered solely on merit, would take up to 40% of the places available, they received less than 20% on the quota basis.

This was one example of the inter-Regional rivalry we witnessed. It was not a matter of tribalism, for the Ngoni who were related to the Zulus, and were considered to be a dominant tribe in the North, also dwelt in Ntcheu in the Centre Region. This was one aspect of Malawi I failed to comprehend. I could understand rivalries on a tribal basis, but not those based on a Colonial subdivision of the country. I have dwelt more on the North in this section because this seemed to be the one Region which suffered the most from Regionalism. The South and Centre appeared to get on well together, but the North seemed to arouse hostility from both. With this one not insubstantial exception, the Unity that Dr. Banda exhorted was intact.

The inter-related qualities of Obedience and Discipline were taken as an essential component of the system. The President explained to us at our first audience with him that he did insist on these qualities at all levels of human development. Children must honour and obey their teachers, the authority of leaders in the church and community must be acknowledged, the Party and the Government must be honoured, and above all, the President must be revered. In particular, as he often stressed, this latter requirement of submission to the President applied to the Civil Service, the Army and the Police.

This policy had some very good effects. The discipline practised from childhood led to a most hard-working population, and the Malawian work-ethic, already quite strong prior to Independence, became renowned in this part of the world. The philosophy continually driven home in the President's speeches, of hard work in the fields, did mean that agricultural production was much better than it might otherwise have been, and the rapidly expanding population was almost able to feed itself and produce substantial export crops. The University did undoubtedly benefit from the political importance of hard work, and most students made exceptional efforts to do well to the extent that very few dropped out of studies, and only a few repeated a year, (only one repeat as a maximum was allowed for this relative failure). The pass rate each year was in my time always greater than 95%. The students themselves had low regard for those who did not work, and little sympathy for their few colleagues who failed their exams and were thus excluded from any further association with the University. On one occasion the Chairman and senior officials of the Students' union made an appointment to see me on an urgent issue. Their complaint it appeared was that I had actually accepted an appeal made by one or two failing students who pleaded particular extenuating circumstances which I found acceptable.

Up to a point this national discipline was impressive but in many respects it stifled initiative and development. The Agricultural policy of achievement by sheer hard work tended to ignore modern methods and put too great a burden on the soil. Despite the growth in population, the annual production from this subsistence sector remained virtually static while the rate of growth of the tobacco and tea estates was always vibrant. The expansion of population put increasing strain on the quantity of land which could be shared, and the majority of families reduced to less than half a hectare, could not grow enough food to last the whole of the year.

The hard work done by students was good for passing examinations, and particularly helped a University which was largely vocational in character, but the incentive to original, creative work was lacking, and in any case positively discouraged by the authorities. It was often necessary to tell students preparing for examinations that studying late into the night was not the most fruitful way to go about the task.

The logical consequence of the concept of Loyalty was that there could be no conceivable opposition to the rule of the Malawi Congress Party, and to the President in particular. The country after Independence and the first elections quickly became a one-party or rather a one-man State. Under the guise of loyalty, Banda allowed no-one to disagree with him on any issue and in a series of so-called 'Cabinet Crises' soon after Independence, managed to dismiss virtually all of those most able people who had borne the brunt of the Independence movement from within the country and formed his first Cabinets. A few years later he had himself designated as 'Life President'. He retained the four portfolios of External Affairs, Agriculture, Works and Supplies, and Justice, and never appointed a Vice-President or a Prime Minister.

During the election campaign of 1987 in which I have described my part elsewhere, I attended the major Party rally in the Kamuzu Stadium, Blantyre. The President used his speech to present his views on democracy and to justify the one-party State. The reason very simply, he said, was that while other parties did contest the first election in 1960, they were just no good. The people did not want them and they gained hardly any seats. So there was no need for any party except the Malawi Congress Party, and that is how it has remained.

Further, after candidates who could not pass the Proficiency in English test had been eliminated, each constituency was free to choose from a list of candidates whose loyalty to the party and the President was unquestionable. 'And if that is not democracy,' concluded the President, 'then I don't know what is'.

It might have helped underline the President's point if results of this democratic election had been published, showing the huge numbers of the population who had voted and how their choices had been made. Unfortunately, this was not forthcoming. There was just a radio announcement to tell us that vast crowds had thronged the polling booths, and a picture in the *Daily News* to show us one or two of the electors, but no real information to indicate the success or otherwise of the campaign.

While it is true that the other parties made a poor showing in the first election, and rapidly disappeared from the scene, any move to introduce a new party since that time, has been put down with great harshness. It is illegal even to distribute leaflets, and in one solemnly worded edict I found in the official Gazette, there is a total ban on the wearing of 'Subversive T-shirts'.

The consequence of the application of these four cornerstones of Unity, Loyalty, Obedience and Discipline have been that on the more positive side there does exist a unified nation which is administered in a reasonably efficient manner. The crime rate is low, international debts are paid back regularly, the annual budget is almost balanced, and despite the handicaps of the lack of mineral resources and transportation problems caused by the closure of routes to the sea due to the endless civil strife in Mozambique there is a healthy economic growth rate. The people are well dressed in the cities, the litter is removed, the grass is kept short, and one can even enjoy an international football match without feeling threatened.

The President does enjoy enormous popularity. This is largely due to the most effective propaganda machine of the one-party State, boosted by the lack of opposition, and which succeeds in persuading most visitors to the country to make their usually unsolicited contribution to the adulation. But it is also due to his personal style of leadership, in which he concentrates on his own country with little attempt to enter the international arena, the downfall of many other African leaders. His crop inspection visits at the height of the rainy season, even if heavily stage-managed by the Party, are greatly appreciated by the villagers who probably see much more of their President than would be the case in most other countries. It is significant that when he appears at a public function, he is surrounded not by armed bodyguards but by dancing women. He is a great showman. He knows how to handle a crowd, how to make the right gesture, how to make the appropriate remark, all with faultless timing. His speeches are not great, but he knows how to throw in the one-liner which will be remembered, and using the technique of repetition, he usually manages to communicate the point he wants to get across.

It is accepted also that a ruler has to be single-minded, beyond contradiction and quite ruthless in carrying out his purposes. His decision is always accepted as the final word. I have talked to a number of people who have been demoted, dismissed or even imprisoned at the direct wish of the President, and many retained their personal loyalty to him, even when outside the country.

It is regrettable but apparent that there are circumstances, particularly when rapid national development is needed, in which a dictatorship is more effective than a democracy. Britain, for example, had many centuries of one-party dictatorial rule before enjoying the blessings of democracy. It could be argued that Banda's type of leadership is just what a country like Malawi needed to begin its new life of Independence and under him the country has obtained a good measure of internal stability which has been internationally recognised. Malawi has been seen as a bastion of stability in a volatile part of the world, and has often received international support on the grounds that aid is more likely to be effectively used in these conditions. The country has also benefitted from the President's most firm anti-communist stance at a time when neighbouring countries embracing all or part of this creed have experienced initial prosperity turning to economic disaster. Now that communism is no longer fashionable, the attention of donors is drawn more to countries going through the withdrawal symptoms from this malaise. In addition, countries like South Africa and Israel which the President befriended when they were almost alone in the world, are now looking for other and more prosperous friends elsewhere. The emphasis of the donor community is now to look on Malawi simply for its own merits, and to see instead of the old reliability, the ever present backwardness and poor record of human rights. It is clear that the new picture is not an attractive one.

My own critique of Dr. Banda would be to assess him not by modern standards of democratic procedures, not always successful elsewhere and not necessarily relevant to the immediate needs of Malawi, but rather by what he has attempted to do using, as far as I am able to discern, his own idiosyncratic approach to independence and development. By these standards much has been achieved, and I have tried to demonstrate some of the major ways in which the country that at the time of Independence in 1964 through undoubted colonial neglect and exploitation possessed only two secondary schools, about sixty kilometres of tarred roads and a population of just over two million which it was unable to feed effectively, has been able to make significant advances.

Certainly as the President has often repeated in his speeches, the country is now unrecognisable from what it was then. At the same time I would assert that despite all the advantages of dictatorship without opposition, a hard-working and intelligent population, and the goodwill of the world donor community to provide whatever was lacking in the fulfilment of ambitions for development, the potential has not been achieved.

This can be seen by taking a cursory glance at basic aspects of the nation, looking in particular at Education, Health, Industry, Agriculture and Government.

As Education has been much of the theme of this book, it will only be necessary to underline certain observations made elsewhere. The fact remains that a large proportion of the population, (almost 50%) receive no education at all, the rate of illiteracy is high, and Primary Schools have large classes, (sometimes over a hundred), with poor pay and conditions for teachers and few books or furniture. The opportunities for Secondary Education are few and at a rate of 4% of the age cohort, Malawi according to World Bank figures, is one of the lowest in the world at this level, together with Tanzania and Rwanda. The University has struggled through its own efforts to grow over the last four years from two to three thousand students, which in a population of nine million places Malawi far back in comparison with the Government-led opportunities being provided at tertiary level by countries not much wealthier. The Gweru vision of a University has not been actively pursued after the initial impetus. Whenever the President speaks about Education, he usually refers only to Kamuzu Academy, and I have offered my critique of this Institution elsewhere.

The Health record of the country is poor. Malawi has one of the worst records of infant mortality anywhere in the world. The official tragic figure of 167 per 1000 live births is considered to be an underestimate of the real state of affairs. The malnutrition rate among children under five is correspondingly very high.

These figures reflect a country in which Health Services are not given a sufficiently high priority, where over-population abounds and poverty in both rural and urban settings is widespread. One reason for initiating a Medical School at the University was the extraordinary lack of doctors in the country. There were just over one hundred for the whole country, of whom the majority were expatriates on short term contracts and just thirty were Malawians, with quite a number of these employed as administrators at the Ministry of Health. Many young Malawians have been sent abroad for medical training, but few have returned, most likely because of poor remuneration and the adverse political climate. We had to argue with donors that the best intervention to help the ailing system of Health was at the level of Medical

Practitioner as is discussed more fully elsewhere, but everywhere else, in provision of nurses, paramedicals, medical assistants, technicians, equipment, beds, hospitals, there were gross shortages. While there were many valiant struggles by those in the health profession to offer a service of some quality against the appalling lack of resources available, some of the best work was provided by the Mission Hospitals supported directly by missionary societies abroad.

The great reliance placed on the Agricultural sector had the effect of limiting the diversification of the economy and the building of a strong industrial component. There were a few service and manufacturing companies to be located in Blantyre and Lilongwe, mostly of an agro-industrial type but investment from within, and particularly from abroad was lacking, and this has remained a small part of the economy, under-resourced and discouraged by unfavourable taxation policies. The only extractive industry is coal, but the mines are located in the far north, away from the major roads, the railway system not having developed much since Independence. It is normally asserted that Malawi suffers through lack of mineral resources. It does not have the advantage of copper like Zambia, or of diamonds like Botswana. However, I did hear some most reliable reports that significant quantities of gems such as emeralds, and deposits of rare earths had been located. As yet, neither of these has been exploited for the benefit of the nation.

The questions about Agriculture have been raised earlier. Much good has been achieved but there is equally much more to be done. The vast supply of water has been little utilised for irrigation purposes, and potential growth industries like Food Processing and Fisheries have barely begun. Widespread subsistence farming by traditional methods continues and is unable to provide the food requirements of an expanding population. The Estates are successful and growing, but the reliance placed on tobacco as the main crop and leading export is worrying when world demand for this questionable product may be seriously diminished through health legislation. Neither in the University nor in the Agricultural Research Stations is Biotechnology being much used, and to keep pace with developments elsewhere in the world, it may be necessary to take this approach rather than wait, for example, for a new synthetic and safer tobacco to emerge elsewhere, superior to the natural product.

The major failure is undoubtedly with respect to Government. As indicated earlier the first able group of politicians were dismissed for failing to agree with the President, and all subsequent Cabinet Ministers, Members of Parliament and Party Leaders have been more noted for their unflinching loyalty to the President than for their political or intellectual ability. Those who have unexpectedly demonstrated such latter qualities have not remained in office for long. In practise, the President makes all the decisions, large and small, and the function of his Government is to implement these. In this impossible situation in which initiative is continually stifled, and the agendas for both Party and Parliament become increasingly trivialised, the vacuum of decision making is filled in two ways.

On the one hand there is the Civil Service with the Government Departments located in Lilongwe, and the burden of decision is unnaturally placed on those whose work should be that of implementation. Further, the task is a hazardous one, for any proposal has to be endorsed ultimately by the President, and there are penalties for those who would venture to take independent action, or offer advice unacceptable to him. Consequently the incentive to decide, or to take any action at all, is not strong, and so vital decisions which urgently need to be made for the benefit of the country can be very easily deferred. One person particularly disadvantaged by this vacuum is the holder of the post known as Secretary to the President and Cabinet. He has to perform this dual function of serving the President normally in Blantyre, and running the Civil Service in Lilongwe, spending much of his working time being driven between these cities, two hundred miles apart. In the absence of anyone else to perform this function, the role of Prime Minister is virtually included as an unwritten part of the job assignment. It was most fortunate for the country that this impossible task during my four years of residence, was performed by two superb SPCs, Sam Kakhobwe and later, Justin Malewezi. I found both to be most able, dedicated and humane men, ready even in the midst of their huge responsibilities to let me talk to them about the University and to give me valuable advice. Regrettably the many jobs included in the position of SPC does not include that of Lord High Executioner. That privilege is reserved for someone else, and since the work carried immense responsibility but little power, both these admirable gentlemen were dismissed at the height of their achievements. Both in turn I would suspect had done something to displease the second set of vacuum fillers who I can now introduce in an appropriate context as 'The Family'.

During the President's transitional period in Ghana, after leaving Britain and returning to his own country, he was joined at some stage as his personal nurse by Cecilia Tamanda Kadzamira from Malawi. On return in 1958, she remained with him and has done so ever since. She has been given the function of 'Official Hostess' and the title of 'Mama' so that when she came to University functions I would introduce her as 'The Official Hostess, Mama C. Tamanda Kadzamira'. Legend has it that at one stage the popular song 'Cecilia' was actually banned in Malawi. Now she prefers to be just plain 'C'.

We had many contacts with Mama, and on every occasion she was pleasant and charming, an excellent conversationalist, most concerned about how we were settling in Malawi, and always remembering to send a Christmas present to our daughter Claire. She is all you would expect a Hostess to be. I am well aware that other much less flattering things have been said about this lady, but our direct experience of her, always cautioned by her probably sinister role in the country, was most positive.

Her association with the President, who appears to have very few relatives of his own in Malawi and who I will state in fairness have never taken advantage of their closeness to him, and neither has he given them preferment, has helped to draw her own family nearer to the centre of things. Her brothers and sisters all have key positions in the country, but most significant of all, her uncle, John Tembo, became involved in the Government from the time of Independence.

I have later reserved a whole chapter to John Tembo, but sufficient for the moment to say that he is the only survivor from the first Cabinet, and that since the early days, his influence in the country has become quite dominant. He is in effect the President's right hand man, often making decisions on his own, but his thinking and reacting has become so aligned to that of Dr. Banda that it is hard to tell the difference. He is undoubtedly a talented, decisive and exceptionally hard-working man, and with almost all others who could be described in this way being either exiled, imprisoned or returned harmlessly to their villages, it is a matter of common speculation as the President becomes older, the extent to which Tembo, or even Mama, is actually running the country now. From this follows the second order speculation that in the previously unthinkable event of Banda stepping down, whether it will be uncle or niece who seizes the throne. The President did actually make reference to this delicate question at the Annual Party Convention of 1987 when he stated that the Party would decide his successor as the time arose according to the laid down Laws of Malawi. He added in this context that Mama herself had no political ambition at this level. As in fact a reading of the Laws of Malawi will indicate, the process of appointing a new President is far from straightforward, and there is the real danger that the procedure could become dangerous through its indeterminacy.

While the President retains a good measure of popularity amounting to a sense of awe, the same is not true of the Family who are universally disliked. It is only by clinging to the President that the Family has any credibility, and it would seem quite impossible for them to lead the country once his umbrella is removed.

The existing set up which has carried Malawi for better or worse through the first nearly thirty years of Independence, is clearly on its way out. The movements for a new democracy have begun and no amount of repression will stop the flow. At the time of writing, the Catholic Bishops have risked their lives to proclaim the need for reform; Chafukwa Chihana has nobly returned to place himself at the mercy of the authorities so that even if his life becomes forfeit, others will receive the benefit of democratic rule; the students at the University, the workers on the Estates, and the people on the streets of Blantyre have made it clear that they want change and expect it to happen soon. The President is still revered and this factor will slow the process of immediate change. But clearly the people want a freely chosen regime, the release of all those who have been unjustly interned for untried 'political' crimes, and the return of the many talented exiles who have had to flee the country. They want democracy; they do not want the Family. Many have already died for this cause, and those who remain will not be dismayed, but will persevere until a real change is made.

It would clearly be in the best interests of everyone for the

Family to recognise from the way events are happening throughout the world, the inevitability of a new Malawi which cannot have a place for them, and to withdraw quickly from the scene. Otherwise they face the prospect of having to answer for the many serious allegations that have been made against them. This would be one positive gesture to compensate in some way for what they have done to Malawi.

Whether or not this is heeded, the change will come but it needs to come quickly because the increasing ungovernability of the country means that many will suffer, many will starve unless rapid action is taken, and wise leadership restored. In this sense the donor community has a great responsibility as the only external body able to make some impact on the regime. It is a further criticism of the present regime that the country is still so dependent on help from abroad. In this sense, real Independence has not been achieved, and worse still, a mentality of donor dependence has been generated. The donors should now make it clear that aid except for carefully defined humanitarian purposes so that it does not reach the wrong hands, will cease immediately until human rights are restored and multi-party democracy is initiated. This would certainly cause suffering to the Malawian people which any donor would be most loathe to allow, but all the indications are that the people are willing to undergo this, if it will lead to the desired end.

When the new regime comes, it will have enormous problems to solve as a legacy of what has happened before, and some of these have been indicated. At the same time the first regime has done many good things which can be built upon. The unity of the country is a great achievement and all must co-operate to ensure that this will continue. The emphasis on Agriculture as a basic priority must be not only retained, but with modern farming methods applied, the fertility of the soil and the use of irrigation techniques will enable a much richer harvest to be reaped. With international co-operation, and encouragement even of the multi-nationals, the potential for profitable new industries can be developed. The very able graduates from the Engineering and Business Faculties can, given the chance, make a major contribution to the growth of a new commercial base.

The great emphasis placed on the need for discipline and hard work resulting in the Malawian work ethic is a great asset to the country. Many Malawians are rightly shocked by the laxity of standards in the western world. The President has striven to see that such harmful practises are not imitated in his country, and any future leaders, consistent with the cultural norms of Malawian society, would be well advised to ensure that Dr. Banda's stance on these issues is firmly maintained.

The new Malawi will need much help before it can become truly Independent, and is able to battle on its own against the forces of poverty, ignorance and disease. To achieve this with the present lack of natural resources and any number of handicaps to economic growth, the greatest asset the country has is its people. I have great faith in the potential of the people of Malawi because they have at least five major qualities. They are able to work hard, as Dr. Banda has continually exhorted; they are able to learn, as my experience of their success at the University and other Institutions has demonstrated; they are generous as the way in which they have received the refugees from Mozambique has shown; they are spiritual as their reception of the Gospel from the first missionaries onwards has indicated; and now, recent events have made it clear that they have demonstrated the courage to put it all into practice. The country has good prospects.

Ultimately, the question is not an economic one but a spiritual one. Can those, the majority of the nation who have so freely received the Christian faith, be open to the leading and direction of the Holy Spirit to apply themselves for the benefit of others, and for the real building up of a people? The temptations manifest even in the early church to put one's own interests ahead of the interests of Christ and others are always there, and not easy to resist. But if this basic spiritual battle can be fought and won, then I believe that the more temporal battles can also be won.

Chapter Four
London

Before continuing with the African story, it is necessary to indicate more of my British background, and to describe briefly the ideas, institutions and people who had major influences on me prior to our departure for Malawi. Almost all of these were located in London. I studied at Kings College, University College and the Institute of Education, all part of London University, and I worked at three of the London Polytechnics, Thames, South Bank and North London. As at one stage I almost despaired of ever leaving London, the escape we eventually made to Africa was all the more spectacular.

My first experience of Higher Education was as a student at Kings College London where I graduated in Mathematics. I became interested in the idea of the then Colonial Service as a career, but National Service followed, and during the next two years as an Education Officer in the Royal Air Force, the wind of change had begun to blow and there was not much of the Colonial Service left. Then a related opportunity arose. Immediately after completing my time in the RAF, even forgoing my end of service leave in order to get started, I took my first job as an Assistant

Lecturer in Mathematics at Woolwich Polytechnic. I had been interested in Woolwich for some time, since at St. John's Church, Blackheath, which I had been attending for some years, we were concerned about missionary work, and grasped the logic of ministering first to those who had come from abroad to our own doorstep. Woolwich Polytechnic offered internal degrees of London University, mainly in Engineering and Science, but also a very popular 'A' level programme which students often took as a preliminary to degree work elsewhere but a good number preferred to stay on at Woolwich, building up a good community spirit over the years. At this time there were over fifty nationalities represented at the College. This was the community to which the church attempted to relate, with some success, even to the extent of building a large Overseas Students Hostel in Woolwich, and from my point of view it meant that I already had many friends from abroad, especially from Nigeria and Malaysia. If my earlier ambitions to join the Colonial Service and go to places like Nyasaland now seemed unlikely, Woolwich appeared to be the best alternative.

This choice did mean that I returned to live in Blackheath, cementing my ties to South-East London, but I enjoyed the transition from the fairly easy bondage of service life to the more strenuous liberty of being a civilian again, and I worked hard on my new lecture courses to students who actually wanted to learn, and relished the individual contacts I made with students from abroad in my role as personal tutor.

At Woolwich it soon became apparent that it was necessary to undergo further study. A first degree was not sufficient for what was beginning to look like a rather longer career than initially envisaged. At Kings I was essentially a 'pure' mathematician who tolerated 'applied' only because it made up the syllabus, and at Woolwich my specialism became the most abstract of all undergraduate studies, that of real analysis. It seemed natural to study, at Master's level, in something equally abstract. I went off to Bedford College once a week to be delighted by a series of postgraduate lectures on mathematical logic. Much as I loved this double helping of abstraction, it became clear that this was not aiding my social development. My tendency to become reclusive and remote from people was only being reinforced. A different approach was needed. I then remembered a friend in the RAF who had told me about a most interesting M.Sc. course he had taken at University College in the History and Philosophy of Science. At the same time, my mother had been urging that what I really needed was a course in car maintenance. I pondered this dilemma for some days before making the great decision, and not surprisingly I registered for the more academic option. My mother was a source of great wisdom and normally right about these things but I think the car maintenance class was full, and to some regret and considerable financial loss I have subsequently never taken any course in this area.

However, the course at University College was the most user friendly for a teacher that could be imagined. The lectures were presented from 5.30 to 7.30 on two to three evenings per week and the examinations were held at the end of September so that the normal long vacation period could be used for preparation. This idea of presenting a part-time course to be as convenient as possible for the most likely clients was forward thinking indeed for the early 60s.

It was also, as my friend in the RAF had said, a most stimulating intellectual experience. We encountered all the sciences from the earliest civilisations to the present day, followed the developing perceptions of mankind about the nature of the Universe with the consequent religious and sociological implications and discovered how humane is the study of Science. There was also a research project which gave the excitement of studying original texts, often in different languages. This really proved to be just the sort of study I needed, and I went on to take both the M.Sc., which was very demanding, and the Ph.D. which I found to be rather more straightforward.

The work in the History and Philosophy of Science seemed to lead from one thing to another in ways I never could have anticipated. The first paper I published led to an introduction to Professor G.J. Whitrow of Imperial College, and from this an invitation to give BBC broadcasts on the History of Mathematics for the then new Open University. While working on the Ph.D., I was invited to give the lectures in the History of Mathematics on the M.Sc. course at University College London.

Then I was invited to write a book which came out in 1970 as *Development of Modern Mathematics*. The book was not a great success, although in some places it is still being used today, but it was read by Arthur Morley in Nottingham who wrote and suggested we form a society. I met with Arthur in the buffet at St. Pancras Station where we agreed to convene a national meeting which led to the formation of the British Society for the History of Mathematics. Initially Arthur became Treasurer, I became Secretary and Gerald Whitrow agreed to be President. It was thought that there might not be enough interest to sustain such a society for more than a few meetings, but in fact it is still active in 1994, and several other national societies in this area have been started.

My own research was concerned with the work of Charles Babbage, known chiefly for having had the concept of the modern computer a century before its time. Babbage's work was not known or taken at all seriously until B.V. Bowden in *Faster than Thought,* his 1957 book on the early history of the computer, drew attention to this most remarkable man. Since then much study has been put into the many-sided nature of this eminent but neglected Victorian, and it has been my privilege to share in the modern revelation of this British genius of near Newtonian stature.

There was another major dimension to our lives at this time. We had become very involved in the life of our active parish church, St. Andrew's, Sidcup, and I had become an Anglican Lay-Reader in 1965. The Vicar, Philip Lenon, who was a great influence in our lives, had become interested in the Charismatic movement which was flowing through the more traditional denominations at this time. I was most sceptical at first but eventually became convinced and committed, but that is a story for another time. Philip introduced us to Harry Greenwood, an Irish itinerant evangelist with a teaching and healing ministry. Harry in turn invited us to visit his home base, the South Chard Full-Gospel Church in Somerset.

This was the first of many visits to this west-country fellowship which effectively became our spiritual home. It was a most remarkable church with its open worship, open pulpit and emphasis on the reality of the Holy Spirit. The pastor, Sidney Purse, had given up his farming in order to implement the vision he had of a New Testament based church, and my purpose in introducing Chard, is to say more about Sid and his influence. In particular I would lay emphasis on one aspect of his ministry that he would not have said much about, and that was his management style.

It was very noticeable that despite being the Pastor, there were many services and meetings at which Sid would sit in the background, silent. There were several in the congregation who could give stirring messages and a number who, like Harry, had a worldwide ministry. But there was no doubt that this diminutive man was in charge. His was an enabling ministry which encouraged others to go out in confidence and fulfil the gifts and calling they had been given. Sid was there to return to, to assess, encourage and direct, and under his quiet but unquestioned authority, other ministries could flourish. This seemed to me such a refreshing contrast to the majority of churches where normally one man performs it all, and no one else is able to develop a ministry except on a minor scale. Sid, in contrast, demonstrated that to share the ministry is in no way a threat to the authority of the pastor, and that instead the authority is enhanced and the church grows much more rapidly and effectively through the release of this plurality and variety of ministries.

This struck me as a most valuable example not only for the operation of the church, but for my own profession as well. The essential job of the Head of Department, or Dean, or Principal, or Vice-Chancellor, is not so much to pursue his own work, but to provide the optimal conditions and encouragement for others to be productive. Anyone who takes on academic leadership must be prepared to sacrifice his own academic advancement, and to a certain extent the reputation that goes with it, for the greater satisfaction of seeing a department or faculty or university achieve its larger purposes. This became the motivation for what I was to experience at South Bank and in Malawi.

Woolwich had now become Thames Polytechnic, the academic structure had been changed, and I was appointed the first Head of the new Division of Mathematics. This was my first taste of management. I asked a good friend in the Management Department if I should take a course with them but he advised me instead to keep well away, and manage according to my own experience and understanding. So I started putting into practice my own ideas, and particularly those from Chard which certainly served me very well for the next twenty years of educational management.

A year later I applied for and obtained the position of Head of

Department of Mathematics at the Polytechnic of the South Bank. I had been at Woolwich for fourteen years, the time Jacob had worked for his Rachel. Certainly I had my own Rachel who was now five years old, but what had made me stay at Woolwich for so long? I can only say that I felt called to work at Woolwich, that I had enjoyed my time there immensely, and that there was so much change and development taking place that it was never the same institution two years running. In the era of the CNAA (Council for National Academic Awards) there was so much opportunity for innovation that Polytechnics became exciting places to work in, and in many cases surpassed the Universities in educational ideas and the quality of the programmes offered. Now this is all being recognised, and places like Woolwich are at last due to receive their deserved University status. What started for me as Woolwich Polytechnic and then became Thames Polytechnic, is now to be known as the University of Greenwich.

I think I was badly in need of a change from Woolwich. The latter years I spent there were becoming frustrating until the new stimulus of leading the Division of Mathematics arose, but before this task could be properly developed, the opportunity at South Bank emerged, and I have never for one moment regretted this decision to change.

After fourteen years at one place of work, one approaches a new job with some trepidation. In practice it took only a few days, or maybe just a few hours to virtually forget about Thames and commit myself fully to South Bank. In the end I stayed there for another fourteen years, and for much the same reasons.

On the surface it might appear that there was little change to anticipate. It meant continuing in Sidcup, and instead of commuting daily to Woolwich, commuting to a part of inner London that tourists do not often see; it meant moving from one Inner London Education Authority Polytechnic to another one, and from leadership of one group of mathematicians to another. Further, while the Thames Mathematics Department was acknowledged as one of the best in the public sector with a range of degree, postgraduate and HND courses, the one at South Bank had only half the number of staff, and until as recently as 1970, two years before my arrival, had been concerned only with servicing the other courses of which Engineering predominated.

However it was this small staff group which gave me my initial stimulus at South Bank. My predecessor had done valuable work in starting off some courses in Computing at a time when this subject was still considered only an adjunct of Mathematics, and had initiated the planning of a new degree to start, given the approvals, in September 1972. Also he had put together a staff whose average age was only thirty-one. I had the privilege of working with a most able and highly motivated group, determined to revolutionise teaching and learning methods, devise new curricula, respond to community needs and maintain a healthy research output. Many of these younger people have subsequently become leaders in the academic field, and as a stimulus to all of us in this department, we were fortunate to have a mathematical superstar, David Singmaster. David is an American who has settled in England, and he has remained in the department for over twenty years. He is a prolific researcher who has gained a great reputation as a populariser of Mathematics; among other things he is the man who introduced the Rubik cube to Britain. His encouragement was a major factor in the department; not only did he make his own contribution to the advance of Mathematics, but as our range of specialisms increased, he proved to be the one person who was versatile enough to present courses with confidence in almost every one of these.

It was most stimulating to work with colleagues such as these; in the course of a few years we had produced our own degree in Mathematics and Computing which we later revised to include a route for teachers of these subjects, we designed an M.Sc. in Mathematical Education which proved to be so innovative that the CNAA organised a national conference to discuss the curriculum, and we introduced the first national course in Computer Education, intended for teachers of other subjects to convert to this area.

One consequence of all this for myself, which I took to be a recognition of the progress of the department, was the invitation which I received in 1979 from the CNAA to become Chairman of the Board for Mathematics, Statistics and Operational Research.

Whether by accident or design, the initiating of the CNAA has turned out to be one of the most successful innovations in British Higher Education. The Council was established for the purpose of ensuring that degrees and other awards offered by colleges in the public sector were of comparable standard to those of the Universities. The process of validation was normally to receive documents which defined the course proposal, scrutinise these through the appropriate subject board and then follow with a visit to the institution to discuss the submission in some depth with the staff concerned. This method of peer group review proved to be the ideal vehicle for the new Polytechnics. The often sharp and resented criticism provided by the visiting party was most valuable in setting standards which in many cases were higher than those of the Universities. The CNAA panels normally included University representatives, and several of these expressed doubt if their own courses could pass such a rigorous scrutiny.

The process of review every five years encouraged both old and new courses to innovate, and with more Polytechnic staff being selected to join the boards and panels, new ideas and improved practices were transmitted from one institution to another. It was generally agreed that the major strength of the CNAA lay in its subject boards, each one being a carefully balanced selection of experts in the relevant areas drawn from the Universities, Polytechnics and Industry. What was not so effective were the quinquennial Institutional Reviews in which a wide spectrum of board members and CNAA officers descended on a college, stayed for nearly two whole days attempting to assess the general academic health of the institution and made judgements which in many cases were sweepingly wrong.

It was my privilege to lead one of the most active of these subject boards over the next three years. This was the period in which the CNAA introduced its new philosophy of Partnership in Validation, and as we travelled around the country on visits to Institutions offering undergraduate and postgraduate degrees in Mathematics, we did our best to adapt to a variety of styles of validation as proposed by the Colleges themselves, avoiding any set pattern of course proposal and being open to new ideas from the proposers. The great majority of visits provided a most stimulating intellectual experience as we listened to fresh ideas being proposed and argued constructively towards their improvement.

In 1980 two events took place which changed me in a number of ways. At this time my career seemed to be developing well. The department was growing in reputation and to become a Chairman of a Board was a rare achievement. I had suffered something of an aberration in the mid 70s when we left the Anglican church to join a house-church, but now we had returned to the safer haven of the parish. We had moved to a larger house, but still in Sidcup. There was a slight danger of complacency setting in.

Then the Director of South Bank Polytechnic decided to retire, and I was voted on to a selection committee to look for a successor. This task proved to be harder than expected. Two sets of competitive interviews were held, no suitable candidate emerged and we began to wonder if such a person existed, relative to the magnitude of the problems and the unattractiveness of the salary. Then, at the third attempt, John Beishon, Professor of Systems at the Open University came along and demonstrated that he was by far the best person for the job and, to our immediate relief, he accepted the position.

This relief quickly changed to anxiety. The new Director was very different from the former one and totally unlike the currently popular image of a Polytechnic leader. He appeared out of sympathy with the work being done and openly dismissive of what most of us thought were respectable achievements. In rapid time he succeeded in alienating most of the staff, and there were even attempts to have him removed. He ignored the mainstream of the courses being taught, and seemed to concentrate more on peripheral activities.

Having, I thought, achieved so much in the department, it was certainly not pleasant to have this man come along to a staff meeting and decry our best efforts. As he left the room I felt I had to tell my colleagues that, despite what we had heard, we should continue, relying on our own integrity to do what professionally we knew to be right.

Early in 1981 it was necessary for me to see the new Director; a most gifted and dedicated colleague, Gareth Pugh, had died of a brain tumour at the height of his career. I found John Beishon to be most sympathetic and helpful, and it seemed from this point that my own attitude to him began to change. I started to understand at last that by his challenging of the existing assumptions and demonstrating alternative approaches, even if in a characteristically abrasive manner, we were being motivated to look at the educational process in a more fundamental way. Without having any previous experience of work in a Polytechnic, here was someone thinking again from first principles about the role of a Polytechnic in the 1980s. Increasingly I saw John Beishon as an educational visionary whose thinking and achievements have proved to be most influential. At a personality level we were quite incompatible, but professionally I am grateful to John for having caused me to re-think my own educational philosophy, and helping me to criticise my own attitudes and performance at a time when I might have sunk into the dungeon of self satisfaction.

Early on in his time with us I remember John saying to me that in his observation South Bank Polytechnic did not exist. He explained that what he saw instead were thirty independent departments squabbling with each other over relatively trifling issues, without any sense of corporate identity, and even less of any responsibility to the outside world. He encouraged us to stop worrying over parochial matters and instead to concern ourselves with the acute social and economic problems of the world around us, in particular those of South London. It is a good illustration of our attitudes at this time that in 1980 there were the serious and much publicised riots in Brixton. As I read my copy of the Scarman Report on the causes over a year later, it dawned on me that Brixton was less than three miles from the place where I was working, yet we were so out of touch with the community that the riots hardly even caused staffroom discussion let alone any sense of responsibility. We needed the sharpness of a Beishon to remind us most forcefully of this need to recognise and respond.

For academic organisation of the Polytechnic with the need for more corporate thinking to take place, the emphasis was removed from the departments to the faculties. Gradually the benefits for building the corporate identity of the Institution became apparent. In particular the new mode of organisation continued to challenge previous assumptions and enabled an atmosphere of fundamental debate to emerge. My own part was to be elected first as the Dean of the overly large Faculty of Science and Engineering and, when we succeeded two years later in dividing into two Faculties, based around the emerging concepts of Biotechnology and Information Technology, I was re-elected as Dean of the latter, somewhat misleadingly named the Faculty of Engineering.

These experiences as Dean meant that I now had to part direct company with Mathematics, especially as my three year association with CNAA finished in 1982. Instead I found myself drawn into a different world, initially as an unwilling arbiter of disputes mainly over resource allocation, but then into the new intellectual fascination of Engineering Education.

In 1985 the Polytechnic of North London went through a crisis of such magnitude that the institution was almost closed down. This had always been a most turbulent college since the former Northern Polytechnic and North-Western College were merged together in 1970 to constitute the new Polytechnic of North London. There were student demonstrations against the appointment of the first Director, Terence Miller. The Director rightly survived but the Socialist Workers Party managed to secure a stranglehold on appointments to the Students Union Executive, and the clash between a determined administration and this militant student group caused a continual struggle which often led to strikes and closures of the Polytechnic. There were also strong hints of undue left-wing bias among the staff, which in turn aroused hostility from Conservative Ministers of Education.

The troubles reached their height in 1985 when it was discovered that the Polytechnic had a student who was a prominent member of the right wing National Front. The Students Union organised protests against his continuing in the Polytechnic, which led to violent confrontations and even to interventions into College property by the police. The Union were demanding the expulsion of this student, but as he took care to see that his undesirable activities were confined to outside the Polytechnic and committed no offence inside, there were no grounds to consider this demand.

The Polytechnic administration, much more pacific than those of earlier days, was quite unable to handle the situation. It became necessary for the local authority, the ILEA to intervene. They did this first by providing early retirement for the current Director, and then by persuading John Beishon to relinquish his post at South Bank and move to North London on a temporary basis to attempt to sort out the chaos.

With a combination of firm action and subtlety, John managed to bring some sort of peace to the Polytechnic in the sense that normal work was able to continue and the student at the centre of the problem was actually able to complete the final year of his degree. However, it became clear that through the continual hostility between students and administration, with a generally poor standard of management, there were many more problems than simply those of pacifying a militant group of student officials. To help with the academic consequences of this almost continuous decline, John invited me to join him at North London on a half-time basis.

I greatly welcomed the opportunity of this new challenge and especially the prospect of working again with John Beishon. My particular task was to draw up an Academic Plan for North London in consultation with the staff at the Polytechnic. South Bank was by now a highly successful and well regarded institution with an increasingly well motivated staff, and I managed to keep my work there ticking over while spending two or three days a week at North London, a task which I found immensely satisfying.

A major part of my work was to spend time with senior staff, the Deans and Heads of Department, to learn about their work, their problems and their ideas for future development. Their very friendly reception surprised me. I felt that if someone from another Polytechnic had visited me to discuss my aspirations I might have reacted differently, but the people at North London seemed only too willing to discuss their ideas with me, I suspect because no one had done this before. I also drew the conclusion that much of the student disturbance could be attributed to their uninspiring academic diet. A small group of militants cannot command the support of the mass of normal students unless there is a general discontent shared by all. It seemed to me from my discussions with staff and from my CNAA knowledge of North London that very little attention had been paid to curriculum development. Rather the general style was to present University type degree courses in the hope that the institution might be singled out for University status. The effect was that, lacking the type of resources or learning environment associated with a normal University, the Polytechnic was only able to offer second rate undergraduate education without the stimulus of the normal Polytechnic ethos as compensation.

Through discussions with staff it was possible to draw up an acceptable Academic Development Plan and as a related part of my job to convince the funding body, the National Advisory Board for Higher Education (NAB) to keep the Polytechnic in business, even saving the Education Department which had been under the greatest threat of closure. My work at North London having now finished, I returned to full-time work at South Bank for the whole of 1986.

By the end of 1985, John Beishon had decided to stay on at North London. His Deputy at South Bank, Alfred Morris, became Director of Bristol Polytechnic, and we were left somewhat short staffed at the top of the organisation. It proved not to be easy to find suitable replacements for these two, and so the two remaining Assistant Directors, Doug Hykin and Maxwell Smith were appointed Acting Director and Acting Deputy Director respectively, and I was brought in as Acting Assistant Director. It was again very good to work with Doug and Maxwell, and I thought we did a very good job between us. However, by the end of the year my thoughts had turned to Africa, and there was not really time to think out what the job might have involved. It was still a happy and valuable experience.

But I must return from this long digression about colleges south and north of the river in order to describe the second major turning point of the year 1980.

We had been scanning through a Christian magazine looking for holiday ideas when I spotted a somewhat unusual advertisement – 'Wanted, Honorary Pastor for United Reformed Church in St. Pauls Cray, Orpington.' I knew little about the URC except that it had come about through an amalgamation of the Congregational and Presbyterian Churches in England. I deduced also that the church that needed this help must have been the one known locally as Giggs Hill which was only two miles away, and where my children had recently been to some lively youth meetings. Veronica persuaded me to phone the number given, and rather than receiving my tentative request for further information, the voice at the other end almost offered me the job at once. I suggested it might be better if we first met together and learnt more about each other.

When we met with Alf Kensington, the church secretary, and his wife Lily, he explained to me that this church, built in the late 1950s had first flourished and then declined in the mid-70s to such an extent that it had been virtually closed and merged with the nearest other URC at Petts Wood. However during this time of exile a good youth group had developed, mainly from the young people of the more affluent Petts Wood area and the Boys Brigade, more attractive to downtown St. Pauls Cray had emerged, to the extent that the remnant from the former church had pressed to be independent again. The surviving congregation consisted of young people and older people with no one in between, and together there were far too few to justify the expense of a minister. Hence the agreed need for an Honorary Pastor.

For the second time we had been feeling the need to move on from St. Andrews in Sidcup, and this prospect of increased responsibilities seemed to us and to others the right sort of direction. We therefore expressed interest and were invited by the church meeting to begin in September 1980. Apart from any spiritual credentials which seemed acceptable to our new friends, we had the advantages that our ages were half way between the averages of the two groups, providing the formerly missing middle, and we lived near enough to require no help with housing or transport. It was disconcerting to discover that, even after we had started, the advertisement still appeared in the monthly magazine where we had first seen it, but they explained that they had paid for six successive months in advance, and wanted to get their money's worth. It was that sort of fellowship!

The youth group disappeared very quickly. Almost everyone had a University place, and while they were able to turn up during the vacations, it was normal to move to another part of the country after graduation. We quickly learnt how to say, not 'Our congregation is declining', but 'We are a church which sends people out!'

This departure meant that for the majority of our time the church consisted of people who had lived in St. Pauls Cray for many years, were attached to the place and intended to stay there. In order not to interfere with my contracted work I agreed to be present every Sunday, preaching at one of the two services, and also to take responsibility for the mid-week Bible study and Prayer meeting on Thursday evenings. Sometimes more time than this was involved, but I never found any clash of time or interests with my daily work. By the grace of God it proved to be possible to concentrate properly on both assignments, and even to take one as a healthy relaxation from the other.

Whatever the church received from this arrangement, it was certainly a very great blessing for us to be associated with our new friends. This was a fellowship in which openness was the order of the day. There was none of the hypocrisy or secrecy normally to be found in middle-class congregations; rather there was an unwritten rule in this church that there was to be no gossiping or backbiting, and any newcomer quickly learnt this. It all provided an atmosphere in which there could be reverence for the Bible as the Word of God, in which it was expected that prayer would be answered, and in which the Spirit of Christ could move freely to teach, direct and transform. We were greatly helped to grow in this way by my overseer, Richard Wells. Richard was and still is, the Minister of Swanley URC, and we had the arrangement that the church at St. Pauls Cray would come under his supervision.

It would be difficult to imagine a happier outworking of such a relationship, and it could be that it worked all the better because I was a part-timer. Richard's role was to be supportive and any problem or difficult visit or interaction with the denomination could be handed over to him. He had a most dedicated style of living, totally committed to serving the people entrusted to him. He believed and practised that all church life was subject to the sovereignty of the Holy Spirit. Whenever we had an elders' or church meeting, if there was the slightest suggestion of disagreement, Richard would stop the meeting and call for a time of prayer, and not until we were all of one mind would he allow the meeting to continue. I took to Richard as the equivalent of a spiritual director, and I still refer to him over important personal matters.

One great benefit I discovered of having a part-time ministry is that people in the church are much more willing to share out the jobs that have to be done. These include not only the more menial tasks, but also ministries of teaching, preaching and evangelism which develop more easily because they provide no threat to the pastor who is in a similar position himself. We were able together to arrange two evangelistic missions and made a number of visits to every house around the area. It was noticeable that while we received some excellent visiting evangelists, the greatest fruit came from the preparation for these missions, as we mobilised our resources to proclaim the Gospel.

Then, in 1984, we received what pastors never like to talk about but secretly hope will happen, an increase in the size of the congregation. The numbers doubled in this year to nearly three figures in the morning service and to almost fifty in the evening. Most encouragingly, the mid-week meeting drew over thirty, and I would always emphasise how important it was to attend for this time of fellowship and prayer.

Then in the next year we found that the previous advance was followed by a time of trial in which virtually every key member of the church found him or herself facing a deep personal problem. I learnt through this that the only attitude to take is to dig in firmly, to trust God against all appearances to the contrary, take on the armour of God, and stand.

The very mixed experiences at Giggs Hill provided among other things, a remarkably good internal preparation for what followed. It had been my initial intention to do this work for three years, but in the event we stayed at Giggs for six. In the early part of 1986, I began to sense that while I found no difficulty in doing these quite different things at the same time, and certainly nobody from the church or the Polytechnic ever complained about any lack of commitment, this dual life was not a feasible long term prospect. What I was now looking for was an occupation which effectively integrated my academic and pastoral interests. Then in the middle of the year, the opportunity from Malawi emerged!

Chapter Five
The University

Having earlier described the history, location and size of the Colleges which together make up the University of Malawi, the aim in this chapter is to look more closely into the character and operation of the Institution.

The University was founded by the President and he has remained as Chancellor since its foundation. In the early days of development he took a close personal interest in the growth of the institution, holding regular meetings with the first Vice-Chancellor, and frequently coming to address the students. Now that the University is a more established institution and, as I describe in a later chapter, his educational interests have diversified, there is less direct contact, but still the Vice-Chancellor has the privilege of open access to the President.

It was thus relatively easy to obtain an appointment with the President and in any case I had one regular meeting with him each year to request that he sign the certificates of graduation. On other occasions we would discuss matters such as the progress of the Medical School, but generally our meetings were friendly, brief, and served the purpose mainly of assuring him that the University was still alive and active. Once when I tried to raise a specific matter with him, he replied that he just wanted us to be happy in the country, and if I had any problems I should take them to Mr. Tembo.

The Honourable John Z. U. Tembo was the Chairman of the University Council, and my relations with him and, by implication, the Council as a whole, are described in a later chapter. In common with other Universities, we had a Council as the Governing Body and a Senate as the chief academic authority, although the relation between these two bodies was somewhat different from that which normally prevails.

The University included four colleges at some considerable distance apart with no less than ten distinct faculties and as many as forty different departments, rather many for an institution which in 1987 had barely 2,000 students.

I would emphasise that despite the diversity and the scattering of the four constituent colleges, it is a single national University. One essential part is the University Office, located in Zomba, where the Vice-Chancellor, Registrar, Finance Officer and their assistants all have their offices, but at a safe distance away from Chancellor College. We were able to extend this orthodox range of functions to include a Planning Officer, an Information Officer and a Research Co-ordinator, but this was essentially the residence of the senior administration. It was a matter for debate whether this centralisation exerted too much power over the Colleges, and whether this was healthy for the academic life of the institution, but we worked within a committee system which did ensure that resolutions could be made and acted upon by the Office. While in the course of time, as each College is able to grow, it may be that we have four potential new Universities, I never heard any serious consideration given to providing more autonomy for the Colleges. The formal and informal channels gave sufficient opportunity for communication, and the advantages of working in the same way in one University seemed to outweigh any disadvantage.

I arrived at the University at the beginning of 1987, armed with ideas generated from my time at Thames and South Bank, reinforced by the Beishon influence. These ideas were, in my opinion, in advance of those to be found in other British

Polytechnics let alone British or overseas Universities. The Polytechnic ethos has now become much more the orthodoxy in British Higher Education, but immediate acceptance in Malawi in 1987 was too much to expect.

Contrary to this, my early impression of the Malawi University was that some old-fashioned and unhelpful academic concepts were dominant. There was much that could be described as academic arrogance, the diploma disease, and worst of all a sense of intellectual colonialism.

To describe first the more serious of these symptoms, the colonialism manifest as an over-reliance on western based thinking at the expense of developing a proper African philosophy originated initially from a sound and successful policy. When the University started in 1965, there were only a handful of Malawians who held first degrees let alone the type of academic background to be expected of a University lecturer, a reflection of how Nyasaland had been treated in the colonial era. With Independence and the founding of the University, which the President believed an essential component of a new nation, it became necessary to quickly advance those who were capable to further levels of academic attainment.Those who succeeded well from the initial intakes to the first programmes offered by the University were then sent abroad to take higher degrees. The general pattern which still prevails in Malawi and other African Universities is that a graduate is selected for staff development, sent abroad in most cases to Britain or America to do a Masters' degree, returns for a time to lecture and then goes abroad again to do a doctorate. After the second return, the aim of most is for the further opportunity to do a post-doctoral fellowship.

In Malawi this policy had worked successfully in that, given the relatively short time available to make the change, it had been largely achieved. Whereas in 1965 over 90% of the staff were from abroad, by 1990 the situation had been reversed and up to 80% of the staff were Malawians. Half of these had achieved their doctorates, many were working overseas for higher degrees and still more waited for the opportunity to arise.

While this success implied that staff were both well localised and formally well qualified, it meant also that the majority of local staff had spent much of their formative academic lives in other countries.In many cases these overseas experiences were taken as the definitive intellectual formation, and return to Malawi often perceived as not too exciting a prospect. This was particularly the case with Ph.D. training. The study normally involved four or more years away from the country researching into an ever narrower field, often divorced from anything ever likely to be taught at the University with the knowledge that Malawi would not have the facilities to continue that research there. For many of the staff, it was the location of the years devoted to the doctorate which provided not only nostalgia, but the real intellectual homeland against which the limitations of working in Malawi became only too apparent. With colleagues in the same position the feeling that little good could come out of the local University was reinforced, and the resulting intellectual colonialism was a major, continual challenge to anyone who would seek to give direction to the institution.

In addition, those returning from abroad would sometimes bring bad academic habits with them. That research was superior to teaching, that pure research was superior to applied, that class contact hours should be minimal, that promotion came only through the accretion of published papers, that administration had to be treated as a chore, that sabbaticals were a right, and the best a University like Malawi could aspire to, would be a third rate imitation of an old-fashioned British or American University.

This feeling of mine may have been a gross exaggeration of attitudes, but right from the start I was very conscious that here lay a major obstacle to progress, and one that had to be vigorously contested. The best way to do this was to discover a vision and a purpose which could give a direction against which all activities could be assessed.

It then occurred to me that even in London it had been possible to determine the mission to which most of the concerns of the institution could relate. At South Bank, the Polytechnic could be seen essentially as a major technological institution, and the large Science, Engineering and Building Faculties, together with Technopark provided the reason for the existence and growth of the institution with other disciplines not immediately in this sphere encouraged to develop in the context of this technological environment.

Further, on the day I started work at North London Polytechnic, one of the first things I asked John Beishon was if there were any general theme to which it might be possible to tie the academic planning.His response was that the major characteristic of the work was its relation to community development.It was then possible in consultation with the staff there to make this the key idea from which the plan could be developed. Having identified this, it then became possible to work out new curricula, especially across former subject boundaries, initiate interdisciplinary research projects, and establish centres to concentrate on specialised work, in conformity to this underlying theme, and drawing on the resources from related areas which already existed.

In Malawi it was not necessary to search widely for a mission. The President had already given the lead when he selected the establishment of a new University as one of the essentials of the new country. The immediate need might be to localise the key positions in the Civil Service as the colonial rulers departed, but beyond this was a vision to inspire and unify all our diverse skills and activities. The magnificent theme of the University as having a key role in National Development, devoting its talents to the building of the nation, for the advancement of the people, as a leader in Education, Culture, Society and Technology in the forefront of the battle against poverty, ignorance and disease; this was the theme, the inspiration, the mission which as appointed leader I had to declare.

The concept had its enemies, some of which I have already identified, and many preferred to go about their work without such direction, but this was the message which to staff, students, the government and the general public I continually proclaimed and often preached. To the traditionalists I would always argue that this concept of the University did not devalue in any way the accepted norms. Rather it extended the boundaries of normal rigorous scholarship by raising new questions whose answers in terms of national requirements would be, if anything, more intellectually demanding than any traditional academic problem. There might be time and funding for an ivory tower sometime in the future, but for the present the University had the opportunity to identify itself with the needs and aspirations of the people, the great majority of whom would never have the privilege of a University education.

68

To reinforce these ideas I made a discovery early on which seemed a fairly obvious one, but whose implication did not seem to command much thought. That was the realisation that the institution was in fact already, and had been for a number of years, a Vocational University.

This was an immediate consequence of the far-sighted decision made early on, that the University should include all higher education in the country, with the Colleges an integral and equal part of the whole. Three of these Colleges, the Polytechnic, the College of Agriculture and the College of Nursing, were by their nature vocational, preparing students for entry to specific professions. Even Chancellor College included the Faculties of Education and Law with about half the students in the College, so that it could be asserted as a matter of fact, not opinion, that over 80% of students in the University were on vocational programmes, a ratio to be further increased as the Medical School grows to full capacity.

From this observation I concluded, although it would have upset people if I had stated it at the time, that the University was in fact more like a Polytechnic than the normal concept of a University! Now that in Britain and elsewhere the folly of the binary divide and the achievements of the Polytechnics have made them officially equivalent to Universities, I can make the point more loudly, the main consequence being that without using the emotive word, the Polytechnic ethos was much more applicable to the Malawian situation than its academic alternative, and this I attempted to apply, consistent with the general philosophy just outlined.

My concept of the ethos as it might be applied in a Malawian context, was to be responsive and pro-active towards educational needs, to develop the educational means to achieve what was required, to develop professional as well as academic abilities in a democratic environment, to conduct appropriate research, consultancies, advisory services and short courses, to interact freely with all branches of society, to set professional examples by the efficient operation of the institution, and always to be open to appraisal, evaluation and criticism. It will immediately be recognised that not all of these were possible within a Malawian context, but inside the microcosm of the University we did our best to operate in this way.

The opposition, however, should not be underestimated. The Chancellor, himself, took the traditional view of the idea of the University, and I am grateful that he never encouraged me to discuss educational philosophy with him. The Chairman would largely follow the views of the Chancellor, although he was supportive of new programmes considered to be developmental. Some of my predecessors had also taken the traditional line, and what was the most difficult, some of the Principals without whose support it was almost impossible to achieve anything new were also inclined in this way. Then there was the body of staff, mainly at Chancellor College, who preferred to see the traditional role of the University being maintained.

It was most interesting to observe how the difference of educational philosophies manifested itself in a number of ways. One aspect was the perennial question of staff promotion. We were fortunate that on this important and emotive issue, plenty of promotions were available, but the question always arose about how they should be distributed, and by what criteria.

The traditional method of University distribution is by means of published research papers. Like most other places we never actually said that when inviting applications. Rather we announced that due account would be taken of teaching ability, curriculum development, community service, invited consultancies and conference addresses, and even attempted to design formulae to weight these different factors, but found that in practise it is easier to count the number of publications rather than make too much allowance for these more unquantifiable activities. Unfortunately there are some areas of work in which it is easier to publish than in others, and some which in Malawi, for example, Physics, in which publication is almost impossible.

The problem accentuated differences between Colleges. In much of Chancellor College, and to a certain extent Bunda, a doctorate followed by a string of papers was the normal means of academic advance. In the Polytechnic and the College of Nursing, where we would wish for evidence of professional as much as academic achievement, it was not fair to expect a similar profile to the other two Colleges. The issue raised the point sharply about the purpose of the University. I argued that whatever the objectives of the University might be, then promotional awards should go to those who most evidently contribute to the achievement of these objectives.If the aim is to write papers for journals, then clearly those who write the best and the most should receive the credit; but if there are different aims to be fulfilled then awards should correspondingly be given to these achievers.

I tried to resolve the issue by inviting each of the four Colleges to put forward its own criteria, but even then, as much depended for comparison purposes on how an application was presented and defended by the College Principal concerned, Chancellor College who were the experts at both of these activities, usually seemed to gain the most promotions.

Another traditional influence was apparent in the class-room. Despite the very practical and vocational orientation of the University, I strongly suspected that most of the action in teaching was on the black-board.Students would quietly and patiently write it all down, then commit it to memory, and in the frequent assessments and examinations, repeat back to the teacher what he or she had told them, and normally do this rather well.

It was encouraging that the University had a Committee for Teaching and Learning, and that each College had its own sub-committee in this area. As the concept of vocationalism took more of a grip with the implications for varying approaches to the teaching and learning process, it was gratifying to observe the titles of some of the seminars considered by these groups.There were in the different Colleges, discussions on the value of open-ended problem solving, evaluation of industrial attachment, the art of curriculum development and the value of research to the teacher. With this type of attitude, I was sure the standard of teaching in accordance with the real needs of the University would improve.

Allied to this philosophical contest is the phenomenon identifiable as the Diploma Disease. In one sense the idea is justifiable, because when educational opportunities are severely restricted, care must be taken that these are allocated to those who can be expected to make the most of them, and earlier success is the most apparent criterion to use. It is much less justifiable that educational qualifications are made the basis for level of appointment, salary scale and promotion at work.

This disease is manifest at the University not only in the question of appointments, academic or otherwise, but also in the selection and assessment of students. The achievement or non-achievement of a student at school remains, even if many years have passed since school was finished.

We had the case of a new course we had been asked to run by the Ministry of Health, to give management training for a year to senior members of the Nursing profession. When the qualifications of the applicants were examined, it was noted with pleasure that all but one had obtained a pass in the Malawi Certificate of Education, the minimum entry standard for the University. The one exception had only passed the Junior Certificate of Education, normally taken at school two years earlier than the other Certificate. Despite the fact that this lady had subsequently travelled abroad, and had been a Sister in the wards of a Scottish Hospital, her performance as probably a teenager was still looked on with doubt. Fortunately the decision was made after much discussion to take a chance on the lady, and I was delighted to hear subsequently that she had passed the year and was third highest in the class.

I had a similar pleasure when I signed a part-time lecturer's contract on behalf of Black Pweseli. Black was Malawi's first recording artist many years ago. Now probably into his seventies, he gives guitar lessons to a group of students at Chancellor College. Almost certainly he has no educational qualifications, and probably did not even attend school. It was therefore all the more satisfying to be able to welcome this talented man on to the University staff!

Then there was the problem of academic arrogance. It is still a very rare thing for a Malawian to be able to attend University. Comparing the number of graduates with the size of the population it becomes evident that so far less than one in a thousand have had this privilege, and only one in forty thousand has been a University lecturer. Coupled to this there is the danger that the country is developing a class system, and one clear route to the highest class is through association with the University. There is therefore a strong temptation for staff and students to become arrogant towards the less fortunate, and for these unhelpful attitudes to be expressed even within the University. In accordance with the principles for University development laid out earlier I try to make it a point to draw attention to this matter when giving public addresses.

It is so vital to the health of the nation for those from the University to share their privileges and to work for the benefit of the other 99+ per cent. When I make this point to Christian gatherings, the response is good. When I address students generally on this matter, I am not so sure of their response! It was most encouraging, however, to discover from the Tracer Study we made of our former graduates (reported more fully in a later chapter) that a large majority agreed that the University had encouraged them to be of service to the community. This was much larger than the numbers who were willing to admit that the University had helped them to earn a good salary. In my own time it was a cause of great satisfaction to see how many graduates had chosen a career of direct service to the community.

It is a fairly obvious matter of experience that when attempting to lead a large institution, it is much easier to achieve change in one's first year than later, when the ability to achieve something different seems to decline in inverse proportion to the amount of time spent on the job. The ability diminishes almost to zero during the last three months. On the other hand time is needed to understand how a large system operates, what is acceptable to it, and what is impossible to change, so that any intervention may be effective.

Quite apart from coming into an unfamiliar continent and culture, I had to adjust like the Vicar of Bray to some very different expectations of the approach I was expected to take. In South Bank under John Beishon's direction, democracy (apart from dealings with him!) became the accepted way of life. The Dean of Faculty was an elected position held for three years and the constituency included all members of academic staff with a good representation of technicians, administrators, secretaries and students. Having been elected the Dean was now accountable to this large constituency through the open Faculty meetings, the elaborate system of committees, and in representing their interests at the protracted negotiations for institutional resources.

Largely from these experiences I drew the conclusion that the major benefits of democracy are that people feel more included and accepted, and do participate more in sharing their ideas. The weaknesses I perceived are that the decision making processes are slowed down, often at the very point when swift responses are needed and that it can promote mediocrity. When arguing for example about resource allocation, it becomes much easier to agree to equal shares all round, rather than the harder process of arguing out where the resources should go for the greatest benefit to be obtained.

It was even possible to experiment with democracy. One department in my Faculty needed a new head of department. The members reasoned that the functions expected of this office, to be manager, research leader, course development leader, laboratory developer, liaiser with industry etc. were not to be found in one person. We agreed that they could split these into individual responsibilities so long as there was a departmental chairman whom I as Dean could recognise as leader. The department went ahead under this people's democracy arrangement, and from a former state of inactivity, became one of the most successful departments in the Polytechnic.

The state of democracy at South Bank was carried to further excesses by the left-wing Inner London Education Authority and its parent body the Greater London Council. When we left London in 1986, at the zenith of their influence, it seemed that under this type of political doctrine it was not so much education but rather anti-sexism and anti-racism that were the fundamental purposes of places like South Bank. These eccentric attitudes did make life less attractive at the Polytechnic, but they had no influence on our decision to go abroad.

I mention these things at some length in order to make the point that this was the political atmosphere when we left England, immediately prior to starting in Malawi. The political atmosphere we found in Malawi was somewhat different.

In fact the contrast was very great indeed. There was comparatively little democracy to be found in Malawi and as a result comparatively little to be found at the University. In contrast to what I had just experienced in England where in approximation to Mao's doctrine, it is the people who are really powerful and the leader carries no particular respect in regard to his position, the reverse was the case in Malawi. Further, the tremendous regard in which the Chancellor is held, is expected to trickle down a little on to the Vice-Chancellor. I was expected to lead the University, not merely to chair its democratic decision making processes.

As examples from all around the world clearly demonstrate, the transition from democrat to authoritarian leader is not at all difficult to achieve. In many cases it even seems a natural sort of individual progression. I now had this opportunity on a limited scale before me, and took the attitude which I hope I was able to sustain, that to have this type of authority could be very useful in tackling immediate problems, but that nothing of lasting value could be achieved unless the staff could be persuaded to develop their own ideas and contribute to a participatory process. It was therefore my policy to try to achieve as many necessary reforms as possible in the early days while at the same time encouraging colleagues to do their own thinking with the promise that all worthwhile views would receive a hearing and support.

Among the first problems to be tackled were those of Research, where despite the importance of this area for individual promotion, there was no coherent policy or even ambition for the University as a whole, Consultancy where the approach of lukewarm interest accompanied by suspicion had to be replaced by positive encouragement and appropriate incentives, Programme construction and validation, External Examiners and Advisors, Performance Indicators, and a number of issues arising from the academic work of the Colleges. Problems like academic structure and student assessment were also considered at this stage, but these proved to be more intractable.

For the longer term purpose we set up several informal working groups concerned with such matters as Consultancy and Short Courses, Internal and External Communications, Women in the University, Distance Learning, Vocational Education, Graduate Evaluation, Staff Development for non-academic staff, Community Relations, and invited membership simply by interest in the subject. As with much informal work, many of the ideas generated by this means fell by the wayside, but others proved to be strong enough either for immediate implementation or at any rate a passage through the more formal committee channels.

This last sentence betrays a hidden question which became more apparent over the years. That is the dichotomy between the formal and informal ways of decision making. Most of the ideas like those generated from the working-groups could be taken up immediately, especially with the help of a donor. The idea for a graduate study was ripe to take up with the HRID scheme of USAID as indicated in a separate chapter. Distance Learning was handled by inviting a Consultant from the Commonwealth of Learning. The suggestions made by the group on Communications were immediately followed by consultations with the Malawi Broadcasting Corporation which led to a regular Saturday evening half-hour for the University. In contrast those taken up through the normal committee structure travelled much more slowly, often in circles, and seldom reached their destination.

This contrast I found even more accentuated when dealing with our major donors. The British ODA came every three years and the aid they provided in terms of staff supplementation, training places and equipment was eventually worth over a million pounds sterling per annum. The World Bank also arrived at comparable intervals and donated generously but often towards less obvious areas of development. These substantial inputs were always most welcome, but inevitably carried policy implications. Since speed was of the essence in responding, it was not possible to set up the formal mechanisms to debate these sometimes new issues. My own preference was to gather up a group of senior staff to handle the immediate questions with the donors, adjust policies where necessary and report to Senate or Council at a later time. This concept of executive action is, I believe, both necessary and legitimate, but it left the unresolved question of how Senate could remain the proper decision making body when it seemed the really important discussion was taking place outside its hearing.

One unwelcome consequence is that the meetings of Senate and its committees can become routine and boring. On at least one occasion I cancelled a meeting of Senate because I could not bear the thought of distinguished academics taking a day off from work and travelling long distances in order merely to endorse such uninspiring material as our agendas were providing. As a believer in Senate, I took it as a major responsibility to make its meetings more meaningful and exciting, with an increasing number of open-ended items appearing on the agenda, but in the end I reached the view that accountable executive action is the better way to do University business.

As illustration I would refer to two things that happened in 1989. This was a year in which the country received a succession of highly distinguished visitors from abroad. First the Pope, then Mrs. Thatcher, then the Archbishop of Canterbury and the Moderator of the Church of Scotland all came in rapid succession. The University's own main visitor at this time was Professor John Ashworth, then Vice-Chancellor of Salford University and now Director of the London School of Economics. The purpose in inviting him was to explore if the unique methods he had supplied at Salford in which through interaction with industry, the University was generating over half of its annual income, could be adapted to Malawi. His short visit aroused much enthusiasm, and some opposition from the traditionalists, and after informal work we put together a proposal to go through Senate to Council to initiate this type of interaction with industry in Malawi.

To my dismay, Senate responded by asking for more time for discussion and in particular to obtain the views of the Faculties. The feedback from the Faculties turned out to be favourable, but it took nearly a year to come back to Senate and by then initial impetus of the idea had departed. In contrast, a dynamic Egyptian member of staff, Omar Selim, had the idea at the same time for an international computing association which he called CISNA (Computing in Southern Africa). With my encouragement but without formal approvals, he simply went ahead and launched the society with himself as General Secretary and myself as Chairman. Since then CISNA has organised two international conferences in Blantyre, one in Namibia, and another in Botswana, has started a journal, has obtained international recognition and worked with great energy in the Blantyre area to advance Computing in education and business.

While greatly satisfied at the success of an enterprise which started at the University, I can only lament by comparison the demise of the efforts to build on John Ashworth's ideas. If we had not worried about going through the official channels, I am sure this would have been a most successful enterprise.

One policy which did receive support throughout the University was the need to increase its size. Early on I had felt that a national University of only two thousand students was surely inadequate for a country with a population of more than nine million. This view was brought home much more vividly at the end of my first year.

The obstacles to growth were financial and physical. It had been policy up to this point that all students should be accommodated in the Colleges. The boarding and feeding of the students placed a severe burden on our finances, but as they were recruited from all over the country it was necessary that such accommodation should be found for them and so hostels were built for this purpose. I did raise the question of students living out, particularly in Blantyre and Zomba, where suitable accommodation might be available, and on investigation it has been found that probably at most a maximum of two hundred such extra places could be found.

It appeared that there were severe physical limits to growth, and this factor was being additionally strained by some otherwise encouraging developments. The first was that there was a distinct improvement in passing end of year examinations. The pass rate in 1987 increased to about 95% and has either remained or improved on this figure ever since. But with only a fixed number of residential places available, the high pass rate meant that students would be returning in large numbers and would not make any new space for entrants!

Further there was a distinct trend to increase the average amount of time a student spent while at the University. The earlier pattern had been that the majority of students graduated after three years with a Diploma award. Only the top third of any class would continue to complete the degree in normally five years. The trend which started at Chancellor College and which I was very happy to continue was to phase out the Diploma, and thereby give more students the chance to obtain a degree. This seemed a laudable move since the country needed more specialists and to finish higher education only three years after 'O' level seemed a wasted opportunity. Chancellor College was in the process of changing the three/five year pattern to straight four year degrees, and this was completed by 1990. The Polytechnic similarly changed the pattern of its Business Administration/Accountancy degree, and without changing the Engineering time format, gave many more opportunities for diploma holders to move on to the degree, especially after the reform to create more specialised routes. Only Bunda College stuck to the existing structure, and I warned them that unless they were willing to either offer four year degrees as an alternative or increase the proportion going on to the degree class, they would not attract students who clearly would not wish to take the risk of finishing only with a diploma when much better degree opportunities existed at the other Colleges.

Consequently the average length of stay at the University was increasing and this in turn meant even fewer places for new students. At the same time information from MANEB was showing that the number of students passing the Malawi Certificate of Education and qualifying for the University was increasing by over 10% per year. There was even a good success rate among students who, unable to obtain Secondary School places, had embarked on the hard road of studies through the Malawi College of Distance Education.

Putting these factors together, I announced to Senate that we had a major crisis on our hands. The response was very positive. All agreed that the policy of extending degree opportunities was right, and that we should make every effort to ensure not only that no less places were available for new students but that in view of the increasing demand, we should strive to make extra places to meet the need. Following this decision, the College Principals and the University Office made every effort to expand the availability of places. It was agreed that students could be accommodated outside the Colleges where possible, and new hostels were acquired either by renovating buildings used for other purposes or finding boarding places from schools which no longer needed them. The consequence of all this was that the student population increased from about 2,000 in 1987 to very nearly 3,000, four years later, with the pass rate still at its very high level. Thus productivity had been increased by 50%!

I would emphasise that this growth was achieved entirely by the University. I used every opportunity in public speeches, often reported in the press, to stress that there was this fundamental need for expansion. I argued that not only was there a demand from Malawi Certificate holders which we could certainly not meet, but also in view of the vocational nature of the University nearly all of our graduates were destined for jobs of vital national importance where there was always a need for more graduates. Regrettably this was one area that donors did not respond to. They were not interested in financing new buildings; my counter-argument that donations of hardware, software and liveware cannot achieve much without the brickware to house them went unheeded. Also the Government did not seem to place a high priority on this type of growth. This was in contrast to stories we had heard from neighbouring countries where the Government, understanding the importance of a sizable force of graduates, had actually taken the initiative, and ordered the growth of the Universities.

From World Bank figures, Malawi has with the possible exceptions of Tanzania, Rwanda and Mozambique, the lowest ratio of tertiary places to population of any country in the world. In paying tribute to my colleagues who have captured the vision of what is needed, and probably done all that is possible without help from outside, I would express the hope that future governments and the donor community as well as the commercial sector in Malawi will see the importance of this issue, and make growth to a realistic level more possible.

Because opportunities are so few, to the extent that we only have room for one in every seven qualifying for entrance, our selection methods have to be stringent, and as a result we are able to recruit a most able and hard-working set of entrants. It is not altogether surprising that the difficulty of entrance together with the Malawian work ethic produces students who very rarely fail the courses. It was one of my complaints that students are over-assessed and tested during their time with us, but the general view of the local staff is that as they were treated in that way and survived, why should today's students not be subjected to similar rigours? The method certainly works in terms of the results at the end of the year, and we have good reason to believe that the standards attained have international status.

On the one hand it is our policy that all subject areas have external examiners normally from abroad, and these are carefully selected not only for their academic record but also for their knowledge of standards in other countries both in Africa and beyond. These examiners do provide comprehensive and critical reports, and almost without exception they are highly complimentary about the standards being attained. In order to give the staff more of a chance to learn of subject developments elsewhere we do encourage these visitors to stay for a week or more in order to fulfil their second role as academic advisors. The reports they produce are taken very seriously, and discussed at departmental, faculty and committee level, and in particular, any adverse comments are thoroughly debated with those affected by them. We also encourage external examiners to write directly to the Vice-Chancellor if they have particular matters of concern which they would like to keep confidential. I only ever received one such report!

Some of the better students can be appointed as staff associates on graduation, and interviewing these gifted young people who are normally most articulate is one of the greatest academic pleasures we experience. The more fortunate among these will be sent abroad immediately, mostly to Britain, to take a course at Masters' level. It is another indicator of the standard attained at graduation that such students will be able to take the Masters' degree successfully without requiring any more time than postgraduates from British Universities will need. The preparation they have received from Malawi is equivalent to that in Britain.

There is a quirk in the selection process which has a positive as well as an immediately negative consequence. During my first months I received a directive from Government on how to select students for the University. Having read it quickly, I told the Registrar that this would not work. Later I made the same comment, giving reasons to the Ministry of Education, but the common response was that we should still give it a try. In fact the directive was a political resolution which the officials were fearful of disobeying.

The basic proposal was that while the selection would continue on academic merit, interpreted in the normal manner as performance at the MCE examination, there had to be in addition, an even spread of places across the country. This is a concept which is used in other developing countries, and it is difficult to find fault with this interpretation of equal opportunities when it is recognised that through the inequalities of colonial government, some areas will have been disadvantaged educationally relative to others.

However, the way in which the places were to be distributed, according to this ruling, was a clear discrimination against the North. Prior to this directive, places at the University were distributed in equal shares between the three Regions, and our statistics showed that although the population of the North was much lower than the other two, students from this Region obtained over 35% of the degrees and diplomas. The new regulation would mean that the North would in future have its quota of the intake reduced from 33% to about 15% at most.

It would have helped the instigators of this new plan if the performance of students from the North had conveniently declined, but unfortunately the first year we operated the system, the reverse happened. In fact if we had been allocating places on merit alone that year, the North would have received about 40% of these.

When the University Council met to decide on the allocation, I had a prior meeting with the Chairman in which I pointed out to him that we simply could not turn away students whose performance in any year before this would have put them among the first to be chosen. He accepted the point and agreed to do what we could, but the solution which he proposed and was naturally accepted, was that we make use of the newly introduced policy that students could live outside the campus, and give these extra places to these students from the North. It did mean that the Region now received 22% of the places, well above the new quota, but well below what they had been accustomed to or deserved on merit. Further, it was a hardship to live outside the campus, as the University had not yet worked out the financial implications of this mode of attendance.

There was however one positive aspect of the matter. The converse of well qualified students being denied access was that students fortunate enough to come from Districts of lesser ability, obtained places which on strict merit they were not entitled to, and yet at the end of the year, there appeared no significant difference in performance by these students relative to the better qualified at intake. The deduction I drew from this, and used publicly as a further argument for the expansion of the University, was that if students of this lower calibre of entry performance were still able to succeed, then if we were able to expand and offer many more places, the successful rate of graduation would not be affected.

I tried to make a point of meeting with students at their Colleges and invited questions to help understand how they perceived the University, and through these gatherings it was possible to anticipate and take action on a number of issues. There was

82

always an element of restraint at these meetings as with staff meetings also since the general repression in Malawi does not encourage people to speak freely on any issue. Just occasionally a student would confide in me that he belonged to an alternative and therefore illegal party, but generally political thinking, and following that, most attempts to be creative were considered too risky. The Party might have its reporters anywhere, and students unnaturally had to keep their thinking to themselves. However, such thinking cannot be suppressed indefinitely, and it is gratifying to learn that students from the University have joined freely in the movement for democracy along with the bishops and the trade-unionists. There has already been persecution of the students with Chancellor College in 1992 closed for the first time in its history.

In my time we were able to maintain the record of the University never closing throughout its twenty-five years of existence. I claim no credit for this; clearly the causes of this unusual record of 'discipline' were factors outside my ability to influence. The price to pay for this record was the suppression of any political thinking. I was left to meditate on the paradox that while one could easily deplore this unnatural repression among young people, at least we could get on with the job. While students in more democratic countries not far from Malawi seemed to be perpetually at odds with the University and national authorities, and constantly suffering closures, missing whole years, sometimes receiving military intervention, our students worked on without hindrance and graduated in the normal time with good degrees in areas of vital importance to the development of the nation.

I cannot answer the paradox. There must be some middle way whereby a University can be creative, disciplined and productive. In Malawi we scored two out of three.

Chapter Six
The Donors

An important, enjoyable, frustrating and absorbing part of the Vice-Chancellor's job in Malawi is to seek support from the variety of international donors for the University. It is a task which gives scope for initiative and enterprise, and opens up a new world of interaction. Sometimes it is successful and the University gains much, and sometimes four years of hard canvassing and form filling leads nowhere.

It is however a necessary job, because in a relatively poor country there is barely enough money to pay the staff and supply basic necessities. To provide that quality without which higher education can be virtually useless, the additional funds have to be sought elsewhere. This task becomes possible because in the third world there are numerous organisations, international and multi-national who have funds and are willing to help.The art is to locate the right donor for the particular project you have in mind, and then win their confidence that if supported you are able to make good use of the provision. This is the pleasant part of the dealing as it usually involves policy discussions with ambassadors and mission directors, relating the needs of the University to the interests of the donor. The harder and more bureaucratic aspect is then to convince Government, through whom the formal request has to come, to give your proposal priority over other national claimants to the funding available.

As with any enterprise of salesmanship/begging, the first thing is to make yourself known, and I decided to start with the Embassies. The countries which will have Embassies is in direct relation to the foreign policy of the host nation. External affairs was always one of the personal portfolios taken on by the President, the others being Agriculture, Works and Supplies, and Justice. In pursuing his overall policy of good neighbourliness with contact and dialogue as the way to solve problems, he had made what was for that time, a rather unusual bunch of friends.

As a pro-westerner who had rejected anything to do with Communism, his leading friends included Britain, U.S.A., France and Germany. Nearer to home there were the neighbouring countries of Zambia, Zimbabwe, and later Mozambique as relations with Malawi which at one time were tense, had now much improved. The President had early on rejected the overtures of mainland China, and consequently made firm friends with the Republic of China, Taiwan. He also had good relations with South Korea at a time when this nation was generally not popular, but oddly still maintained a link with North Korea.

At the time of the 1973 Middle East crisis and the subsequent oil boycott, most African countries were persuaded to break off all ties with Israel. But Dr. Banda insisted that Israel had never done Malawi any harm, and he would not have his foreign policy dictated by others, so almost alone among the more than forty African nations, there remained an Israeli Embassy in Malawi.

Even more controversially, Malawi was the only black African country to have diplomatic ties with South Africa. At the time of Independence, the President wanted to build a new capital city at Lilongwe, more to the centre of the country than Zomba, the colonial capital, or Blantyre, the largest city. Finding the British and others unwilling to finance the operation, he turned to South Africa for help, and obtained what he wanted. He used to state that while apartheid was loathed as much in Malawi as anywhere else, the best way to obtain change was by maintaining contact and dialogue rather than confrontation and sanctions, and to a certain extent this policy has been vindicated. South African Presidents at the worst times would listen to Banda, and his conciliatory views probably did as much to cause the eventual downfall of apartheid as the more direct methods of others. He would add that Malawi always related openly with South Africa, while the other front line states did so secretly, as he put it, like Nicodemus, coming only by night.

The idiosyncratic selection of friends implies at the same time the selection of those who will not be friends, and this determined the Embassies not to be found in Lilongwe. Since Israel was there, there would be no Arab countries. Since South Africa was there then the Nordic countries were not present. The entire Eastern bloc, the Arab world and most of the rest of Africa with the exception of the neighbours and Egypt, were left out, and including India, there were twelve Embassies to relate to.

So early in my first month, I made appointments to visit the Ambassadors of South Korea and Israel. I had never met any sort of Ambassador before, and did not know quite what to expect. In the event there was no need to worry. It is a necessary function of an Ambassador to make visitors welcome, and it was always a pleasure to meet with any of them.

The first call was on the Korean Ambassador. I charged in with the shopping list I had worked out – hostels, computers, scientific equipment, library books, sports gear, etc. Well, this was all new to me, and I learned very quickly that this is not the way to do business. The poor man whose tour was coming to an end quite soon, just nodded at the mention of each request. I discovered afterwards that his English was not too good, so he probably had understood very little of my ideas to boost the University.

Keyed up by this first triumph, which in reality led to nothing except maybe some calculators, I moved on through heavy security to meet the Israeli Ambassador. Here I was met by Zev Dover who with his wife Alisa became very good friends in the year in which we overlapped. He opened the door and all in one breath it seemed, gave me his opening greeting, 'welcome, welcome, I knew your predecessor well, we are a poor country, we cannot give help to anyone, please sit down.'

Clearly I had to forget about my shopping list with this man and instead we talked about Israel. He told me about his part in the

Entebbe raid when he was in Kenya; he told me with great relish how as a young boy in 1947 he had hidden weapons in his shirt to use against the British; and then we talked about his country's remarkable achievements in irrigation, and how useful this might be to Malawi if the Lake could be utilised for this purpose. We did later manage to set up a meeting between Israeli and Malawian Water Engineers at Bunda College, but primarily we valued the friendship and advice which Zevy gave to us. I could ask any question about Israeli policy and always receive at least a half-hour speech in response. He was most astute on Malawian politics too, and I am grateful for the moderating advice he freely gave me which as much as anything enabled me to complete the four year contract without it ending prematurely.

Soon after these first meetings, we encountered the German Ambassador, Dr. Theodora van Rossum. We were fortunate to have had this privilege because Theodora was in her penultimate year as a diplomat before taking retirement. She was tall, blonde, elegant, formidable, the rare type of person you could address correctly as Your Excellency, and sometimes mean it. She was a lady of immense energy, sometimes seeming to be in different parts of the country simultaneously, and devoted to her task with a commitment that remained even to the day when she retired. Her aim was to gain as much help for Malawi as she could, and if there was any slackness in the agencies of her own country, she would go back to Bonn, and thump the tables until the poor officials would comply. As a measure of her success, I remember a day in her office when she showed me a newspaper report of current British Aid to Malawi, and told me in triumph that German Aid now exceeded this figure. Those who had been in the country longer told me it was not always like this. The assistance from Germany had not been so great until this dynamic lady came on the scene.

The other way in which she made her mark was at the official State occasions attended by the President. The custom was that invited guests, including the diplomatic corps, should be in their seats up to an hour before the great man arrived. This period of waiting time was, however, complicated by the additional time taken by the President to make his way through the crowds of adoring, dancing, singing, ululating women who, some voluntarily and willingly, others by compulsion, always barred his entrances to the major occasions. The President himself was in no hurry. He enjoyed adulation. The songs were all about himself, and the great things he had done, mostly 25 years ago, but still fresh to the faithful, and he would actually wave his fly-stick in order to conduct the singing. On occasions he would sing himself.

These spontaneous outbursts of loyalty made the prediction of waiting time complicated and precarious. It would be dangerous to attempt a late arrival at these functions based on a wrong calculation of adulation time. However, Theodora managed to solve this arrival problem, and at almost every waiting occasion as the compliants like ourselves resigned to the hour plus of inactivity, her place would be empty. Then just five minutes before the President's entry, Theodora would sweep in. The purpose of this most skilful manoeuvre was very clear. It was so that the assembly could receive the vision of Theodora's resplendent new hat. This was a most charitable gesture on her part, because the company became so uplifted by this revelation that it was now ready to face anything, even the speeches.

Towards the end of my first year in Malawi, I received a phone call from Theodora. 'Why have you not answered my letter inviting you to a conference in Berlin' boomed the voice of command. 'Because I don't think I have received one from you' I answered timidly. 'They are very stupid in Berlin. I will speak to them' she said, and I felt for whoever would receive her call. As I began to think how I could excuse myself from time out I had not planned for, she added that if I went, she could arrange for me to return via London. This sold the idea completely. I had been out of England for eleven months now, and although I felt no regret about this, the opportunity of seeing the family again, and my first grandchild, was irresistible.

We arrived in Berlin and as I was shown around the city on our first night and saw the opulence, the Christmas tinsel, the beer halls and the sex shops, the western world I had been parted from for nearly a year seemed most decadent and unattractive. But for the promise of the family visit, I would willingly have returned quickly to Africa. The one thing which I did enjoy was the extreme cold. I had no idea of the lost pleasure of being really cold, so easily taken for granted in Britain, and I went for long strolls in the grounds of the Villa Bersig where the conference was being held simply to bask in the coldness and the whiteness.

The gathering of heads of ten Southern African Universities with German and British experts to discuss staff development was successful in that it paved the way for many following conferences in Germany and Africa which for the most part proved to be effective. We later held a particularly stimulating conference at Bunda College on staff motivation with German and British support.

The time eventually came for Theodora to retire, and this was done in a grand way with parties in her honour in all the main cities, culminating in the final one in Lilongwe which lasted for twelve hours. The party in Zomba was largely taken over by Chancellor College which she had done so much to help, particularly on the Arts side. The musicians even composed a song 'Theodora, we'll miss you', and seldom can an ambassador have so won the hearts of a people to have been given this type of send off. I do not know what her former excellency is doing now, but I am sure she is still excellent.

Inevitably the Embassy I had the most to deal with was the British. This was due to my natural affinity, the extent of British Aid, particularly with supplemented posts for the University, and the number of organisations concerned. There was in Lilongwe, the British Council, the British High Commission and the British Development Division for Southern Africa. These three organisations overlapped to a certain extent, and I don't think I ever grasped the actual difference of function. Almost invariably if I wrote to one, it turned out it should have been one of the other two. Eventually I would send copies of my correspondence to all three in the hope of striking the right target sometimes.

Because of the relative shortness of the tour, I overlapped with three successive High Commissioners. I will only mention the middle one of these, Denis Osborne, since we had three full years at the same time, did much work together, and met with our families on numerous social occasions. Denis was not a career diplomat; in fact he was an academic who had lectured in Physics at a number of African Universities, so that he was a constant and welcome visitor to our four Colleges. Before coming to Malawi he had been a Professor at University College London and then worked in the Overseas Development Administration (ODA) in

London. It was probably an advantage not to have been a professional diplomat since Denis was able to bring new ideas to the work and achieve much through the new energy he brought to this potentially major position. Equally, Christine Osborne proved to be no conventional diplomat's wife, and one of her achievements was to set up a national toy-making competition to stimulate children to play more in a creative manner.

One of my first contacts with Denis was an arithmetical one, an interest in which we had much in common. I had just received through the post from London, a glossy booklet on British Aid to Southern African countries. It all looked most impressive, but I have this unpleasant habit that whenever I see a set of figures, I look for another set from a related area to divide into them, and see if anything significant comes out. In this case it was easy to do something interesting. Given the total aid over the last five years to Botswana, Lesotho, Swaziland, Malawi, Tanzania, Zambia and Zimbabwe, what could be more natural than to do what the pamphlet had not done, and just divide these totals by the respective populations of the countries? I did this and obtained the answer I had anticipated which was that in terms of aid per head of population, Malawi was at the bottom of the list and well down on the second worst treated country. Further when I investigated the statistics to see if this might have been because of Malawi's greater wealth, I found on the contrary that in terms of GNP, per head of population, Malawi was the lowest of the seven.

Denis was grateful for this information and said it would help make the case better in London. Whether or not these facts were used, Denis showed great energy in bringing more aid to Malawi, and I think in overtaking German aid again. I asked him why he thought Malawi had been so badly treated relative to the other countries when unlike others in this list, it had never threatened to leave the Commonwealth, and had even sent boxers to the 1986 Commonwealth Games which most of the others had boycotted. He replied that it just illustrates the way we treat our friends.

We did not always agree on issues of aid, and I recall one issue I took up with him where I still think there is a general case to be made. It arose out of an interview Denis gave to the *Daily News* in which he talked about the 200 scholarships being awarded for Malawians to study in Britain at a total cost of twelve million kwachas. What struck me when I read this figure of twelve million, was that this was almost exactly the annual recurrent budget of the University, and we educated two thousand students for this money.

So I wrote to Denis to ask if it would not be much more effective if the money, or a substantial proportion of it, could be used instead to build up the local University so that it would not be necessary to send so many of our students to Britain. As this example showed, we could be ten times more cost effective, and this ought to please the British tax-payer as much as the country receiving the extra benefit.

I took up the same issue with the British over the Medical School. As will be described in a later chapter, starting in 1986, twenty students per year were sent to study pre-clinical medicine in Britain at an average cost, I discovered of 11,000 pounds sterling. These students were intended to stay in Britain for three years so that after a time there would be three cohorts totalling sixty students, at a cost of 660,000 pounds per year. My argument was that if this flow of funds could be diverted to Malawi, it could go a long way, using local prices to build our own Medical School.

To my regret I soon discovered that the officials Denis referred this question to, took a negative view which suggested to me that the purpose of much of British Aid, and this goes for other aiding countries too, is to aid the donor as much as the receiver country. In particular it seemed a useful device to divert funds through the Foreign Office to help support the underfunded British Universities. However I remain idealistic enough to still believe that the best use of aid is to build local infrastructures rather than to spend it much less effectively on British institutions and individuals.

The second great British institution in Malawi was, as ever, the British Council. This particular branch of the Council played a major role in promoting British culture through its regular programme of films, exhibitions, plays and individual performers as well as the popular daily films of Britain in the library. The Council paid for short-term scholarships and visits to Britain, and for prominent British visitors to come here. We received some memorable visits from musicians, actors, historians, computer scientists, and as I describe in another chapter, a significant visit by John Ashworth then of Salford University. One of my unfulfilled ambitions was to persuade the Council to bring over a British Chess Master to help develop the very enthusiastic players at the University, but I hope this has been achieved after my departure.

The British Council was also responsible for the link arrangements we had with a number of British Institutions, which normally led to an annual exchange of staff visits. In a national University where travel abroad is not easy, and academic contacts are few, it was always a great encouragement to work with staff from abroad through these links. Mention has already been made of the Bunda link with Aberystwyth which had lasted successfully for over twenty years, and the Huddersfield link with the Polytechnic. In addition to these we had a Nursing connection with Ulster University, Economics with Bath and Biology with Newcastle Universities. It is only fair to add that we had other connections with Universities in the U.S.A., France, and Switzerland, but because of the regular financial commitment provided by the British Council, these links seemed to continue and endure long enough to build up significant relationships at both institutional and personal levels.

The third member of the trio, the British Development Division in Southern Africa, the local arm of the ODA, became more prominent to us at the time of the triennial visits. I have referred to one such visit shortly after my arrival, in January, 1987. Now three years on in January 1990 we were due for the next visit.

This review was, with one exception a great success. As has been mentioned, British aid to the University focused on what they considered to be the developmental areas, in our case, Engineering, Accountancy, Business, Mathematics, Computing and Science Education. We were able to demonstrate that good progress had been made in all these areas, with considerable increases in student intake, and excellent examination performances. The report issued by the visitors was most encouraging. They indicated that the University was being very well managed with strong performance indicators such as the input-output ratio of intake to number of graduates, and promised to step up aid to over one million pounds per year through additional supplemented staff, scholarships in Britain at the rate of ten per year, with books and equipment to support.

This was all wonderful news, but I have to mention the one

exception, and that was that it took so long to materialise. I left Malawi a year after this visit, and several months even after that I was remonstrating with BDDSA about just when these promises were going to be put into practice. I understand that now most components are in place but as I discovered from colleagues who were supplemented by ODA, this is an organisation which moves slowly and with much bureaucracy.

Then there was Dr. Feng, the Ambassador from the Republic of China, Taiwan, by far the longest serving diplomat in Malawi. It was always pleasant to call on him in Lilongwe and drink tea together. The conversation was always of a general nature, and if it ever drifted towards help for the University, Dr. Feng's understanding of English seemed to take a sudden change for the worse. We used to receive a weekly news bulletin from Taiwan which focused on the remarkable economic growth and prosperity of the land. Whenever there was a piece about computers, usually to underline prowess as the third highest producer of microcomputers after the Americans and Japanese, I would write a note to Dr. Feng congratulating him on the achievement, and asking in so many words if there might be any to spare from the annual production of over two million. The same applied if there were an article on aid to developing countries, and eventually the tactic worked. The Faculty of Engineering has now been given a number of computers by the Chinese for use in Computer Aided Design. The Chinese took a great interest in Agriculture, fully funding a lecturer at Bunda College, and to the great delight of the students at Chancellor College, brought over, every year, a troupe of young singers, dancers and acrobats to perform in the Great Hall.

The last Ambassador I will mention was the South African, George Stroebel. I took the view that as Malawi had good diplomatic relations with South Africa, and my job was to do all I could to help build up the University of Malawi, it was quite legitimate to seek aid from this source as well. So I made an appointment to call on the then new South African Ambassador. I took to George immediately. Although confined to a wheel-chair through an accident, he still moved very swiftly round the room, and as I discovered soon afterwards, he also moved round Malawi most rapidly, contributing to and initiating many aid programmes.

He proved to be immediately helpful to us, contributing

books and prizes, and arranging for short term visits to R.S.A. by members of the University. I benefited from the first of these, and in the course of ten days visited the Universities of Stellenbosch, Cape Town, Witwatersrand, Pretoria, Medunsa, Vista and the University of South Africa. This was a stimulating visit because in late 1989 one could sense change in the air. De Klerk, the formerly mistrusted Minister of Education, and often the target for University protests had become President and immediately started on his process of radical change. He had begun to talk to leaders like Buthelezi and Tutu, declared that apartheid was a dead policy, and started to release the ANC political prisoners. There was the suggestion that one day even Mandela might be set free. An unexpected but most moving moment for me was when I touched down at Jan Smuts airport on the way from Cape Town to Pretoria, and arrived at just the same time as Walter Sisulu and eight other long term prisoners who had just been released. The joy of the hundreds who had assembled to greet these now quite old men was something very precious; and as The Economist put it, what a stroke of totally undeserved luck for the South African Government that these men who had suffered for so long, turned out to be so mellow and constructive in helping to work towards new understanding, and paving the way for the release of Nelson Mandela a few months later.

The experience of going round the South African Universities was stimulating in many ways. The thinking in these places about the future South Africa was years ahead of the Government. The Universities had suffered both from the cultural boycott for which they were not to blame, and from the withdrawal of funding as one consequence of the Sanctions campaign, but still in the case of Cape Town and Witwatersrand and probably others, funds had been found from somewhere to finance special programmes for disadvantaged black students. In both the vigour of the academic programmes and the innovative ideas of administration, the isolation from the rest of the academic world did not appear to have weakened the Universities, and I returned to Malawi with an abundance of new ideas. I also returned with a refreshed view of South Africa. There are immense problems to be solved, entrenched attitudes to be changed, fundamental economic, political and sociological questions to be answered, but the fact that these exist and real attempts are being made to solve them, makes the country to my mind, one of the most exciting in the world. The potential which this country has for leadership in this most disadvantaged region of sub-Saharan Africa is enormous, and what has for years been a source of oppression, of destabilisation, of enmity could become a haven of peace, of blessing and prosperity for its long-suffering neighbours. It is significant that among all races there is much revival among the churches, and as the vast human resources are released from the need to battle with one another, to cooperate in building a unique new country, there is despite all appearances to the contrary, a real hope for South Africa.

There is here an immense spiritual struggle and the country is in tremendous need of prayer support. The forces of destruction are clearly evident, and in this pointless violence we can see the legacy of apartheid, the work of darkness in opposing the progress which undoubtedly is being made. There will clearly be much pain in bringing about the so-called new South Africa, but of two most moving books on the subject, I believe in the cautious optimism of Michael Cassidy's *The Politics of Love* rather than the resigned pessimism of Rian Malan's *My Traitor's Heart*.

In addition to the Embassies, there are the International Agencies whose influence and assistance are often greater than that of the friendly countries. Among these the first place must go to the World Bank, for not only is this potentially the largest supplier but also the most influential on the other donors. My recollection of the Bank is the contrast between my almost continual arguments over its policies and the very good friendships we made with their representatives. There was initially the difference over the value of third-world tertiary education which we encountered in Harare, and the themes discussed here seemed to reappear in subsequent visits from the Bank, especially when Mrs. Shields, their mission leader from Nigeria, insisted that the student loan scheme must go ahead, on penalty of all Bank Aid to Malawi coming to an abrupt end! Over the years we argued about Education and the proposed Medical School but we developed a very good relationship, and eventually Mrs. Shields was persuaded that the next major Bank loan for the Education sector would go largely towards the building up of the University. Unfortunately for both of us who now shared a view of the great potential of the

University, this could not happen until 1993, some time after I had finished.

Then there was the UNDP which supported projects and provided staff in the areas of Demography and Statistics, financed the Community Health Department of the Medical School, and during my last two years we were negotiating a million dollar deal which would have provided laboratory and computing equipment, grants for poorer students and funds for differential staff salaries. These are all most worthy causes, but I was particularly interested in the latter one as this seemed about the only hopeful source of supply. It is a most difficult problem but one which must be tackled by Universities like Malawi. As a University which I believe rightly aspired to have a strong vocational component, we faced the problem of not being able to offer competitive salaries in certain subject areas. This was particularly the case in disciplines like Accountancy, Computing and some branches of Engineering where the private sector was able to offer two or even three times our salaries. In order to ensure that we retained a minimum number of staff in these areas, and that these were not all expatriates or those who could not secure jobs in their own profession, it was necessary to take some action, and to do so in a way which would not cause resentments among staff in less financially rewarding areas. The first approximation to a solution was to liberalise our rules on consultancies and provision of short courses, the idea being that the greatest demand for these type of services would come from the wealthier types of profession so that those teaching the corresponding subjects would have a natural salary differential over the others, and which would be a function of how well regarded they were by fellow professionals. The second line, since this first approach could only partially solve the problem, was to seek additional funding not from within our own resources but from an outside source, and who better than an organisation like UNDP to express an interest in the continuation of such vocational disciplines being presented. I can only hope my colleagues have been able to follow through on the idea.

I would also mention briefly our other international donors such as DSE (Germany) who took an interest in staff development, and in addition to the Berlin conferences, financed a number of workshops in Southern Africa, including an excellent week at

Bunda College; VVOB (Belgium) who provided a number of fully-funded staff including the whole of the Classics Department; NUFFIC (Netherlands) who worked with staff at Chancellor College to provide an in-service programme planned to reach all Secondary School teachers of Mathematics and Science; the U.S.Peace Corps who provided at one time up to twelve short-term lecturers in a variety of shortage areas of work. The way I negotiated this particular deal set up one of my major differences with the Chairman of Council, but these volunteers proved to be so able, experienced professionally and well motivated that I felt it was well worth this altercation, especially as their salaries cost the University nothing! The French, German, and Chinese Governments as well as the Church of Scotland each supplied a fully funded lecturer in a field of their choice, and in another chapter I tell about how three sports coaches were provided by the Southern Baptists of the U.S.A.

Among all the aid provided we had at one stage almost thirty members of academic staff working for us at no cost other than housing for the University. I greatly appreciated the combined efforts of all our friends without whose help our performance would have been greatly diminished, but of all these donors the one I would single out as the most helpful of all was the USAID (United States Agency for International Development), and I do this not so much for the quantity which was considerable, but for the way in which they went about it. I refer elsewhere to the way in which they had the Bunda Road built for us, but here I would like to describe their Human Resources and Institutional Development scheme referred to as HRID which seemed to me a model way of providing aid to a developing country.

First a team of consultants visited the country in late 1987 whose purpose was to assess the major professional needs in both the public and private sectors. This was followed by a discussion document produced by Richard Shortlidge, the Deputy Director of the Mission in Malawi, and now the Director in Namibia. The document analysed the professional needs as reported by the consultants, discussed training and other support requirements to help these professions identified as being mainly in Accountancy, Agriculture, Engineering and Technology, but distinguishing between those which certainly should be supported and those considered of lesser importance but for which a case could be made. The essence of the programme was that a sum had been agreed with the Government, $18 million over an eight year period, and under certain guidelines defined in the document, institutions would make bids to gain funds for particular projects. The great advantages were that since the overall sum had already been agreed, there was no need to convince Government Ministries each time a new project was proposed, and that any such proposal was scrutinised and assessed by a peer group which included representatives of USAID, Government and the relevant sector. There was to be bidding and competition for funds which were known to be available, and this seemed to me a more satisfactory way of doing business than the chancy, arbitrary and often undeserved way in which other donor funds were often allocated. A further advantage of a bid led system is that evaluation is always possible, and the ways of procedure can be improved in the light of experience.

There were also a few gifts in the script. One of the resolutions in the defining document was that there should be support for women to enter into any of the professions, and this was to be achieved by offering scholarships to women students in non-traditional subject areas at the University. Since there could be no competitors for this award, I put in a bid as soon as the scheme was declared open. The only difficulty we had was in determining precisely what was a non-traditional area. Engineering clearly qualified as up to this point we had never had a woman student in this field, but beyond that we had some difficulty. Eventually we had over sixty women in the scheme, about a third of them in Engineering, and each year we had a most pleasant and well publicised ceremony in which the lady Director of USAID came to present the students with their awards. One unexpected by-product of this project was that when we started an M.Sc. in Applied Chemistry, the difficulty that it was hard to find enough students who could be sponsored, was overcome by providing qualified women students through this scheme, and this valuable programme was able to begin.

Among other projects we were able to launch through HRID, we made a study of the place of women in national development. An expert was recruited from America to lead the scheme, we organised a national conference bringing together all those concerned, and followed by introducing a Masters' programme in this new subject. We were able to identify long and short term scholarships abroad for staff in the Colleges of Agriculture and Nursing with staff replacements from America while they were away, and again with American help, strengthened the Economics Department to offer a wider range of options to undergraduates and design a new M.A. in Economics. It was through this HRID scheme that we were able to do the Tracer Study of our former graduates which is described elsewhere.

Another idea I had formulated early on was the need for postgraduate conversion courses. In particular I was concerned that students were withdrawing from the Humanities Faculty for what they considered to be lack of job opportunities, and at the same time the country had an acute shortage of personnel in certain vital professions like Accountancy and Marketing. The idea was to offer one year professional courses in these subjects to graduates from areas of lesser employment opportunity. The conversion course could only be a starter into a new vocation, but employers welcomed the idea since the students they would receive already had a good general education as opposed to narrowly specialising in these fields. This would have remained simply an idea if it had not been possible through HRID to obtain the funding to put it into practice.

The means of operating HRID was to contract it to the American company who made the best case, and this award went to A.E.D., the Association for Educational Development. Their team was led by Dr. Rudi Klauss, who became a good friend and associate in the implementation of the plan. Rudi would visit us at the University with his team every three months in order to discuss the progress of the various components and help with any problems. He also arranged for evaluation teams to come from the U.S.A. and investigate progress in some depth. We did not always agree with their assessments, but it is always an incentive to know that your work is arousing sufficient interest for evaluation to be taken seriously.

There were inevitably some disappointments in working with the scheme. We had been hoping to launch a much needed MBA programme to support the business sector in the country and made considerable efforts following the visit of a consultant to interact with the private sector, and determine what was required. However, the evaluation team concluded that the University was not yet ready to take the responsibility of the considerable financial support which would be needed to operate effectively at this level, and we had to accept this ruling.

I was also concerned because when I first read the HRID scheme, I concluded immediately that here was virtually a script written for the development of the Polytechnic, and yet as will be seen from the examples given above, very little was received apart from the women's scholarships and the conversion courses, both submitted by myself. The sad fact is that the staff did not stir themselves in time to take this opportunity, and when they did eventually start to put cases, the money had already gone, much of it to the more enterprising approach taken by Chancellor College.

Despite these setbacks I believe that HRID was an outstanding success, and a good example of how aid should be distributed. The system assured that funds went only to the more enterprising, those most able to use it effectively and benefit from it. The continuous monitoring and evaluation ensured that funding was not wasted. I only wish that ten times as much money could have been made available. It certainly could have been used by the many organisations who put in some very ambitious bids once they had realised the value of HRID.

I would not complete the chapter without referring to some of our more local donors. I have already mentioned the generosity of Mobil Oil who opened a trust fund to help Mechanical Engineering, virtually the week I started at the University, and in the course of time other industrialists gave comparable support. There was a very popular fund to support students in need, once at World Bank insistence, a fee of two hundred kwachas per year had to be paid. It was comparatively easy to obtain funds from companies and embassies for this purpose, and several individual enterprises to raise funds were undertaken.

A relatively small donation could also be used effectively if well managed. We received a new gift of five thousand kwachas a year from an insurance company, and this was used by the Mathematics Department to organise a national olympiad for schools, and launch a magazine with the residual funds!

Also we discovered that there are many organisations which

support research especially in developmental areas, and to take our research out into this sort of field as opposed to the ill-funded individualistic efforts which had earlier been the norm, we set up a Research Office and internally seconded a member of staff to run it. It was most fortunate that we had Dr. David Munthali, the Head of Biology, to take on this task, as he worked with great enthusiasm and ability to both encourage staff from all parts of the University to widen their thinking about research, and to visit the supporting agencies to tell them what our staff were able to do. As a result, research became much more active in the very areas which were needed in the country, and with the help of agencies like the Rockefeller Foundation, IDRC (Canada), the McArthur Foundation, the African Biosciences network, ICLARM, the EEC and UNHCR, several million kwachas worth of research funding has flowed into the University.

For the present, donor funding has largely been withdrawn, until human rights are restored and multi-party democracy is permitted. The country badly needs this aid from the donors, and one consequence of the withdrawal already being felt, is that many committed people are leaving as their contracts expire. However, this is a burden that will willingly be borne by the great majority of Malawians who long for change to come, and this withdrawal seems at present the best way to influence the Government to take some positive action on these two vital issues. When this has been achieved, it is my hope that the donor support will be strongly restored. There are few countries which under wise, democratic leadership will be better able to respond effectively to the right kind of donor aid.

Chapter Seven
John

The last three chapters related to matters of general interest; the next four will offer character studies of individual people, three Malawian and one English. Our first study introduces John, a young Malawian, who we came to know very well. He had nothing to do with the University, but his story typified for us the problems faced by the great majority of Malawians who have no chance of entry to University or even of escape from the bondage of poverty.

The pastor at Zomba Baptist introduced me to John after an evening service in October 1987. John was in his early thirties, one of the church leaders, entrusted as a preacher and song-leader in the main church at Zomba, and as an itinerant in the neighbouring villages. He conversed well in English, but as we talked it became clear that John was in very deep trouble. It was also apparent to me that Veronica was much better at handling problems of this magnitude, so I introduced John to her to work out some sort of solution.

John had been working recently as a barman at the Government Hostel in Zomba. It had been discovered that a sum of sixty-eight kwachas was missing from the till. John had been held responsible, dismissed from the job, and threatened with police action if the money, equivalent to a month's salary for him, was not returned. Further, as he was no longer an employee, the accommodation provided with the job had to be surrendered.

We therefore encountered him at a time of great need. He had a wife, Keltha, and five children aged between eight months and eight years to support without home or employment and the threat of prison if the debt could not be paid. The type of employment he would need was very scarce at the best of times, and after dismissal for dishonesty, virtually impossible. The church was naturally aware of his problems, and had decided to help by loaning him the money to pay back the alleged debt. I have to add that this was not a unanimous decision among members of the church, several of whom were not in sympathy with this disposal of a relatively large sum from the somewhat frugal funds.

We retained an ambivalent view of John's guilt in this affair. Certainly his employers had no doubt about it, and official letters of dismissal and eviction followed. It was easy to see how John might have been framed or betrayed by colleagues, a regrettably not uncommon occurrence in Malawi, but no evidence was available to support such a proposition, and we never pursued this line. Instead we felt that, guilty or otherwise, here was a brother in great need, and so we concentrated on the immediate problems of finding a house and a job for this very needy family. We soon discovered incidentally that this debt was almost certainly not the only one troubling John at the time.

The housing problem was not too difficult to solve. There was a vacant house in our staff quarters, and the family were able to move in immediately on a temporary basis. We found a gardening job for John with an expatriate who most regrettably took advantage of his predicament to extract the maximum work for the minimum pay; consequently this arrangement lasted for only two weeks.

At this point of renewed crisis, Veronica had an idea. Noticing John's very good command of English, she asked him if he thought he could teach her Chichewa, the language spoken by most Malawians. We had by then struggled for nearly a year trying to learn this language without much success. My excuse was lack of motivation since the people at the University always spoke to me in English, but Veronica had made many contacts with Malawians through her work with pastors' wives at the Theological College, through the church and the house, and particularly in the market where she was determined to talk to Malawians whether they spoke English or not. We were using a good textbook but could not find a teacher who met our needs, so Veronica asked this relatively unschooled and certainly unqualified Malawian to be our personal tutor.

John proved to be a quite outstanding teacher. He was patient with our difficulties, answered all our questions and had a deep command of his own language so that he was as helpful in grammar and structure as in vocabulary and culture, and the way Chichewa is actually spoken. Soon Veronica was able to have real conversations in Chichewa, and I started to learn the language again. The teaching was so good that we found other pupils for John, and he was able to put together quite a respectable weekly wage from his lessons.

I would make the point here that it is extremely difficult to learn an African language, and most expatriates seemed to give up the struggle quite early or in many cases never began at all. Some heroic efforts were made, mainly by missionaries and farmers, but the majority made little progress. I never reached even conversational mode, but found the little study I made of benefit in two different ways. On the one hand it made me appreciate better the converse problem of Malawians who have to master the English language to advance educationally. Very few children will come from homes where English is spoken, yet from the first year of primary education, English has to be learnt so that by the end of standard eight, when the leaving certificate is taken, all examinations must be written in English. The achievements in mastering English as a second language, particularly the standards achieved in the writing of poetry, were a constant marvel, and the general performance of University students subjected throughout their studying lives to this learning handicap, a cause for much satisfaction.

The second benefit is that even a low level study of Chichewa can give insight into the conduct of a conversation. I noticed early on that Malawians experienced some difficulty of comprehension whenever I asked a question, and then discovered that in Chichewa a question is quite deliberately signalled in advance. Having learned this through an elementary study of the language, I had to try and amend my dialogue accordingly, and especially to re-phrase the type of complicated question I was in the habit of asking at interviews.

John and his family settled into the quarters and related well to our staff, and in our own developing relationship we learnt about his earlier life. His education came to an end half way through secondary school when he had caused a girl to become pregnant. Under the harsh Malawian discipline on this issue, the girl is immediately suspended from the school, and so with equal justice is the boy responsible. John never returned to formal education after this, and he drifted around various jobs, developing a serious drinking problem. At some time in this stage of his life he had a Christian conversion experience and after joining a Baptist church, sought training for the ministry. However, the pregnancy which led to an unwanted marriage and then divorce (before meeting his present wife), prevented him, through church discipline, from acceptance for such training. Instead, he made himself useful as a layman and he was given various responsibilities in church leadership.

We discovered a number of other potential talents in him, and I offer a few examples. The American Baptist Missionary in Zomba, Rendall Day, is a keen and able sportsman, and he introduced basketball and long distance running to the church. For a time, the Zomba Baptist running club was one of the top national teams. Unlike other high altitude African countries, Malawi had not shown much prowess in track and field events, but it is beginning to show promise in long distance running. John was one of Rendall's discoveries in this area, and he began to run full marathons in competitive events with some success.

Unaccompanied choral singing is a major pastime in Malawi. One of the highlights of the year in Zomba is the Choral Workshop held at Easter in Chancellor College. Under an agreement with the German Government, the conductor, Dr. Alexander Sumski, from Tubingen University, came to Malawi each year beginning in 1985 in order to develop Malawian music. From his first visit it became clear that the best medium to work on was choral music, and so began the series of choral workshops which attracted choir leaders from all over the country. Each year the numbers attending increased to well over two hundred. The success of these workshops can be attributed not only to the major skills of our distinguished visitor but also to the dedication and enthusiasm of our American music lecturer, Mitch Strumpf, one of the great characters of the University whose unflagging service to the people of Malawi was exemplary.

The benefits of these weeks have had a multiplier effect on choirs throughout the country. New compositions were encouraged by what became an annual composers' competition and the select Nyimbo choir, chosen by Dr. Sumski from the workshop participants, has given many concerts, radio broadcasts and recordings.

John was one of the choral directors at Zomba Baptist and was delighted to have the chance to take part in the 1988 workshop. Dr. Sumski selected him for the Nyimbo choir and also used his skill in the two languages to help set some European works in Chichewa for the choir. When Dr. Sumski published the Nyimbo choir song-book in Germany, he mentioned John by name in his introduction as having been particularly helpful through his work of translation.

The lessons I received from John usually ended with a discussion of Malawian culture, and on one occasion we developed a possible new approach to religious education. The normal curriculum at school and University is based on the three main religious divisions of Christianity, Islam and African Traditional. In seeking a common basis from which these different approaches could be considered, we observed that the Chichewa language, as no doubt other neighbouring languages as well, is rich in proverbs, sayings and stories, and we concluded that this collective wisdom should form the basis of early teaching and learning. The established religions could then be explored in a more natural way, in relation to the extent that basic human needs were met. This approach also had the advantages that local culture, not normally prominent in school curricula, could be more emphasised, that children would learn by action, discussion and drama rather than as passive listeners, and contrary to most conventional approaches to education, wisdom would have a place in the curriculum.

The residence in our quarters was only temporary, and we were glad that after a few months the church found a house for the family in a village about five miles outside Zomba. This building was adjacent to a small Baptist chapel in which John would have eldership and caretaking duties. A friend from England, Neil Inkpen, who came to stay for a few weeks with us, went out to the village with John to advise him on building and sanitation. After a while Neil and I agreed that John seemed to have turned the corner and that his prospects were now quite good. He had a house, a reasonably sound job with prospects for development, a settled family, a place to exercise ministry to others, and the opportunity to expand his talents and even catch up on the education which had been so seriously disrupted. He need not be dependent on expatriate help much longer.

As part of this new independence, John continued to come and teach Chichewa to us and his other clients. However, at this time two less desirable trends were becoming increasingly apparent. One was his proneness to illness, which seemed to affect him for increasingly long periods. Sometimes he would walk the five miles to our house, a relatively short distance by his standards, and it became at once clear that he was in no state to teach, and needed to rest for some time or to be driven back home. The other trend was that despite having found a means of employment which provided wages well in excess of his previous earnings, and although some of his other pupils were treating him quite generously, he still seemed to have acute financial problems. Either he was paying off other debts unknown to us, or he was attempting a standard of living beyond his means. We found this factor increasingly troublesome, and resolved to have some sort of showdown with him about it.

Then it became apparent that the village church responsibility was not working well. Fellow elders were finding his preaching offensive, and reported the issue to Pastor Gama in Zomba. John claimed that in fact his complainants were unwilling to change their lifestyles. The only time I went to preach at this chapel, he asked me that whatever I chose for the subject I would be sure to say something against drink which he considered to be the basic problem. I followed these instructions but failed to notice any conviction among the congregation on this issue. Whatever the cause, there was no doubt of a deep division between John and his colleagues.

Early in 1989, John's illnesses were becoming more prolonged, and it was necessary to take him into the very fine Malosa Hospital just outside Zomba for two weeks to deal with his acute stomach pains. The Dutch lady doctor in charge of the hospital, who knew of our interest in John, was kind enough to make a visit to our home, and what she felt she had to tell us only confirmed what we had already begun to suspect. Tests at the hospital had shown that John was HIV positive and his condition indicated that he was in a terminal stage of AIDS. He had a very short time to live.

This was our first known personal encounter with AIDS. It was not possible at this time to give an accurate estimate of the extent of this scourge in the country, but certainly our medical friends, particularly those working in country districts, supplied a very gloomy picture, and more recent figures have demonstrated the devastation already being experienced throughout the land. It is one of the most severe problems a developing country can face, and humanly speaking there seems little prospect of defeating this devastating epidemic. However there are some signs of hope. The country is bravely responding energetically to the threat and all means are being used through education, the media, and informal networks to at least provide information and indicate precautions. The Baptist church and no doubt other denominations make the combat against AIDS a central feature of the pastoral and evangelistic programme.

In the University, where we had already suffered some deaths among staff and students, it was possible to speak to the student body to make it clear that the only real answer must lie in a universal change of lifestyle. I emphasise that this must be the generation which defeats AIDS, and that all the resources of a committed Christian life are necessary to maintain the monogamous stance which is so essential. As medical statistics indicated that a good proportion of students are STD (sexually transmitted diseases) sufferers, and therefore all the more vulnerable to this deadlier disease, then the message is all the more urgent that they do respond and change quickly. I have the great encouragement that the country is so open to the gospel of Christ, and that Christian students in particular are aware of the spiritual fight that is needed.

It has to be said, of course, that sexual transmission is not the only way this disease is passed on. There is great danger, especially in a developing country, from infected needles and contact with blood, to the extent that some hospitals already find difficulty in obtaining sufficient supplies of uninfected blood. However, sexual transmission remains the primary cause from which these others follow, and must necessarily be the focus of any campaign.

It is one thing to generalise about AIDS; it is another to see a friend dying from the disease. If we remain at the generalisation level, a first impulse is to be judgmental. Initially it was promiscuous homosexuality which caused the spread of the disease and now, especially in Africa, it is promiscuous heterosexuality that sustains it. These people have defied the laws of God and here is the judgement, so the initial impulse goes. In the case of a friend, as we found with John, the question of how the disease came and who was to blame simply does not arise; nor is it even an interesting issue. The only emotion is compassion for the sufferer. How can we best help him in these last days, and what about his family? Will his wife and then his children be affected in the same way? What sort of ministry can be given to them at times like this? How can their future living needs be met?

John died on Maundy Thursday of 1989 and was buried in his village on Good Friday. The village was only about ten miles from Zomba but the rains had been very heavy that year. The flooding which we encountered all along the route, with the need to make long detours on the road and then to wade through rivers over knee deep, meant that the day became a very long one. As at most such funerals there was much wailing and much waiting, but Pastor Gama eventually conducted the service and invited me to preach the sermon which he translated. The whole village and a busload of people we had brought from Zomba were in attendance. The coffin was carried in procession, over some rough and flooded ground, with continuous hymn-singing about two or three miles from the village to the place of burial. There was no doubt genuine grief at this early demise of a man whose chequered life had indicated signs of great promise and achievement. We could only speculate about what John might have become given more opportunity, but we still had cause to rejoice in a life brave enough to overcome the most severe set-backs, and in a man dedicated, after his earlier problems, to the service of God and his fellow man.

Mercifully, Keltha and the children did not catch the disease, and they have been provided for. Another friend in England, who had received Chichewa lessons from John while staying with us, sent money to build a house for them in her village just outside Blantyre. Veronica arranged for the transportation of all their belongings and I was able to find a catering job for Keltha at the Polytechnic.

John's life may be seen as a reflection of many of the tragedies and hardships experienced by other Malawians. The lack of funds for universal primary, let alone secondary, education prevents many from reaching their full potential, and the lack of jobs without the backing of social security causes many families to live in deep poverty, or at any rate to return to their villages and live by subsistence farming which on the whole provides the average family with food for only eight or nine months of the year.

It can also be stated that John was fortunate to find such help from the expatriate community, and even that he showed some cunning in making and retaining such contacts, most helpful to him but not available to the majority of his countrymen in similar need. On a number of occasions we needed to ask ourselves if we were being cleverly conned, and my answer would be that sometimes this was probably the case. If I had been in his position, I would have probably, out of desperation, acted in a similar way. However I have no doubt that here was a very genuine need which we were privileged to have had the opportunity to meet in a few ways. I have made no attempt to whitewash John's character nor to excuse his faults. Instead I have tried to portray something of the life of a typical Malawian, indicating something of the problems, frustrations, temptations, tragedies and triumphs of these otherwise forgotten people. In doing so we have been able to see something of the consequences of the severe lack of opportunities for talented people and the multiple problems of poverty, now compounded by the scourge of AIDS. At a personal level, from my brief acquaintance over just eighteen months, I can assert that I greatly valued John's friendship and feel that my life has been enriched through knowing him.

To round off I asked Veronica to provide a postscript. This is what she has to say. 'John Maunda was a man on his own, and because of his intelligence became alienated from his friends and jealousies were aroused. This was probably the root cause of the problems with him in his own village. But to provide continually for his family after his death was very difficult. There had to be a point when Keltha had to rely only on her own family. We had done our part. She had the basics of a house in her own village with her mother and brothers to support her and a regular job not too far away. We could only pray that she would remain in good health and maybe marry again some day.

The eldest daughter Grace was a bright girl, and by the age of ten was top of her Standard 3 class. There followed two boys named Princeton and Professor, giving some idea of John's extravagant aspirations for them, a girl named Gloria who had nearly died of measles, a deadly disease for children in Malawi, but had amazingly recovered, and completing this wonderful list of names, the youngest child, Victoria. I was really sorry not to have made more of a friend of Keltha, but lacking John's qualities and with the barriers of language and the huge disparity in material possessions, it was not possible. Instead, through the experience of learning more about the Malawian people from our friendship with this family, I was better able to enter into real fellowship with a most wonderful set of Malawian ladies in Zomba.'

Chapter Eight
Jack

When I first knew Dr. Jack Mapanje, he was Head of the English Department at the University of Malawi, but he was better known as the country's leading dissident poet. No doubt he will tell his own story, and will be able to recount it much better than I have done. However, his experience had such a great effect on our outlook on Malawi, that my own story would be incomplete without reference to Jack.

I had heard about Jack Mapanje before my first visit to Malawi. I mentioned earlier that when I learned of my short-listing for the post I was able, through the Missionary Societies, to contact David Matthews who had just completed seventeen years in the country, and he was most helpful in introducing me to this unknown place. After telling me about the most likely contenders for the Vice Chancellor's position, he added that I should try to meet Jack, who he described as Malawi's leading poet, and a man of great integrity.

I did not meet him during the interview visit, but when I made a preliminary tour the following November, he was introduced to me as the Head of the English Department. At our first conversation he warned me that as I was new to Africa, people would try to take advantage of me, and at our early meetings once I had begun the work, he took a particular concern that I should not do the wrong thing and so end my time in Malawi prematurely.

If there was any hint of trouble whose significance would not be clear to a foreigner, he would come straight to my office to advise on what to do. On one occasion there was some student misbehaviour at the performance of a play in the Great Hall. The editor of the *Daily News* was there and he made this the subject of his editorial comment the next day, not only deploring the drunken conduct, but placing it in the context of ingratitude to the President who had provided the Great Hall for the University. Jack immediately came to see me to warn that this was potentially dangerous because ingratitude to the President was considered a serious offence in Malawi and might cause the Special Branch to intervene. In the event there was no such visitation, but Jack's warning did strengthen my resolve to take the precautionary action of addressing the Chancellor College students immediately on the subject. Having done this, it is most likely that word would have got back that action had been taken, and nothing more sinister was needed.

There had been considerable public concern about the conduct of this College, and the line I took was to explain that the tolerance of such unacceptable behaviour was not in the interests of the students as a whole. If they wanted the reputation of the College to be restored, with all that might imply for their own futures, then they should ensure that such acts of hooliganism could not happen again. It was fortunate that some most responsible student leaders emerged, and from this point there was no further such overt indiscipline at the College.

I found that I could discuss a variety of academic issues with Jack, not only English but even regarding Faculties far removed from his immediate interest. In my early days I was most anxious to discover those on the staff who were ready for the type of change and progression I wanted, and Jack was one of the foremost in this connection. On each occasion he would offer me political advice. He was never disloyal to the President or Government in what he said, but most concerned to see me established in the position, so that I would not make the kind of silly mistake which in an over-sensitive country could so easily lead to the next flight home and prohibited immigrant status.

The time in which we most closely worked together was in the matter of the Parliamentary Election I have referred to earlier. In April 1987, the President dissolved Parliament and ordered a new election. Since English was the official language of Parliament, it was a necessary condition for any candidate that an examination in proficiency in English had to be passed, and, by law, the University Vice-Chancellor was the Chief Examiner. I had just returned from a conference in Harare when the Registrar gave me the news that the test had to be taken in only five days time. Fortunately Jack, as Head of English, had already been warned and he had prepared a draft test for me to see on arrival. At our first meeting we discussed the administration of the test, and we were in fairly continuous contact over the next few days which happened to be the Easter week-end. Jack explained how important it was for the University to do a really first-class job over these tests, and in particular how I must establish my own position by organising this with total efficiency. Otherwise, to use Jack's words, 'We will both have our heads cut off.'

So we worked very hard, (only breaking in my case to watch the football match against Zambia), to set, mark, and organise the despatch of papers, investigation of claims for exemption and invigilation of nearly a thousand candidates at twenty-four District centres around the country. On the examination day, everything was in place, University invigilators had been sent to all the centres, and in the evening they returned with all scripts marked and none missing. Just before midnight I had finished adjudication of the border-line cases, and prepared the results sheet in alphabetical order, which was quite an achievement as over half the candidates had surnames beginning with 'M'. In fact the whole exercise worked without error and in good time. Jack and I retained our heads for another day.

The test had eliminated about a third of the candidates, and the electorate was now able to make its choice from the remainder. All of these, of course, belonged most loyally to the Malawi Congress Party.

The next I saw of Jack was when he came to me with the first edition of the *Journal of Humanities* which he had edited. He had deliberately not included anything of his own writing, but encouraged others, mainly from the Humanities Faculty, to offer some very reputable contributions. This journal, which continued in his absence from the scene, has proved to be a most worthy representation of the University, and increasingly gains international recognition. Jack, ever cautious, told me on this occasion that creative work was becoming dangerous for him and that he intended to stick to critical writing for the time being.

Another enterprise he had initiated was a regional organisation concerned with African Language and Literature. This group had planned an international conference in Harare for September 1987, and as this seemed to be a thriving area in the University, I was glad to authorise eight of our staff, including Jack, to attend. Before he left we agreed that he would attempt to internationalise the *Journal of Humanities* so that it would have a wider circulation, range of contributors and editorial board, with the prospect of obtaining donor funding, and also set up a new journal to cover the activities of the conference.

I did not see Jack on his return, but I do recall going to Lilongwe on September 23, for an appointment with Sam Kakhobwe, the Secretary to the President and Cabinet, the head of the Civil Service, and in effect the nearest to a Prime Minister that the country had, the Cabinet having virtually no powers of its own. I always found it most stimulating to talk to Sam and when we met he always allowed up to two hours to discuss a range of issues. He was greatly interested in the University and the contribution it could make to the development of the country. He was most helpful in listening to my difficulties with some of the senior staff, suggesting how changes might be made, and it was one of my lowest moments in the country when I heard in 1989 that this most able and dedicated man had been sacked by the President over a fairly trivial matter involving relations with Lonhro, an international company with considerable economic and political influence in Southern Africa. The only consolation about his dismissal was that he was replaced by a man of comparable stature, Justin Malewezi, who was similarly removed from office in November 1991.

On this occasion Sam had asked me bluntly what was wrong with the graduates from the University. He explained that he could take on graduates for the Civil Service who had clearly passed all their examinations, but who could show no initiative at work, requiring to be told what to do all the time. I agreed totally that this was a serious educational fault which we must take to heart and work upon. In particular we agreed that our academic programmes were much too prescribed and there was little opportunity or encouragement for students to be creative. This was a difficult problem to work on, especially as it seemed to go contrary to the approach of several of our staff, and in a one-party state, thinking can be a hazardous occupation, but as Sam's criticism matched my own educational philosophy, I resolved to do what I could.

I remember this discussion very well, because only two days later, on September 25, the Registrar brought me the shattering news that Jack Mapanje had been arrested, and taken away in handcuffs from outside the University.

The shock of this arrest was one from which I never fully recovered. Here was the unacceptable face of Malawi brought right home to me. I had, of course, heard many stories of repression, of arrest and imprisonment without trial, of political prisoners detained indefinitely, even of executions and car accidents arranged by the State, and over the next few years learnt of many more atrocities in this so-called warm heart land. But to have Jack, who I knew well and greatly respected as a scholar and a true patriot of his country, taken away in this fashion, left a wound that refused to heal.

At once I wanted to visit him, to discover the charges against him, and learn when the trial would take place. I went to the local police stations and prison but could gain no information. I consulted the Chairman of the University Council, but as I describe in the next chapter, he was no help. So in view of our recent discussion, I went back to Sam Kakhobwe. I asked him how he could talk about trying to make our students more creative when one of our most creative members of staff had been taken off to gaol. He replied sadly that there was little he could do, but he did tell me a little about the arrest. I deduced from what he told me and others I consulted on the issue, that the President had received a letter, most probably anonymous, which had so infuriated him that he called immediately for the Chief of Police, the Minister of Education and himself, demanding the immediate arrest and severe punishment of Jack. The arrest had been made, the office and house of the victim searched, with the discovery of hand-written papers deemed to be subversive.

The causes of arrest, I discovered in the course of my time in Malawi, are seldom very profound. The surprise in Jack's case was that he had not been arrested earlier, for his book of poems, *Of Chameleons and Gods*, which came out in 1981 is most subversive. In his case it seemed most unlikely that this could be the cause six years later. What seems more likely was that an anonymous letter had been the cause, though as there was never a trial or even a charge made, we cannot tell.

As in Jack's case, a letter signed or otherwise, will do. It will be believed and acted upon, without too much worry about whether this might have been the invention of an enemy, particularly as jealousy is a regrettably common vice in Malawi.

I discovered a number of cases of trivial indiscretions leading to outrageous punishments. A relative of a member of staff, loyal enough to be a delegate at the annual Party convention made a silly remark about the number of palaces the President had. He was taken into prison and died there four years later. The country's only brain surgeon made a comment which had him thrown into political prison for more than two years. A lady attending an international Anglican conference at a time when she might have attended a women's political rally, was jailed indefinitely on her return. Orton Chirwa, who had worked closely with the President in the early struggle for Independence, was lured back into the country with his wife and the two have been under the worst conditions of prison for the last dozen years. Orton died recently and Vera was not even allowed to attend his funeral. Amnesty International has in the last year published many other cases of such abuses.

Malawi is not alone in its record of oppression among African countries, nor is it by any means the worst, but still the denial of human rights is appalling. Further, there is no need for it. The type of person jailed as a political prisoner is no threat at all to the state, and serves only as an example to terrify others into conformity. The policy is already acting to the detriment of the country since donor aid is increasingly being made to depend on the state of improvement in human rights. I found continually that when visiting the Embassies, the main thing their Excellencies wanted to know was any information I had about Jack. When the country can realise how important is the issue of these rights to those who support them and without whose help the nation cannot survive, then hopefully it will change this counter productive policy. In recent months there has been some yielding to international pressure, and even the release of about a hundred political prisoners but no evidence that a real change of heart has taken place.

I discovered one particularly perverse consequence of this policy of repression when I began to receive letters from all over the world asking the Malawi Government for the release of, or at any rate a proper trial for, Jack Mapanje. The letters were all most courteous and polite. If Jack had committed a crime, the writers had no wish to condone it, but just to be assured that he would have a fair trial. These I passed on to the Chairman of Council, but no response was made or action taken. Rather the attitude seemed to be that the more such letters were received, especially if they came through Amnesty International, a despised organisation in the country, the more the leadership felt justified in their wicked actions. After all, what better way could the nation's sovereignty be demonstrated than by showing it could withstand all this well meaning pressure from abroad?

Returning to the arrest of Jack, there were immediate things to be done. Veronica went to visit Mercy, his wife, to give what comfort she could, and a lasting friendship developed. I addressed staff at Chancellor College to give what information I could. Our concern was that there would not be a purge of the College staff as there was in 1974 when several arrests were made. I urged staff to remain calm, to understand that Jack had been betrayed by someone, most likely another member of staff, so that great care should be taken. In the event, it was most fortunate that nobody else suffered, apart from a single case which I will describe presently.

Society can be cruel to its political prisoners, meting out its own additional punishments, and in a case like this it was customary that the victim should cease to be paid at all and the house taken away. In this way the punishment extended to the wife and children, who would thus be deprived of money, residence and schooling. When the question arose regarding Jack, I took the line that nobody in Government had had the courtesy to inform me about the arrest of a member of my staff, and so officially, I knew nothing about it. I could only assume that the man was not at work because he was temporarily indisposed, and that there was no reason to withdraw either the house or the salary. This state of affairs remained for nearly a year, giving Mercy some financial security until she was able to take a job as a hospital sister with a house at Ntcheu, about a hundred miles away.

I consulted the Head of Police who told me about three months after the arrest that not only was there no trial nor charge registered, but there was not even any line of investigation for him to follow. He had visited the prison and confirmed that Jack was well, but only he and a medical helper were allowed to visit. After about two years, Mercy was allowed a monthly visit, but under ludicrous conditions. My own attempts to obtain approval to visit were either rejected or ignored.

Prison conditions for the politicals are appalling. Torture, beatings and solitary confinement are not unknown, and no reading or writing material is allowed, apart from three Bibles for the whole prison. It is not possible to send out or to receive letters.

Much is made in the country of the President's own one year term of imprisonment which he suffered in Gweru prison at the hand of the British, but it has to be said that this year was spent in conditions of luxury, relative to those he has consigned to remain indefinitely in Malawian prisons.

After Jack had been in prison for just over a year, a man to whom I will refer as Pascal was also arrested. Pascal was a member of the University, and from the same Department. He had a most unfortunate recurrent illness which at one stage caused him to delude himself that he was a Special Branch agent, investigating why his friend Jack had been arrested. These sad activities put him into Zomba Mental Hospital which was actually the place where he was arrested.

The humane and internationally accepted convention that mentally sick prisoners should be treated in hospital rather than in prison was blatantly ignored by the Malawian authorities. Not only had he been arrested from a hospital bed, but he was kept in appalling restrictive conditions in prison to prevent him from moving and making trouble. In fact he was kept in solitary confinement for weeks on end, much of the time in handcuffs and leg-irons. I learnt afterwards that the leg-irons used in this prison bore the stamp 'made in Birmingham'.

As facilities to deal with the complexities of Pascal's illness were inadequate in Malawi, I had managed just before this to arrange for him to have treatment at a specialist clinic in Zambia, and even obtained his consent to undergo this treatment. Now that he was in prison, this was all lost. The Government would not agree to a prisoner, and a political one at that, going abroad for therapy. It preferred to deal with him in its own way.

Having failed in my efforts to obtain approval to visit Jack I asked instead to see Pascal. To my surprise, permission was granted. This was not easy as I had to go through the proper channels, talking eventually to the Secretary to the President and Cabinet, as the ultimate authority for state security. I assume they must have reasoned Jack was much the more serious offender of the two, and there would be less risk to the security of the state if I were to visit Pascal.

The visit nearly aborted when the head of police in Zomba angrily told me that this request was so out of order that he could not allow it, but eventually he accepted SPC's letter as coming from a higher authority, and arranged for my escort to the prison. Accompanied by members of the Special Branch, I was conducted into the prison, and taken to the Governor's office. Here, with the Governor sitting at his desk, carrying on various telephone calls, with the two Special Branch men between me and the door, a prison officer brought in Pascal in his dirty white garb. I could barely recognise him and wondered if the right prisoner had been presented. I also thought that these conditions, talking across a large room with three men between the conversants, must be those under which Mercy was allowed to visit Jack. After a less than monthly trip of over a hundred miles, sometimes cancelled when she reached Zomba, this was the reception that awaited her.

Depending on his moods, some of my earlier meetings with Pascal had been most interesting; I had cause to admire this most sensible, sensitive and intelligent man, and tried to work out with him how we could best find the right treatment for his affliction. Other times were not so good when he blamed the University for all his ills, and it was hard to prevent him from resigning. My meeting with him in prison was by far our worst encounter. He did not want to see me or anyone connected with the University and

120

made this so clear that there was no point, especially in front of these unwanted spectators, of continuing for more than a few minutes.

The type of response was not at all unexpected, and with the prison treatment that he was receiving, he could only voice the tragedy of his situation. I went away thoroughly dejected, having hoped for more, but not surprised by this total rejection. One word of comfort came when I asked the Governor how Jack was. 'Ah, Dr. Mapanje is a real gentleman,' he warmly replied. Despite this welcome assurance, I watched the prisoners working in the fields as we drove away, and felt I had totally failed them.

As my time in Malawi drew to an end, Jack had now been in prison for three years, the regime seemed firmly entrenched, and there appeared no hope of his release. I did take the opportunity in my farewell meeting with Justin Malewezi to brief him on the state of the University, and to emphasise the importance we all attached to Jack's release. On the day that we left Malawi we stopped for an hour in Ntcheu to visit Mercy, leaving a few gifts including our radio/cassette which we no longer needed and some Sibelius tapes.

Jack was actually released on 10 May 1991, as we heard from our new location in Botswana. The donors had been exerting great pressure over the human rights issue, and about ninety political prisoners were released. It was still not easy for Jack to be included at this time. I heard later of a prominent Malawian who, convinced of Jack's innocence, had three times asked the President in writing for his release. On the first of these occasions Dr. Banda had scrawled across the request the word 'never'. This confirmed to me what friends, including Mercy herself, had counselled me, that I should not take up Jack's case with the President, as the most probable outcome would be worse punishment for him and departure for me.

After release Jack naturally asked to be restored to his University position having discharged whatever debt it was he owed to society, but the Chairman of Council was able to prevent this. Jack consequently had the additional frustration of spending the first months of his freedom sitting at home, but as he later told me, comforted by the music of Sibelius we had left.

After some waiting Jack received the opportunity of a Leverhume Research Scholarship at the University of York in England. At this point the British High Commissioner to Malawi was most helpful in ensuring that Jack, together with Mercy and their three children, were enabled to leave Malawi and travel without hindrance to England.

Jack and Mercy have many friends in England, most of whom had previously worked at Chancellor College, and he was able to settle into the Centre for Southern African Studies. In addition he has been much in demand to give seminars and poetry readings at a number of British Universities. It is our hope that the Mapanjes will be able to stay in England for some time until the present regime is thrown out, and a new democracy emerges which among other things will honour its poets rather than persecuting them.

We returned to Britain for the Christmas holidays at the end of the year, and one of our greatest joys was to stay for a day with the Mapanjes in York. We discussed Malawian affairs late into the night, and tried to work out why Jack had been imprisoned and who had betrayed him. Our suspicion mainly based on circumstantial evidence was that someone quite close to the President was responsible. The more important thing was that Jack was in excellent form, starting to create again with the prospect of another volume of poems to follow soon, and most gracious about his time of incarceration. He told us that prison was the place he had felt most free in Malawi. The prisoners, some of them very long term for 'crimes' they had no idea about, would discuss freely the reality of Malawi, and would plan for the new democracy.

Then he remarked about the success of my visit to the prison. I replied that in my opinion this was an utter failure, but he insisted that it had really achieved something. The word about my visit had gone all round the prison, as the first time a white man had ever come to visit. The feeling was that somebody outside cared about them, and he added that morale had improved tremendously as a result. I felt very humbled about this because my own feelings about what had been achieved were so different, but it brought home that if we follow faithfully what we believe to be the right thing, then God is able (and it can only have been divine intervention to so transform a seemingly hopeless situation) to achieve beyond all expectation.

We spent some time discussing Jack's poetry, and he explained from his book *Of Chameleons and Gods* that almost all his poems were political, on the theme that the first Malawian Revolution had been betrayed by those who had legitimately obtained power but had then abused it. The theme is necessarily presented in a rich imagery which at the same time adds power to the concept while obscuring the meaning from those who would not enjoy hearing these truths.

It is my expectation that the volume to come, enriched by his prison experiences, will be most successful and that Jack will have a major part to play in the building of the new Malawi. As tribute to this great patriot who has risked everything to tell the truth, I quote with his permission, our favourite among his poems:

When This Carnival Finally Closes

When this frothful carnival finally closes, brother
When your drumming veins dry, these very officers
Will burn the scripts of the praises we sang to you
And shatter the calabashes you drank from. Your
Charms, these drums, and the effigies blazing will
Become the accomplices to your lie-achieved world!
Your bamboo hut on the beach they'll make a bonfire
Under the cover of giving their hero a true traditional
Burial, though in truth to rid themselves of another
Deadly spirit that might otherwise have haunted them,
And at the wake new mask dancers will quickly leap
Into the arena dancing to tighter skins, boasting
Other clans of calabashes as the undertakers jest:
What did he think he would become, a God? The devil!

Jack's new set of poems, *The Chattering Wagtails of Mikuyu Prison,* was published by Heinemann in its African Writers Series in August, 1993.

Chapter Nine
The Chairman

It is not possible to be in Malawi for long without realising the enormous power vested in the person of the Honourable J.Z.U. Tembo. He simultaneously holds the reins of almost every key organisation in the country. As Chairman of the Commercial Bank, the Limbe Leaf Tobacco Company, Press Holdings, Ethanol, the National Building Society, Blantyre Press, the National Insurance Company, the Dzuka Publishing Company, Air Malawi, and no doubt many others, he is generally referred to as 'The Chairman'. In addition he is Treasurer of his power base, the Malawi Congress Party, and recent news is that he rejoined the Cabinet in January 1992 as Prime Minister. This latter honour is in reality no new thing because although there has been some lapse of time since he was last officially in the Cabinet, his power and influence has always been far higher than that of any mere cabinet minister. When Malawi has needed to send an important delegation abroad, Tembo has led with a few cabinet people in attendance. When major visitors come from abroad, it is Hon. Tembo they seek out to confer with.

In every way he is the President's right hand man, totally,

unflinchingly loyal, modelling his life, his outlook, his character on that of the President, Dr. Banda. However many times he may deny this on frequent BBC interviews there is no doubt that he would like to be President himself one day, and this cloning of character is to prepare for this event. This is his hope, and he clearly has already developed many of the qualities one would expect of a President. Equally he has many qualities one would not expect of this office, and I share the hopes of almost all Malawians that he will never achieve this ambition.

One of his chairmanship roles is one he has held for over twenty years, that of the University Council. Consequently I cannot give a complete picture of the University without discussing my relationship with the Chairman.

Mr. Tembo's reputation had spread further abroad than Malawi, and as I prepared before arriving by talking to as many people as I could find who were familiar with the country, a fairly common theme which emerged was a warning to keep well away from politics; just keep your head down and concentrate on the job, don't worry about the politics, seemed to be the general and quite reasonable advice. Then this sort of counsel was usually accompanied by a warning about Mr. Tembo in particular and followed with a dire story or two about his infamy and the deeds he was supposed to have done. There was this clear polarity in the minds of my advisors. The Malawians were generally nice people, but there was a villain to be avoided whenever possible.

It was not entirely clear how this man had risen to this level of notoriety. He had been a member of the first Cabinet in 1964 at Independence, and the only one of this talented group to have survived, all the others being dead, in prison or in exile. Much of his influence with the President arose from his being the uncle of Mama C. Tamanda Kadzamira who had first joined the President in his exile in Ghana before returning to Malawi, and who now served at his side as the 'Official Hostess'. Nearly all of this family had achieved positions of influence in the country and together formed a powerful source of comfort and protection for the President. As the question of succession increasingly arises, there is much speculation on whether uncle or niece will emerge the stronger, with both having any number of strings to pull. In reality the tide of world affairs has so changed that, provided Malawians and their democratic supporters in the international community are vigilant for freedom, it would not be possible for either to seize effective power for long.

In the face of all this advice I felt that the best policy was to ignore the stories which were probably mostly apocryphal, and face my Chairman without any preconceived notions. This seemed to me the only reasonable way in which I could work with him for the benefit of the University. Let me then talk first about my earlier acquaintance with this certainly very substantial character and indicate my impressions.

The initial impressions were pleasant ones. He seemed most concerned that we should settle well as a family in this new country. After a few days he escorted us to Sanjika Palace for our introduction to the President, the legendary Dr. Banda. The President told us about the history of Malawi, something about the University and much more about Kamuzu Academy. I asked after this audience if the President was expecting us to speak, but was assured that this was certainly not in order at a first meeting. My subsequent discussions with the President are recorded elsewhere.

On the same day I had my first discussion with the Chairman about the University. I did not discover any vision of what he wanted from the institution, but I did gain one unexpected insight into his way of looking at things. I happened to mention because I thought this would particularly appeal to him, that a major priority of mine would be to raise the standards of the University. He replied that he agreed entirely and then added presumably by way of illustration that recently he had looked round one of the Colleges and seen litter blowing around. This to him he made clear was an indication of the failing standards which he assumed I had come to rectify.

This passion for tidiness and cleanliness was always a very strong factor with him. On one occasion he spoke very highly of one of the Principals, not for any academic innovation, but for having had the initiative to call the painters in to add lustre to his College. There was much to commend in this attitude, and it must be largely due to his approach that the cities of Lilongwe and Blantyre are so well preserved, that public places like the airports are a delight to behold, that the grass everywhere is kept short and tidy. One does not have to travel far from Malawi to note the contrast in other countries, and how fortunate Malawi is in this respect to have this type of insistence on the uplifting value of national tidiness. He is much concerned too about the appearance of buildings, and is most meticulous about the quality of any proposed new building.

While learning to appreciate this unexpected value, it was not possible to observe in the Chairman's concern for the appearance, a comparable sensitivity for the substance. My observation based on many board meetings with him, was a pronounced shrewdness and sharpness in the way he conducted business, but seldom a deep grasp of the basic issues. Like many politicians, he does not like to be confused by facts, and even more so, by figures.

The first two meetings of Council I attended were most instructive. The Council included some major national figures, Principal Secretaries of related Ministries and leaders of commerce and industry, yet all appeared to hold the Chairman in great awe, and when called upon to speak, they all tried their best to please him. If his approval could be obtained by scoring a point off the senior members of University staff present, then we were considered fair game for this purpose. The general discussion on papers of an academic nature did not arouse much interest, but a report on a case of misconduct by a junior member of staff really brought the meeting to life, with everyone having views on how the matter should have been dealt with, and eventually the University officers taken to task for our far from perfect handling of the case.

At the second meeting when I began to present my own papers, I learnt what it is to be set up for an occasion such as this. At the meeting of Senate prior to this particular Council, someone who should have known better raised under any other business, a constitutional question. This concerned the representation of Senate on Council. The rules clearly stated that there should be four such representatives elected by Senate. Why then were these four places taken up by the four College Principals? The answer was that the previous Vice-Chancellor had considered that these four were essential to the work of Council and had nominated them for this purpose. Senate was rightly not satisfied with this. No one objected to their presence on the Council, but surely they should be there in an ex-officio capacity, with the written constitution honoured by proper elections of Senate members. Despite being strongly advised to the contrary, I insisted on this item being placed on the Council agenda, and looked forward to introducing this issue whose justice seemed so transparently self-evident.

It was not encouraging to pick up the agenda for Council to find that this had been billed as something like 'Vice-Chancellor's proposal to increase size of Council.' This was not at all the intention as I explained when presenting the item. The resolution aimed only to draw attention of Council to its own rules and seek the correct implementation.

Council rose as one man against this new interloper. Why did the VC want to unnecessarily increase the size of Council? What did he know about the balance of representation? Why did he not trust his Principals to represent Senate? As vainly without any friendly voice to help I struggled to maintain the constitutional aspect of the issue, the Chairman stopped this totally uneven contest by declaring in words I carried around for the rest of my contract, 'The new VC must understand that in Malawi just because something is written down on paper, it does not necessarily have to be taken that way.' So much for rules and regulations I thought, and resolved pragmatically not to raise a constitutional issue again.

I did however raise many other issues of an academic nature which was, I had been advised, the job to which I should pay my exclusive attention. Through such measures I gradually gained the confidence of Council. With the exception of one issue I will describe in a different chapter, the Council approved virtually every proposal without dissent on the recognition that we had done a very thorough work of academic and financial investigation through Senate before passing it on to Council for approval.

This was also the time at which our personal relations with the Chairman were at their best. In starting to prepare my major address of the year for the annual Congregation at which the previous Vice-Chancellor had set such a high standard, I discussed issues to raise with him, and he was most helpful without in any way prescribing what should be said. My high water mark really came not at Council but at a meeting of the Kamuzu Academy appointments committee which not surprisingly, John Tembo chaired. A point had risen about a new teacher who had recently joined the Academy from England. He had not completed formalities such as handing in his notice in Britain, and his former employers were somewhat concerned. There was also some evidence that there were defects of character which if known at interview would have disqualified him. But now here he was at the Academy without a return ticket, and experienced in teaching a subject very short staffed already. What were we to do?

Then one of the committee made a proposal. 'Mr. Chairman' he said, 'you are gifted with a wisdom quite unknown to the rest of us. You interview this man personally, and we will accept your judgement.' Before I and the rest of the committee could recover from this extraordinary hyperbole, the Chairman who had clearly agreed with the sentiment expressed, said 'Yes, I will do this, but I will need to have Dr. Dubbey with me.'

Encouraged by this confidence we did interview the man together and reached the exceptionally wise decision that as he was here anyway we should let him teach for a term and then review his progress while pacifying his British authorities who turned out to be not too heart-broken at their loss. This was precisely what the Headmaster had already recommended but it did give a valuable opportunity to work with the Chairman and having completed the Kamuzu Academy task, to actually talk a little University business.

The major cloud in our relations at this time, while I was still in my first year, came with the arrest on 25 September of Jack Mapanje. Having made some of my own representations on behalf of the University, it was natural to assume that the Chairman of the University Council, in a far more powerful position, would be much better placed to take up the matter. But when I raised the question he was not helpful. He asserted that this was probably a case of subversion, and when I countered that a poet's mind must range freely over issues of truth, and could not hope to always please the establishment, he replied that it was possible to be creative without being subversive; presumably by just writing poems about love and flowers. The Chairman also gave me a strong hint that I should not bother too much about this case if I wished to remain in the job.

Towards the end of 1988, two silly things happened involving the otherwise hard-working and conforming students of the University. First there was what appeared to be a very serious incident at the normally trouble free Polytechnic in Blantyre. Remembrance Sunday is taken very seriously in Malawi, and the

President was for that year going to attend the service in that city. This involved a full rehearsal on the Friday with the Administrative Secretary of the Party, Hon. Pashane standing in for the President.

However, when the cavalcade including Mr. Pashane's car had reached the crossing in the main road they found it blocked by demonstrating students, and were consequently impeded on their way to the Memorial. This is how the incident was initially conveyed to me, and by Malawian standards this was a gross breach of discipline indeed. The Party was affronted and naturally its Treasurer as Chairman of the University was immediately informed, the Police made a large scale investigation, and the Principal of the Polytechnic had to spend some hours in the Police Headquarters for questioning about the affair.

Knowing what I did about the Polytechnic students, this story just did not ring true with me, and when I was able to talk to the Principal and make my own investigations, it turned out as I had expected to be nothing like what had been reported. How many students were involved? Not a mass movement but just five or six. Were they holding up traffic by crossing and re-crossing the road? No, they only crossed once and quickly. It transpired that about half a dozen girls on the Secretarial course at the Board of Governors in the Polytechnic, without being aware of the rehearsal, had clearly mistimed their crossing at the Zebra. When a few days later I was able to convey our apologies to Hon. Pashane for disturbing his procession, he told me he had not noticed any disturbance!

The point about this silly story is that the Chairman became involved, and he took it very seriously. It was not easy in writing my full report of the incident to convince him of the harmlessness of the matter and he began to suspect that I had that very adverse quality of softness towards students.

More seriously, at the same time a new edition of the Chirunga Newsletter appeared. This is a typical student production, written and edited by the students of Chancellor College. The previous edition which had come out in June that year focused on the mal-administration of Chancellor College. There were clearly breakdowns in relations between the staff, that is the Principal, Registrar, academics, catering, gardening and security staff, and their complainants, the students. I wrote immediately to the Principal and Registrar, urging them to take notice of what the students were saying, which seemed to me a genuine call for help. The College authorities did not reply to me, and nothing was done at all. The November issue of the Newsletter took up the issues again with more vehemence, but unwisely without staff guidance at this time, presented their articles in a way which could have been interpreted by an outsider as criticism of the way in which the State was being run, a quite unforgivable sin. There was even a political element in that there were two poems subtly attacking the Establishment. The Malawi Congress Party had in the previous September held its annual Convention at the College and used the hockey pitch for its exhibition ground. The pitch was ruined as a result and no restoration was offered. So one of the students wrote a poem of lament for the lost hockey pitch with the title and refrain 'Come, Come and Mend'.

This otherwise innocuous title was considered most subversive as the initials of the title were CCAM, the name of the powerful women's organisation led by Mama Kadzamira, as many thought her own power base, and you simply did not make jokes about this movement – or for that matter make any enquiries at all about its activities. It is a fund raising organisation which makes much publicity of how much money comes in, but has little to say about where it goes out.

The point about this student protest which would have aroused hardly any comment in other countries is that no sooner had the Newsletter intended only for student consumption come out, than the Chairman obtained his own copy. After about two months he called me to his office. He was friendly and smiling. He explained to me the difficulty of his own position, how he was constantly receiving stick from Party members (I found this hard to believe but continued to listen). Now there was this matter of the Chirunga Newsletter. Prominent people were asking him, are you going soft with the University? How can you allow this type of subversion to go unpunished? He remarked sadly that unless we did something decisive then maybe the Police, the Party or the Young Pioneers might feel compelled to take matters into their own hands, and it would be far worse for the students concerned if this were to happen.

Placed in this impossible position I had to agree that the students concerned should be suspended for the remainder of the academic year. I partially salved my own conscience by reminding those concerned when I called them in to announce their suspensions, that they knew perfectly well how things worked in the country and the risk to themselves they were taking by writing in this manner.

The next day as I arrived in the office at the normal starting time of 7.30 a.m., I was informed that about 150 students from Chancellor College were marching in protest towards the University Office. I had been fortunate up till then that I had never previously encountered a student demonstration. I felt the best way to deal with this challenge was to come out and meet the group, inviting a small number to come in and talk. We held a difficult discussion for over an hour, but clearly the demonstrators were not satisfied and they continued for some time before dispersing and then venting their wrath on the College cafeteria, a legitimate target for complaint, to shout slogans like 'Dubbey, resign'. I felt very downcast by the whole affair, and thought they were actually giving me some rather good advice.

The College effectively stopped work for a couple of days but there was no support from the other three Colleges or from the University of Malawi Students Union, so the protest had no official standing. When less than a week later I had the task to show Chris Patten M.P., then the Minister for Overseas Development, around the College, normalcy had been resumed and he would not have noticed anything at all unusual.

However while I was with our visitor, an emergency meeting of Council had been arranged in Blantyre. I attended the first hour of this meeting and heard the Chairman announce that earlier in the day he had been to the President to report this incident at the University, and that he as Chancellor of the University had declared that the suspended students were to be expelled. Clearly they were rebels now, and would always be rebels was his pronouncement. There was also a paper placed on the table by the Principal of Chancellor College, which clearly laid the blame for the reaction to the suspensions on myself. Added to this, when I had earlier sought telephoned advice from the Chairman on what to do, he was able to assert from two hundred miles away without ever having to confront the students himself, that I was handling things very badly.

I began to feel that my own position was in some jeopardy and was glad to go back to Zomba to meet our British visitor, so that Council could discuss what to do about me in my absence.

Next morning I discovered from the Registrar that Council had confirmed the expulsions, but to my surprise and pleasure decided to take no action against those who had demonstrated, and said nothing at all about my own position. I was still furious about the expulsions, having given my own assurance that after suspension there would be reinstatement, but there was nothing that could be done.

When I later met the Chairman to discuss the aftermath, our relationship had declined to a low level from which it could never recover. As anticipated he accused me of softness, and even of holding views somewhere to the left of Labour. He added that this was all the more disappointing since the reason why they always appointed British Vice-Chancellors was that they considered the British to be the best disciplinarians! He did however agree with me that what we had seen at Chancellor College was only a superficial expression of deeper grievances which needed to be dealt with. Within days I produced a twenty point plan for what was needed at Chancellor College, sending him a copy as well as the Principal. As was the usual custom at the College these ideas were totally ignored, and no amount of exhortation with the Principal or his senior staff could bring about any change in that institution. It is relevant to add that the Principal was a most able and genial man, but in my experience one who for his own reasons seemed unwilling to exercise his potential for the benefit of the University. He is also the brother of Mama Kadzamira and nephew of the Chairman.

The totally unjust expulsion of the four, coupled with the imprisonment of Jack Mapanje and later Pascal, also of the English Department, cast a dismal cloud over my feelings for the work which otherwise were so positive. I did think about the students' advice and discussed the matter with close friends on the staff, but invariably our thought was whether to resign would serve any useful purpose. At most we felt it could only be a gesture which could not be expected to achieve anything. Having been unwillingly party to the students' expulsion I tried to make what little amends I could by doing my best to see that their education was completed somewhere else. They were all students in or near their final year, with previously unblemished conduct, and by the fact that they were writing for the Newsletter, the kind who were willing to contribute to the community. I think that all have been able to leave the country without difficulty and resume their studies in a more favourable climate.

The rest of my association with the Chairman is too melancholy and tedious to relate. The one issue on which he would never commit himself was the question I raised with him in mid 1989 about his views on the possible renewal of my contract due to expire in December 1990. He never answered this question directly but made it clear in his own way by seeming to take issue with me over almost every matter of University interest from that point onwards. After agonising over the matter, Veronica and I decided that we would not seek a further contract, and I submitted my letter of resignation in mid 1990 giving six months notice. Even at this point I said that when he took this request to the Chancellor, if the President wished me to stay I would be willing to listen, but in fact he never conveyed this message. He responded instead by quickly advertising the position!

It was significant that of the seventeen who applied, all but one was from Britain and not a single Malawian asked for the job. The pressure and very real danger of working closely with the Chairman, was I believe, the major deterrent. The person selected eventually declined the position, and to my great regret the post is still vacant well over a year after my departure.

I have to confess that a couple of months before we left, we had a change of heart because so many Malawians and others had urged us to stay, and I did have an audience with the President to ask if the earlier request could be reversed, so that I could continue as Vice-Chancellor. I have good reason to believe that it was Tembo who on hearing about this persuaded the President not to change his earlier approval of my resignation. This was on reflection the right decision for us, because having worked in this way with the Chairman for four years I could not have continued without either falling out seriously with him, or much worse complying with his ways.

Looking back, my feelings towards the Chairman are not entirely negative even though I am prepared to accept that the stories told about him are substantially true and that he has much to answer for. He has been the cause of untold misery to many Malawians unfortunate enough to cross his path, and by his undoubted influence in removing to the sideline those more able than himself, he has done incalculable damage to his own country.

I could only admire his incisiveness, his extraordinary ability to work and his dexterity in handling so many issues simultaneously, but he did give me something else. Through working with him and seeing through what he did, its absence, I obtained as never before a great love for democracy, for social justice and individual freedom. It is my hope that the people of Malawi, freed of Tembo and his family, will soon enjoy these things too.

Chapter Ten
Veronica

It is unusual in a work of this nature to devote a whole chapter to one's wife. Normally there will be an acknowledgement somewhere in the preface that she made the whole writing possible by her patient understanding, keeping the kids out of the way, making many valuable suggestions, etc. But in this case Veronica's role was so crucial that although she has already been referred to a number of times, this does not give an adequate picture, and it seemed only just that she should receive her own chapter.

Veronica was very much cast in the role of the virtuous woman described in Proverbs 31. She maintained the household and family, went out and did business, woke up while it was still dark, and made provision on her own initiative for the benefit of all those associated with us. It must be something of a record that when we finally left Malawi, even the beggars of Zomba had a whip-round to buy her a present! Veronica responded to the challenge of living in Africa in her own unique way, and while sometimes the family tried in vain to slow her down, there is no doubt that she became a highly respected and loved figure in Zomba and beyond. On one occasion we were with a group of people sitting in a circle and introducing ourselves. When it came to my turn, I said 'you all know this remarkable person the Vice-Chancellor's wife. I happen to be her husband.'

I was very happy to play my part in Proverbs 31, just sitting at the city gate conferring with the elders of the land, and content that I did not have to worry about what could loosely be called the domestic and social side of our work since this was in such good hands.

For continuity of the story, I can relate this chapter to the previous three by indicating Veronica's relation to each person described. I have already described the length Veronica went to help John Maunda and his family, and to give them the opportunity of a real chance in life despite all the odds against them. I would only add that these things came about through her own initiative. She would spend much time working out how best to help meet a person's needs and then immediately step in to do it.

When Jack was arrested, Veronica went immediately to see his wife Mercy, and to give whatever practical help was needed, and despite warnings that prisoners are such outcasts of society, especially the political ones, that you should not be seen even in company with their relatives, she kept up this contact. Even on our last days as we drove to the Airport, Veronica said that we must stop in Ntcheu to offer a few gifts to Mercy, having no idea then of when if ever, Jack would be released.

To indicate her composure with all ranks of society, Veronica even got on well with the Chairman. In our earlier days when our relations with him were at their best, she found herself at a State Banquet sitting immediately opposite Hon. Tembo, and with silent neighbours in the next seats, I heard from the other end of the table, a most lively conversation for the whole of the meal, with the Chairman roaring with laughter at Veronica's stories and the way she told them. On another occasion I recall Mr. Tembo asking Veronica for her advice on his younger children, and as usual receiving something very practical.

To go back to the start, Veronica initially supported the idea of the move to Malawi, and even pointed out the advertisement to me, but when the seemingly improbable outcome that we would actually be going there occurred, that was a different matter. She naturally worried that this was such a new and unknown thing for us, would we lose contact with out three older children, would her mother be cared for, would we find friends in Zomba, was there any danger in this exposed position, was it easy to obtain bread and milk, and above all would she have a proper role to play? These were all potentially tormenting questions, and while the answers to all were very easy once we had arrived, it was hard to anticipate the solutions at this stage of preparation. It was very much a step of faith, stepping into the unknown.

In one respect, the prospects for a meaningful role did not look too promising. Veronica is an Infants teacher whose talent and ability to enter effectively into the world of the young child is only partially reflected in the Certificate she gained from Goldsmiths with first class honours and distinction for teaching practice. She really lives her teaching, and is in great demand from parents. Her career had been much interrupted through the births and upbringing of our own children, and now this contract in Malawi would further disturb it. I had made inquiries at my inter-view, but it did seem that expatriate teachers are not welcome in schools for Malawian children; there are good reasons for this as we subsequently discovered, and the only possible opening would be in the expatriate school which appeared to have no vacancies. My suggestion that Veronica tried working instead with an organisation like World Vision did not seem too practical either.

At one stage Veronica became opposed to the whole project, but as she prayed about the matter she at least became reconciled to the extent that as I seemed to be clear about going, she would be the obliging wife and come along too.

However, the instant we set foot on Malawian soil at Kamuzu International Airport, everything dropped into place, and from that moment she had not the slightest doubt that we had come to the right place, and entered fully into the new life we were going to share.

The immediate tasks were to establish the household, to relate to neighbours and others in Zomba, to support the work of the University and to find some sort of vocation.

Taking these in order, Veronica, like the lady in Proverbs, paid much attention to the staff and grounds. The Vice-Chancellor's Lodge, as we had been promised, was quite resplendent, having been in colonial times the residence of the Secretary to the British Administration, and immediately after Independence, just before the capital moved to Lilongwe, the home of the British High Commissioner. The house, built probably at the turn of the century, and one of the oldest buildings in Malawi, was originally built for three senior but single officers who each had a suite of bedroom, ante-room and bathroom, with as communal areas, a very large sitting-room and dining-room. There was a very spacious kitchen, and in the ground of several acres, there was a circular drive about four hundred metres long, a swimming pool with changing rooms and barbecue area, with a guest-house, self contained to accommodate four visitors. It was the type of residence we would not have aspired to in our own country.

To help keep up this mansion, the University provided two full-time gardeners, Johnson Chikalema and Peter Mbanga. A security guard at night was provided also, John Nkongusa. It was necessary to hire a full-time cook, Emmanuel Makumba and also a part-time housemaid. We did have to change this position once but for the majority of the time we had Ellas Longwe in this job. I should also mention the driver that the University provided for my more than 30,000 miles per year on the road, Biswick Lapuwa.

I mention these names because they all became very much a part of our lives in Zomba. Emmanuel, Peter and Johnson all lived with their families in the grounds of the residence, and right from the start, Veronica made a special point of getting to know them with their wives and children. One of the first things she dealt with was their lack of electricity and since night falls at six o'clock all round the year, it meant almost total darkness for the rest of the evening. The reason for this lack was that some very high bluegum trees had grown just over the staff quarters, and the Electricity Company did not wish to extend their lines to these houses in case the trees fell, which being long and slender they looked like doing any moment, and destroyed the whole connection. In fact the trees seemed a major danger to the people living underneath, and badly needed to be cut down before a serious accident occurred. It was not possible to have this done, so we were told, because it is a serious matter to remove a tree in a country which so carefully preserves what trees are left, and several previous attempts to move the town council on this issue had not succeeded.

It is sufficient to say that when Veronica took up the matter, the trees were cut down and electricity restored within a few weeks. We watched with some awe at the way in which these trees were dealt with. Well over one hundred feet high, one man in the team is deputed to climb this spindly bluegum tree, lop off the upper branches and lash a rope round the trunk. The tree is then cut down by the team simultaneously chopping at the roots and heaving on the rope. We were fascinated by the bravery of the climber in the team, and observed that being officially a municipality labourer, he was probably paid not much more than a kwacha per day for risking his life in this way. One of these climbers named Charles made himself known to us, and to help him stretch his tiny income, we hired him as a Saturday gardener, and he came in almost every week for the next four years. He proved to be a man of exceptional skill and vitality, building us a huge vegetable garden, and a chicken house among many other activities.

The main garden also began to flourish under Veronica's supervision. She always had grand ideas of what she expected from a garden, and with Johnson and Peter to provide the manpower, these could at last be put into practice. Following the success with the trees, Veronica's next major venture in the staff quarters was to have a concrete path laid down. It was most satisfying to note that this path had actually been started some years back by Sir Glyn Jones, the last Governor-General and still a very welcome friend to Malawi. By completing his work, we knew we were in the best British tradition.

This path, particularly welcome in the rainy season, provided a further means for Veronica to increase her relationships with the staff and their families. She was concerned to help them through the many illnesses, especially malaria which they were continually vulnerable to. She did much to help the mothers with their babies, and the older children with their school work. Every week she held a class in English for the children to come to in the house.

Before leaving the staff for the moment, I would like to introduce further, our security guard, Mr. Nkongusa. I emphasise the Mister, because while we normally addressed the other staff by their Christian names, he had that authority about him that could only be addressed in this way. We only learnt that his name was John in our last week in the country. At first sight he did not inspire confidence for the job he was expected to do. He was small and thin, he looked near to seventy, and had few teeth left. How could he, armed with only a wicked looking baseball bat hold off the hordes of armed robbers who would undoubtedly be coming to share our comparative opulence?

The answer was that he was made of much sterner stuff than first appeared. He had served with the Kings African Rifles for many years, and with a hidden knife in his sock, had acquired such a reputation with the local villains for his courage and ferocity, that the only time we ever had even the slightest trouble, was on the nights when he was on leave and a younger substitute brought in. I remember when one of our visitors commented on his apparent frailty, I responded that whatever his appearance might be, he maintained a 100% record in his job, and that was good enough for me.

Seeing him every night, bringing him his tea and refreshments, and occasionally having to say, 'Mr. Nkongusa, you are only pretending to be asleep, aren't you?' we gained a great respect and affection for this most friendly and gentle man. We learned from Emmanuel that back in his village, he was the local story teller, and he held his audiences in fits of laughter as he regaled his stories, especially we discovered about white people! When we left the country, Mr. Nkongusa took his retirement, and he no doubt has an additional fund of Englishman stories with which to edify his friends. We certainly remember him as one of the great characters we were privileged to meet in Malawi.

Veronica always took it as a priority to attend to the needs of the house, our staff and their families, and to extend her interests to the community of Zomba. In particular she sought to make friendships with Malawians. There are, of course, many expatriates living in Zomba, at the University and in the Government agencies in the town, and as farmers and missionaries, and it is all too easy for the new Englishman to seek out the several other Englishmen living there as the main social company. In our first months it used to be a matter of concern that we would go to parties in the town and find only white people present. We had not come all this way only to fraternise with whites, and I made it fairly apparent that we did not wish to support such parties. Fortunately in the inevitable turnover of personnel when short term contracts are the order of the day, most of the more colonial types seemed to disappear from the scene, and with the exception of some pockets of past privilege like the Gymkhana Club, we were able to enjoy a good social integration of races. In her role as one of the leading hostesses in town, Veronica always set a good example in this respect and did much to bring about a change in attitudes in Zomba.

But Veronica was not interested in simply making acquaintances with Malawian people, but with real and lasting friendships, and through these to understand the outlook of people at all levels of society. To this end she took the trouble to try to learn the language so that she could talk to the staff, to the people in the market, in the shops, in their homes, to those who had not had the opportunities to learn English at school. This took some determination because it is not easy to learn an African language where every word is so different to those brought up on Latin influenced languages. As described in a previous chapter it was a great setback when her tutor, John Maunda died, but she still tried to work with other teachers, and to my mind obtained a commendable fluency and vocabulary. This hard work was much appreciated by Malawians, who would often have their laughs at mistakes made, but who had great respect for anyone who cared enough to persist in her efforts to communicate better.

For her friendships, Veronica gained much from her fellowship with a ladies prayer-group which met every week. Initially even this group was whites only with the occasional Malawian attending, but under Veronica's influence, the ratio became reversed. She also made many friends through the Zomba Baptist Church where she was elected a Deacon, the only lady and the only non-Malawian in this group, and through the Theological College.

The academic work of the Zomba Theological College is described in a later chapter. Here our focus is on the College rather than the Theology. The College served the needs of both the national CCAP (Central Church of Africa: Presbyterian) and the Anglican Church in Malawi with rather more of the former in terms of both staff and students, than the latter. There were about fifty students altogether, and most of these were married with children. As a result the campus consisted mostly of family houses with what appeared to be many children running around. There were also, of course, a chapel, library and classrooms.

There were necessarily almost as many wives as students, and the wives' group was given a programme of full time study also. With funds being very low, most of the teachers were part-time volunteers, and this gave Veronica the chance to work with the ladies. Her choice was to teach English, and although at first this seemed far removed from the primary school classes she was more accustomed to, there was a link in that several young children she had encountered in the past and would continue to meet in the future, did not have English as a first language.

Most of the ladies in the class would have known some English, since the language is taught quite early on in the Primary School curriculum, and some might have even achieved 'O' level passes, but the majority had left school long ago, and did not use English much in the villages. A new start from the beginning was what most of them wanted. The purpose of these classes was to provide confidence and fluency, so that in the frequent moves of the clergy and their families, the wife would not feel out of place if the ministry took them to one of the cities where English was much more spoken.

Veronica learnt much from this new experience about teaching adults, and as she used many flash-cards with a word of Chichewa on one side and a word of English on the other, extended her own vocabulary. The supreme test towards the end of the course, was that the wife together with her husband, and another couple, almost invariably with a baby each as well, would come to dinner with us, where the entire conversation had to be in English.

As a result of Veronica's class contacts, these informal 'parties' and the numerous social functions at or around the College, we made some very good friendships with the students and wives. It was always a great pleasure when travelling around the country to come across a former graduate of the College, now with not inconsiderable pastoral responsibilities. It was quite normal to find a pastor straight out of College with for example, four churches and ten prayer houses to care for, often several miles apart, and each with the size of congregation that clergy in Britain can only dream about. Where possible we tried to ensure that the Malawian equivalent at least had a bicycle to cover the vast distances involved. We also continue to receive much encouraging correspondence from our friends in this Ministry.

Then there was the Zomba Baptist Church which we joined about six months after coming to Malawi. There are not many Baptist churches in Malawi compared with the much larger denominations of the CCAP, the Catholics, the Anglicans, the Adventists and the Church of God, and this smallness turned out to be one of the major attractions for us. Normally on a Sunday morning in Zomba, we would go to the Chancellor College service which usually drew over two hundred of the thousand students at the College while simultaneously a similar number was attending the Catholic mass. Occasionally we would go to the CCAP in which normally a full church for the English spoken service at 8.00 a.m. would be followed by a similar crowd for the Chichewa service. The Anglicans also met at the same time so that it was not possible to go there very often.

We were feeling the need for a smaller fellowship outside the University, and then the Baptists came along and were smart enough to put on an English speaking service in the afternoon. Initially the Baptists would meet very informally at one of the Missionary's houses, while the new church building was being completed. We moved into this new structure with the roof not finished, and every week met in some trepidation as the building around us began to take more comfortable shape. The church was in the middle of the town, quite near to the Mosque, used mainly by the Asiatic community of Zomba, and it seemed that no matter what time we held our services, there was always a blast from the Minaret to disturb usually the time of prayer, and give us a reminder of the opposition.

It is our firm belief that wherever we go it is essential to find the right church, and to commit ourselves to the fellowship, offering whatever ministry the church might require that we are able to give. The church might not necessarily follow our denominational inclination in England, and would almost certainly not match our own doctrinal preferences, but we believe that the Spirit has always directed us to the particular spiritual home that is most suited for us.

We are not Baptists in England, and many of our previous contacts with this denomination had not been too positive, but certainly we fulfilled what we took to be the basic condition that we upheld the concept of believers' baptism. While at South Chard one year, we had become convinced of the scriptural case for baptism as a conscious response to faith, and submitted ourselves to the waters of baptism at a public service of worship. The very factor which has subsequently made us uneasy with the practises of the Anglican Church, made us plausible candidates to be Baptists.

What we had not realised at first, despite the number of Americans associated with the church in Zomba, was that these were not in fact the sort of Baptists we had encountered in England, but Southern Baptists of the U.S.A. This was the denomination that had started out with the worst kind of credentials possible, associated in the past with racism and slavery. On a rational decision this was probably the last denomination on earth we would have chosen! However, much had changed over the last hundred years, and now the denomination had changed sufficiently to have become one of the most generous in the world towards the social and evangelistic needs of the developing countries. Their missionaries operated in all the African countries where they were allowed, and they sought to meet in very practical ways the needs which they found. In Malawi, for example, the Southern Baptists were prominent in food provision and distribution at times of need, in supporting more productive methods in Agriculture, and in pioneering an information campaign against AIDS. In this context we felt much more at home in committing ourselves to this small but growing church in Zomba, Veronica as a Deacon, and myself with preaching responsibilities every two or three weeks.

As an indicator of what could be achieved through the Southern Baptists, I noted from their literature how much they spent on mission work which they claimed was the highest of any denomination, and asked the missionary, Rendall Day, what could be done to help the University. I have mentioned earlier, Rendall's great interest in sport, particularly running and basketball, and it seemed that this was a good area to look at, as we certainly had a problem here at the University.

The situation was that the University had only one official Sports Coach, Reuben Malola, and he was responsible for the administration and coaching of all sports in all four Colleges. However, the national football team was currently going through a bad time, and Reuben, a former international player himself, was called in to take over the team on a temporary basis. Under his direction, new players were brought in, and Malawi started winning again, to the extent as I have earlier mentioned, they almost won the Africa Nations Cup. Very soon Reuben was appointed Manager of the national team, and seconded indefinitely from the University. While the national team was now prospering with good wins against respectable sides like Kenya, Egypt and Cameroon, the University was left without any sports coaches.

This was the problem I put to Rendall, and he responded by making inquiries about the Journeyman scheme operated by the Southern Baptists, in which young volunteers would go abroad to do a specific job for two years. The idea worked marvellously, and within a few months three young men had been identified and sent over to Malawi. All three had degrees and much experience in coaching a variety of sports; further they had the Christian commitment and outgoing personalities to do a most effective and much appreciated job with us. We sent Chuck to Chancellor College, Kevin to the Polytechnic, and Mark to Bunda College. They all contributed very strongly to building the corporate life of the three Colleges and raising standards particularly in Basketball and Volleyball to national championship level. Further, their salaries and expenses were all paid for by the Southern Baptists. For good measure, the Church also provided the national basketball coach under the same scheme, and subsidised a few academic staff as well.

The presence of these young Americans at the University was indicative of another factor which amazed and delighted me. This was the remarkable number of highly motivated and committed Christian staff who joined the University during our time. It might be thought that this was a consequence of my own position as chairman of the Appointments Committee, but I always took great care to ensure that every candidate was considered only on academic grounds, and I had no influence whatever, except by prayer, on who would actually apply for a job at the University. This last point I make quite deliberately. If we needed, for example, a new member of staff to take charge of Computing, I would ask the church to pray quite specifically for the right person, and we saw answers to prayer of this nature. Without exception the Christians we appointed, mostly young and receiving only local salary, did a superb job both academically and in contributing to the corporate life of the University and the town. In addition most of them in Zomba attended the Baptist Church and helped to build the fellowship.

The church had its service in Chichewa in the morning and the English one in the afternoon. There is always the danger in this device that there will be two distinct congregations, and even worse that the English service will become a 'whites only' affair. Fortunately, this did not happen. While it was always difficult to encourage expatriates to come to the Chichewa service, the afternoon session always had a good mix of nationalities, especially when students from Chancellor College began to attend in numbers.

The few occasions when I attempted to preach at the Chichewa service were always unusual. It is exhilarating to speak accompanied by an interpreter; the translation gives just the right time to think out the next point. In my case, Pastor Gama would do the interpreting, and as soon as I had finished my address he would continue, and harangue the congregation, presumably to drive the message home. After a time I began to wonder if it was really my message or his own, but whatever he was saying, he always had an altar call, and exhorted people to come forward. Having come to the front, the next stage was to turn to face the congregation and explain one by one, exactly why they had come forward! Then followed the prayer and the ceremony of shaking hands with all the elders.

The afternoon services were more sombre affairs, always punctuated by the intervention of the minaret, and having to stop altogether if it rained too heavily on the tin roof, but usually we managed a valuable time of teaching and fellowship. One major problem which we were never able to come to terms with, was the huge disparity of income in the congregation between the Malawians and the expatriates, some with supplemented salaries from abroad. Certainly a number of Malawians were helped out of financial difficulties through this association as I have described in more detail earlier on, but the disparity raised the uncomfortable question of whether this was the motive for attending the English speaking service.

This was the background to the church where Veronica was elected to the diaconate. Her function was to attend church committee meetings, usually conducted in Chichewa, make church announcements, help with pastoral activities and generally watch how the finances were being administered.

The work also entailed going out to the villages. The main church in Zomba, as I have described in the chapter on 'John', supported a number of village churches over a wide radius, and a journey to one of these on a Sunday would often involve a long cross-country drive followed by a stay almost until darkness. Arriving in mid-morning, the first requirement was to have a meal. As I could never feel at ease with traditional Malawian food, I did not look forward to this part of the day, and devised successively more devious ways to reduce consumption while minimising offence. The meal took some time as the whole congregation took part, and when this finished, often after mid-day, the service began.

It is not accurate to describe it as a service, for usually a number of events took place. On one occasion we started by walking to the river for some baptisms, then returned to the church for a long service of worship. Each church had its own choir who tended to dominate the proceedings from this point, rendering without instruments from a seemingly endless repertoire. After the preaching with an interpreter, the building emptied of people, and then after a short interval, they all came back for a communion service. When we were told that there would then be a time of dedication of infants, we looked at the impending sunset, thought of the difficulty of driving over country in the dark, and made our farewells all round.

These incursions deep into the country gave the opportunity to see the Malawi which most expatriates do not see, and for me a welcome break in my normal weekly routine of travelling up and down the main road connecting Blantyre, Zomba and Lilongwe. However as might be predicted, Veronica was much more at home in the villages than I was, and there were occasions when she would travel out on her own to teach, preach and relate in her inimitable way to the scores of villagers who came out to the services. Whether in the village, the market, the theological college or on the street, Veronica could integrate naturally with Malawians in a way which was very rare to see. When confronted with the many beggars who largely congregated around the supermarkets in Zomba, she would always make the effort to seek out the genuine needs, among the undoubted rogues who also lined up for the cash, and as I have said earlier, on the day we left the country, they had a collection to buy a present for her.

Then there were the friends of Zomba Hospital. A very tiny but dynamic hospital administrator, Mr. Ndala, who I had also first met at South Bank, encouraged Veronica and some of her friends of the need for such a group. Veronica was appointed secretary, and was thrust into the front-line of a new activity for her, that of fund-raising.

This is a very popular and necessary activity in Malawi, and there are consequently many competitors in the field. The object is to think of a new way to raise money which no one else has thought of, then organise quietly lest the secret be piratised, and quickly rush out your publicity, using the radio and newspaper if necessary, put on your function, count the money, and try to put it to a useful purpose. This latter point is not always as easy as it sounds, because sometimes after all the other work is successfully completed, the money cannot be given away without difficulty. The particular stunt chosen to raise the funds can seldom be used again, because if successful, all the other fund-raisers will use the idea until both the novelty and the profitability are lost.

It is also a recognised unfairness of this type of activity that the best ideas will not necessarily raise the most funds. However there is always the component that the other purpose is to provide some fun for the community whether the money rolls in or not, and with Veronica's organisation, the Friends of Zomba Hospital always provided this value.

Other than a public film show, a ladies' coffee morning and the auction of our property as we left Zomba, the Friends put on a Dance and a Cultural Show. The Dance which featured the renowned Police Band with their soloist whose massive leaps, wiggles and gyrations earned an Elvis type response, drew in the crowds at all levels of society in Zomba, raised K1500 without much effort while the Cultural Show in which Veronica organised some of the most renowned artistes in Malawi, together with the Chancellor College Rock Band and half a dozen local choirs in the Great Hall brought in just K400.

Having raised the money, there are still two major obstacles to overcome. One is that committees who are talented at organising new activities, are not always so good at deciding which among the multitude of good causes available is the one to support, and the other is that any transfer of such funds has to be accompanied by a proper ceremony. The Zomba Hospital Friends tended to specialise in the provision of blankets, and soon discovered that these could be locked away in hospital cupboards if a ceremony had not been held.

On one occasion I was reading the daily newspaper when I came across a small section describing how Mrs. Veronica Dubbey had presented blankets on behalf of the Friends. Her speech was quoted, as was the response from the Matron. When I showed this item to Veronica we were both puzzled because this had not happened at all, and a little worried about what the chairman of the Friends, a Scottish doctor working in Zomba, might think. When we rang him with the news, he just laughed. He told us that rather than the effort of organising a ceremony, it would be much easier to make one up, so he had sent in this piece to the newspaper and had it published! The Matron, who had entered into the fun, was now able to actually allocate the blankets to the patients.

When I think of Veronica's role in Malawi, whether in supporting me at the University, with the staff at the house, in the Theological College, the Zomba Baptist, the Friends of Zomba Hospital, the Sir Harry Johnston School where she taught from time to time, the villages, either with the church or with a World Vision project, I am reminded about something that our good friend Rev. Stewart Lane wrote in one of his articles. Stewart, an American Anglican Minister who had lived in the country for many years, and became chaplain at both the Polytechnic and Chancellor College, wrote a weekly column for the daily newspaper, and in one of the first I read from him, he was writing about various expatriates who had come and gone over the years and what they had achieved in Malawi. He said that many would hope to be remembered by what they did, but in fact those who were remembered at all, were remembered not for what they did, but by what they were.

I tried to do many things in Malawi. Some worked out, and others did not. I hope Malawians will acknowledge those that did achieve something. But I have no doubt that Veronica will be remembered.

Chapter Eleven
The Academy

Kamuzu Academy was founded by the President in 1981 as the intended embodiment of his educational ideas, the chief of which is that no education is of value unless based firmly on the Classics. This was his second educational foundation after the University, and from his public statements and my private talks with him, clearly the one closer to his heart. Right from my first audience with him, he found it much easier to talk about the Academy than the University, and very clearly he saw it as one of his most important achievements for the country. In the spirit of Plato's 'Republic', he genuinely hoped to prepare an elitist group of philosopher-kings to help him lead the country. Consequently no expense was spared to provide this superior type of education, and even if it meant diverting badly needed resources from all other sectors of education, he considered that this most ambitious aim justified the expenditure.

In this sense I could identify with Dr. Banda's thinking because I often found myself justifying the existence of the University on similar grounds. Given that funds were not available for the comparatively vast expense of universal education even up to primary level, it seemed at this stage of development more appropriate to pursue an elitist policy rather than spreading the funds out so thinly that very little benefit would be obtained by anyone. The difference was that while we prepared our elite in the vocational sense, the President's approach was classical, following the tradition of the British Public School.

Certainly the Academy was a most intriguing concept, and it did succeed in capturing the imagination of a worldwide audience. The BBC televised a half-hour feature entitled the 'Eton of Africa' and gave a most sympathetic presentation of the Academy. The title was well chosen, as parity with schools like Eton was the ambition of the President. To this end, exchange visits were organised, and sometimes a member of staff or a sixth form pupil would be seconded for a year from Eton to work at the Academy. While Eton might have been the ideal, visits to and from other public schools and their equivalents in Britain and Germany were also undertaken.

The Academy became a much more prestigious institution than the University. There was never any question, for example, of the BBC wishing to feature the University, and when Heads of State or the equivalent came to visit Malawi, Kamuzu Academy was always included in the itinerary, but hardly ever the University. At first this worried me, but eventually I grew to see the advantages of not being in the national limelight so frequently. It was easier to do a job without such publicity or public expectation.

My connection with the Academy was as a member of the Board of Governors, as a sharer in the provision of education beyond the equivalent of 'O' level, and as a partner in the two institutions founded directly by the President. There was a great fascination in being involved in the progress of this unique institution in which all pupils had to study the Classics, and all the academic staff were British.

I often wondered if for some reason the President had become disappointed with the University. We too had our department of Classics, and on one of my earlier audiences with him, the President told me that if he had the money he would have liked to build a new Faculty of Humanities to specialise in the Classics and ancient African languages. The first Vice-Chancellor, Ian Michael, told me that Dr. Banda had been contemplating the new academy even in his time, so it could be that his plan was to support classical education at both levels.

Certainly Classics did not do well at the University. This I think was due to the fact that since Latin and Greek were not taught in schools, it was difficult to find the right sort of staff who could both teach an elementary crash course and maintain the academic credibility to be expected of a University.

Certainly the two academically inclined young men entrusted with the Classics department when I arrived, admitted to me that they were quite unsuitable for this work and I agreed with them and made no attempt to encourage them to seek another contract. When they left, only about seven students had opted for Classics, and it was most difficult to find any new staff. For a whole year the department was run by a part-timer, Rodney Hunter, who taught at the Theological College and a staff associate waiting to go abroad for higher level study. Maybe the President suspected that this might happen eventually in the University, hence his greater enthusiasm for the school.

However, in 1989 our problem was solved by the recruitment of a Belgian couple. The wife, who became Head of Department, was an established scholar in the field, and the husband had been a teacher of Classics in school, so together they provided the two halves of what we had been seeking. Further their great knowledge and enthusiasm for the subject together with a third Belgian who joined them, meant that students once more took Classics into consideration, and all the courses and programmes were revised to give a more attractive presentation. One of my last activities at the University was to give to their growing department two lectures on the importance of Mathematics to the Greeks. I left with the knowledge that Classics at last was in good hands at the University.

The Academy was built under the President's close supervision as near as possible to his own village in the district of Kasungu. Visitors can see the kachere tree under which Dr. Banda received his first lessons and the remains of the first school built on this site. Because of its location it is not easy to reach the Academy, but after travelling just over 100km. north of Lilongwe to Kasungu, a cross country journey of about 30km. over often very muddy roads ends suddenly with the resplendent sight of these new buildings on which no expense has been spared. Everything possible has been done to make Kamuzu Academy look like a British public school and to ensure that the staff recruited and facilities offered also resemble those of the British proto-type. In fact it is generally harder for staff to qualify to work at the Academy than at the British equivalent. As a minimum they must have an honours degree, (a pass will not do), three years of teaching experience and whatever their subject, at least an 'O' level in Latin.

It is this latter requirement which throws most would-be applicants, and sometimes the selection committees as well. We have spent much time on the Board and its committees looking at border-line interpretations of this ruling. Does it apply to the Physical Education teacher, the Home Economics staff, the Bursar, the Librarian etc.? More seriously, how can we expect to obtain Science staff of the right calibre when so few have studied Latin at school in England? In the important latter case the ruling was amended to include those who have studied the subject for at least three years without necessarily having taken an examination.

At its opening in 1981 the Academy took in three streams of pupils, from the Primary School leaving certificate for the first form, the Junior Certificate of Education for the third year and the Malawi Certificate of Education for the fifth year. For its second year of operation, all six years were running. Initially, the President's hopes were justified by the successes of the first students, and before I ever thought of working in Malawi, I had an indication of these accomplishments while at South Bank.

We were greeting new students to the Faculty at the beginning of term in 1984 when one of the course tutors asked me to come over and meet some recruits from Malawi. The very presentable three boys and one girl had come through the British Council with several 'A' Grades in Advanced level between them and even a few passes in Latin which was most unusual among our students. These four were clearly among the first graduates of Kamuzu Academy. I was able to follow their progress through the four year course in Electrical Engineering, and then met them again in the Capital Hotel, the day they returned from England. Subsequently two of them were recruited to the University staff in this subject. Through this initial acquaintance I formed a very positive impression of the Academy.

These were the better days of the Academy, and former students I met from this period all seemed to have not only the qualification, but the air of self-confidence and social assurance which comes with the best type of education. Certainly the earlier days produced the type of graduate the President had intended.

As the Academy grew larger, and pupils were admitted only after the Primary School Examination, the standard of academic achievement seemed to have declined, and a large part of my function as a Governor of the school was to help determine why this should be and what could be done.

One cause became apparent before I had first visited the school. On departure from Lilongwe after my interview in 1986 I picked up the well-presented Kamuzu Academy magazine and was greeted on the front page by a photograph and a word from the new headmaster. Yet when I returned in November, I was introduced at the University Congregation to the new headmaster who was clearly a different person from the man I had earlier read about. On investigation it became clear that the Academy had difficulty retaining its headmasters, and in fact the first ten years had been graced by no less than six of these gentlemen.

This was in contrast to the University which had had only four Vice-Chancellors in twenty-five years. It is clearly of great importance for a school to have the continuity and stability provided by the presence of a good headmaster who stays for a significant amount of time, and clearly there must be a basic weakness when men who have been carefully selected as suitable for this task are unable to stay. It is not impossible to continue for several years in Malawi as the contrasting example of the University has shown. I have to say, having known two of the six heads very well, that after a good start when work is appreciated and support is given, a rapid process of disillusion sets in so that seldom can there be a desire to seek a second contract.

The basic complaint is that of interference. The Academy is so great a symbol of national pride that its reputation becomes a matter of high political priority. The Board and its committees are filled with cabinet ministers, top civil servants and other major national figures, who in their desire to do the best they can to help the President achieve his educational desires, become directly involved in the running of the school in ways they do not understand, and this makes the work of the staff much more difficult. This type of unhelpful intervention could be seen in the Appointments Committee where often the Headmaster's advice would be ignored and an inferior candidate selected, and in the academic development committee where the local governors insisted that the Cambridge Overseas 'O' level was not good enough for the Academy, causing any number of problems subsequently in choosing the most appropriate Examining Board for particular subjects. Then there was the frequent problem that it is hard to run a school effectively and at the same time show it off as a national symbol to all important visitors to the country.

The Academy has declined since its earlier days in terms of academic performance. The 'O' level results are good, but in terms of average pupil performance, not significantly better than those of the secondary schools taking the Malawian equivalent examination. Kamuzu Academy is possibly the only school anywhere in which both Latin and Greek are compulsory at 'O' level, and the performance in these two subjects is surprisingly good. There is much more of a problem with English. The traditional Malawian approach to the teaching English is to put great emphasis on grammar and sentence construction which probably accounts for the success in the classical subjects. By taking the British 'O' level however, and more recently the GCSE where great emphasis seems to be on vocabulary and expression to the exclusion of grammatical accuracy, the pupils are clearly handicapped. It is estimated that the average British pupil taking this exam will have acquired a vocabulary of about seven thousand words while the average Malawian for whom English is a second or even third language will have learnt about two thousand by that time. In contrast, the grammatically oriented examinations in Latin and Greek provide a fair competition between Malawian and British students.

Despite this difference, the results in English are satisfactory but inconsistent. In one year the pass rate will be as low as 50% and the Board will be up in arms demanding to know the reason why; the next year, without a significant difference in pupil quality, it will be back to 100%. As a response to the vagaries of the British system of marking English, a cunning headmaster will hedge his bets by putting the class in for two different examining boards. One year this worked remarkably well and at the same

156

time caused a total lack of confidence in the precision of the examining boards when the result from one was almost the reverse of the other. The pupils all obtained a pass from one at least of the boards which was the required result, but the spectacular loss of any correlation between the two performances was a worrying reflection on the objectivity of either Board.

If the 'O' level results were tolerably good without in any way suggesting that here we were dealing with the cream of the country's youth, the 'A' level results were most disappointing and the more so since, as has been mentioned, they were so much better in the earlier days. The University of Malawi admitted students on the basis of performance at the equivalent of 'O' level and the ruling at the Academy was that pupils passing at this level could not enter the University directly but were required to continue at the school to 'A' level, with a view to entrance to higher education abroad. Not all would succeed in this and some would join our University with appropriate exemptions of one or two years from our degree programmes. We found after a time that despite having 'A' levels it was not practicable to give more than one year of exemption.

In these circumstances it was necessary to set a minimum entry standard, and this was set fairly modestly at five 'A' level points. However the standard at Kamuzu Academy became so low that few were able to reach even this level. In one not untypical year that I recall, out of thirty-five who took the 'A' level at the Academy, only eight achieved even the qualifying standard the local University had set.

One basic cause of this decline had been identified by successive headmasters, and on this issue the very people who were normally so keen to intervene in the affairs of the school, surprisingly did not give much help. This was the very basic issue of entry to the Academy.

In the first years of the Academy, selection was made on the basis of performance in the three Malawian examinations, and at the two higher levels this seemed to provide an objective and reliable guide to subsequent performance. It was easy to pick out the best of Malawian students and reward them by this high quality education on offer at the Academy. The subsequent results in terms of both academic and personal growth were very good. The Academy could have been developed as a superb sixth-form college, which still might be the best use to put it to, but instead it was extended to a secondary school to comply with the doctrinaire commitment to classical education for all post-primary ages.

This meant that selection now took place at the end of primary education, and this opened the door to a number of abuses which it was left to the staff rather than the Board to combat. Initially the students who had done best on the Primary School Leaving Certificate were chosen. This should have been a good criterion, but it was found that many selected in this way were quite unsuitable for the demands of the Academy. The reason was that it was by then customary, since this was the door to any secondary education, for pupils to return to retake this Standard 8 examination, where questions were standardised and predictable, over and over again until their mark put them in the qualifying category. As Kamuzu Academy was so much more prestigious, the desire to excel even more by this means became apparent. Michael Maloney carried out a survey of the entrant's class and made the discovery that the average pupil had taken the Standard 8 test no less than 3.8 times!

The answer it seemed was to devise a test specifically for entrance to Kamuzu Academy, and an objective verbal reasoning test was constructed for this purpose. Students were only allowed to take this once, and initially selection was based on the combination of this test and the Standard 8 examination. It had one good effect immediately; by the old method of selection, pupils entered the Academy at the ages of 15, 16 or it was suspected, considerably older in some cases. Now, more reasonably, students aged 11 or 12 were joining the school.

Then the Academy made a bad mistake. Instead of setting a new test every year, they tried to stick to the same one, and this encouraged the phenomenon of cheating on quite a large scale. It was of such vital importance for a child to receive all the benefits implied by a Kamuzu Academy education that parents would do anything to provide this opportunity. It was prestigious for headteachers also to win places for their children at the Academy, so potential collaboration was possible. The existence of a test paper whose answers could be known and memorised was too great a temptation.

It is not easy to prove a case of cheating but less difficult to observe the effects. The new intake based on the Kamuzu Academy test was generally a better group but still there seemed a number who were out of place in this company. The Headmaster responded by giving exactly the same test again but under proper supervised conditions, and found that at least twenty of this new group scored significantly worse than they had previously. These were removed and replaced by students from the reserve list.

The following year a further improvement in selection was made. Thanks to MANEB marking and releasing the results earlier there was ample time before term began to call in the top 150 on the list for a two day selection procedure at the Academy. By repeating the test it was again possible to eliminate a number who had been 'helped' in some way, and an oral test in English eliminated others. As a result the school felt it could be confident that about fifty of the students called up in this way were worthy of selection, and the other thirty who completed the intake would be acceptable but academically at risk. The year after this the top three hundred were called for this selection, and hopefully a worthy cohort of eighty was selected.

In these circumstances and with the original papers taken by the candidates available, it was possible to analyse the extent of the malpractices. One school for example had as many as eight students at the Academy for selection, and on inspection it was found that all their original answer papers were identical. Needless to say, only one at most from this group survived the more searching test at the Academy. Many other examples could be found of specific schools which must have colluded in some way to inflate their pupils' performance.

It was most annoying that having exposed these schools to the Board, compiled of very senior Malawians who were only too pleased to interfere with the work of the Academy on other occasions, no action seemed to be taken, and the same rogue schools were prominent in the same way the next year.

I state these facts quite strongly because by condoning this cheating, the Board was not being faithful to the wishes of the President. It was his intention that Kamuzu Academy was meant for the best young people in the country, not for a random collection lucky enough to have parents and/or teachers who connived to get them places at the expense of the more talented children who should have been there.

The last Board meeting I attended had most of these prominent people present. A proposal had been put forward that there should be a school visit to England the next Easter. This would involve sending football and netball teams who would play a few friendly matches and then take part in a national schools' competition. This meant that a party of about thirty would travel and spend about two weeks in Britain playing games and undertaking educational visits. The total cost, which I thought was an underestimate, would be about a quarter of a million kwachas, well over £50,000. With so many powerful political figures in the room, it was not easy to express dissent and nobody did. So Mama Kadzamira, the official hostess spoke. She said she was so glad there was such unanimity on this issue, and that we were so concerned that this educational and sporting visit should be successful. Therefore she suggested that we should further demonstrate our commitment by sharing the cost between us!

The room went completely silent. I quickly counted the number of people in the room, divided this number into the cost and went into a cold sweat. Whatever happened I was not going to give up this sort of money for already over-privileged children to go on a jamboree to England. Then Mr. Tembo, who was probably no more inclined than anyone else to part with his money, saved the situation for all of us. He said that while we all supported the suggestion, there was no need for anyone to pay anything. There were in the country several large tobacco and tea companies who would be only too glad to sponsor this trip, and he would see to it.

Despite the misgivings expressed in this chapter I enjoyed my association with Kamuzu Academy. I was glad to be able to contribute to the Board as very frequently the members needed to know about the British educational system, and I was able to help in this respect, not least in attempting to press home just how serious were the 'A' level results and to seek the steps to be taken by staff to improve on these. I made some very good friendships among the two headmasters I knew and other members of staff. We had much in common in our work in Malawi and the three hundred mile journey to visit the Academy from Zomba was always most worthwhile. However I have to say that I do not believe the country was obtaining value for money for all the funding poured into the Academy, and which by implication was being taken away from other educational sources. It will probably improve as, thanks to the efforts of staff, the problem of selecting the right children is being gradually overcome, but the most essential reform to be made is that if the country has sufficient confidence in British staff and British headteachers to run this type of school in the best way possible, then they should be allowed to do this without continual intervention from the Government. It will be helpful too if more Malawian staff are able to work in the Academy, and with more Malawians in the administration, as at the University, there will be no need for the type of interference which has been the despair of so many gifted headmasters to date. The University has managed without this level of political intervention, Vice-Chancellors have been able to stay and establish their work, and by all criteria, the University is a more successful institution than the Academy.

Ultimately, I would be surprised if the Academy were to continue in its present state. Several suggestions could be made, such as an Army station, an hotel, a management centre, or even as a College of the University, but in view of its having been built as a school, the best future would be to revert to what in effect it might have become in its earlier days, a sixth-form college. In this way many more young people will have the chance for high quality post-'O' level education, and in this way I believe the Academy has a real future. The source of funding has been a controversial but unspoken issue, and with the present size of the Academy the bill is now up to eight million kwachas per annum. This money, which is supposed to come mostly from the President himself, but at the loss to alternative forms of national development can then be used to benefit more effectively many more talented young Malawians than the fortunate but less able students who have been in occupancy for the last few years.

Chapter Twelve
The Medical School

One of the most appealing aspects of leadership in a University is the enormous diversity of the work. There are so many things happening in the life of each department and each section, that even someone whose style is only to react to crises will find a rich assortment of demands, while those Vice-Chancellors rash enough to want to initiate some of the action themselves will find life exciting and sometimes dangerous.

I described my work in one farewell speech as like that of a juggler. There are always about twenty or thirty balls in the air at once, and each one draws attention to itself at different times. Some drop embarrassingly on the floor and are only fit to be kicked away out of sight. Some are snatched away by others in mid flight and never seen again. A few drop sharply and painfully on the head of the juggler, but just a few keep in circulation and actually are able to achieve something. I want in this chapter and the next, to describe some of these balls that I juggled for most of the four years.

First there was the Bunda Road. I choose this one because the story is fairly uncomplicated, and it was one of the first real issues

I heard about, from the Bunda visitors club in Aberystwyth. As mentioned earlier, these gentlemen made very clear to me the neglect of the Bunda Agricultural College by the University Office, over a hundred and eighty miles away in Zomba. There was no piano in Bunda, there was no decent staff-room, University administrators hardly ever visited, and what was being done about the dreadful Bunda Road, the last ten or so of the hundred and eighty mile journey? This untarred road, impossibly muddy and potholed in the rainy season, throwing up clouds of continuous dust in the dry weather, made the approach a powerful deterrent to visitors, and the daily journey into town, a necessary task for many of the residents, a constant source of irritation.

My first encounter with this contentious highway was in the November before I started. The driver knew the road by heart, drove on the left, right or middle to miss all the bumps and holes, shooting through at an average of nearly sixty miles per hour so I wondered what all the fuss was about. Recalling the other criticism of the lack of interest by senior staff (not justified as I discovered), I made sure to register an attendance by signing the visitor's book and resolved to return as frequently as possible.

The next visit brought home the problem much more clearly. Having started the work in January 1987, I decided that in the first month I would visit all the Colleges and give brief addresses to the different audiences of the students, the support staff and the academic staff. The tour began in the north and seemed to go reasonably well at KCN before moving on to Bunda. The first talk to the students began ominously. I opened with a fairly banal remark which the audience found to be hilariously funny, and they rolled in the aisles for what seemed like quite a few minutes. So I immediately followed up with what I thought was rather a good joke, and this fell totally, embarrassingly flat. Somehow I finished the rest of this initial exhortation, and gladly moved on to speak to the staff. This was quite fun by comparison, but then to my dismay, the chairman announced he was sure I would be delighted to answer questions.

This was still my first fortnight in Malawi, but fortunately the first few questions were fairly conventional and not too difficult. Then a more senior man rose to his feet. 'We are all so glad the new Vice-Chancellor has made the effort to visit us at Bunda. We are so glad too that he has brought the first rain with him, and we are all so sad that because he has come this far, and because he has had to drive through the rain, his car has got splashed with mud. So my question is, just when does the new Vice-Chancellor propose to do something about tarring the Bunda Road?'

So I received the message. Something had to be done about the Bunda Road. There were other things which needed to be done at Bunda. The large commercial farm was incurring a loss every year, the size of the library and most laboratories were quite inadequate, new hostels were needed, the primary school for staff children was only half built, and while a consignment of equipment under Japanese aid was imminent, there was not a computer in sight. It was possible to deal with some but far from all of these problems, but what had emerged very clearly was that of all the questions to be faced, the Road was the prime issue.

The problem of the farm was solved quite easily. The manager it transpired had been seconded from the academic staff and paid his normal salary, so that questions of profit or loss did not seem to trouble him too much. We also discovered he had his own farm which strangely was able to make a profit while ours was making a loss. The simple answer was a swift change and we appointed a man for his farming ability rather than his academic qualifications, made a share in the profit a substantial part of his salary, and under this new leadership the farm once again prospered. But the Road was much more intractable.

Returning to Zomba with this question foremost, I composed a letter to the Principal Secretary of the Ministry of Works. The arguments followed the line of the potential value of this Agricultural College as an international centre for research and professional development if linked by a proper road to the capital city and the airport, the deprivation suffered by the existing community, many of whom needed to go into Lilongwe daily, and the wear and tear on the many official vehicles having to use this route. For good measure we discovered a potentially large market supporting a substantial population a little further down the road, who would also benefit greatly from a decent connection to the city.

The Secretary, a most genial Scot named Charlie Clarke who had lived in Malawi for many years, sent back a very nice letter saying he agreed with all the points made. The only slight problem he had was that of cost. It was then estimated to be about eight

164

million kwachas. If I happened to have this amount to spare, or could suggest someone else who did, he would be only too glad to authorise the tarring of the Road.

This simple principle having been established, the answer came surprisingly easily but had to wait for another three years. Throughout this time I consistently campaigned through public addresses and private canvassing for the University to grow physically and for Government or the international community to help with capital provision. This was not easy for at this time both donors and politicians had other priorities on their spending, but one man who accepted the University argument was Richard Shortlidge, the Deputy Director of the USAID Mission, and author of the excellent Human Resources and Institutional Development scheme.

He encouraged me to put out the arguments for specific physical developments of the University, and then came up with the financial answer. The Mission had been carrying out a number of projects in the country in which dollars had been injected and kwachas generated in return to the extent that they now had many millions of kwachas at their disposal. Approval was still needed from the Government whose concern was that agreed public spending should not be exceeded, but eventually Richard was able to inform me that there could be something in the order of ten million kwachas available for our development plans, and that as USAID had always had a close relationship with Bunda, they would like it spent on this College. Faced with possible alternatives, I had no hesitation in giving the prior claim to the Road, confident that this was an expression of the main desire of the staff there.

Even with the money available and the Government approval to build the road, progress was far from swift. The funds had to undergo some bureaucracy before becoming available, the consultancy had to be established, tenders received and evaluated before work actually began in October 1990. Then the company, having started with just a few hundred metres quickly completed, seemed to disappear to do another job, and I never saw the work anywhere near completed. However the news in early 1992 was that the Road is now finished and all the benefits I had advocated in earlier writings on the subject, are now being enjoyed by the Bunda community and beyond.

Then there was the saga of the Medical School. This was by far the most ambitious project I became involved in. For many years Malawi had thought about the need for a Medical School, and each time had been deterred by the cost. But the longer the project was put off, the greater became the cost implications, and it was decided, a few years before we came to the country, that there was no sense in deferring the matter any longer. The cost of this most expensive of all academic disciplines might be prohibitive now, but next year it would be even worse, so the logic was to start as quickly as possible. The longer the delay, the greater the shortage of doctors. As recently as 1990 when the population had expanded to nine million, probably swollen to ten through the influx of refugees from Mozambique, there were little more than a hundred doctors in the country, one of the worst patient-doctor ratios in the world. Further, the majority of these were expatriates on short term contracts, leaving only about thirty Malawian doctors working in the country, and quite a few of these in administrative positions in the Ministry of Health. Students were sent abroad for training, but for a number of reasons, few of these returned to work in their own country. There was therefore a major need for a home based Medical School which could supply about twenty new doctors each year.

Two positive initiatives were taken in 1986, the year before I started. A team of Malawian, British and German Medical Educators were drawn together to work out the location, organisation and costs of a School in Malawi, and to recommend a curriculum. This curriculum aroused great interest in the Medical world, as it sought to lay considerable emphasis on the delivery and management of Primary Health Care, emphasising the role of the doctor as the leader of a district team, and as it attempted to integrate the clinical and pre-clinical components of the programme. The other was to begin the project immediately by sending off the first of an annual batch of twenty students to study in UK, ten of these to University College Hospital in London, and the other ten to St. Andrews University in Scotland. The idea, funded by the ODA, was that the pre-clinical studies would be taken in Britain for three years, followed by a similar period for clinical work in Malawi. One consequence of this plan which overcame the earlier inertia and actually started something happening, was that all subsequent planning was dominated by the thought that students would be returning in 1989 with three years of British training behind them, and expecting to find something comparable back in Malawi.

This was a good positive start but soon after I had arrived and settled, and noticed the glossy curriculum document on my office shelves, I asked the Registrar what was currently being done to prepare for this return. He agreed this was a good question. In fact it was several months into 1987 before anything started to happen. First, Dr. John Chipangwi was appointed Medical School Project Co-ordinator, and then an official Medical School Co-ordinating Committee was set up with the Vice-Chancellor nominated as Chairman. But before describing the activities of this Committee, it is necessary to say something about John Chipangwi.

John was a specialist gynaecologist, well known already for his dedication to serving the health needs of his countrymen. He had served on the original group who had devised the curriculum, and more than any one he could see the great need for a Medical School, and was determined to do all he could to make it succeed. He was also a Governor of the University, and one of the two lay members of the Appointments Committee, where his wise and humane contributions were greatly valued. When he decided to retire early from the Health Service to take on the full-time work of co-ordination of the Medical School Project, he was an ideal choice for the task. His dedication was tested early in that while civil servants were taking an inordinate time to define the job, the salary and the taxation, he actually worked without pay for several months with myself as Chairman of the Committee becoming increasingly angry on his account, before the matter was resolved. As I got to know John through our work on the School, and as we shared moments of encouragement and many more of despair over the progress of the project, I gained an increasingly high regard for him, and would attribute any success of the project to John's unfailing devotion, wisdom and determination to see it right through to fruition.

But chairing the project committee which was my job, was something different. The art of chairing academics is not too diffi-cult to acquire and I had much experience. After the first complete year as Dean at South Bank with our new committee infested structure I worked out that I had chaired 113 meetings, and I defined a meeting as an assembly of any size with formal agenda and minutes, and lasting at least two hours. In London a matter could always be settled by taking a vote, but this method was quite unacceptable in Malawi where consensus had to be the order of the day. This does have the advantage that no one need ever demonstrate the courage of their convictions by raising a hand, a potentially dangerous thing to do in that society, but it does impose a disproportionate strain on the chairman who is thereby required to express the sense of the meeting and attempt to make a sensible summary of the diverse opinions around the table to the extent that all can smile and move to the next item. Even then the task is made much more difficult because after trying one's best to make the required balanced statement, someone will invariably then make a small point which has the effect of throwing the delicate conclusion out of balance, and the debate has to resume and eventually a different summary has to be devised.

The difference with the Medical School Coordinating Committee was that the majority were senior and highly experienced Civil Servants, and this represented an unfamiliar culture for me. They knew the way the Government worked, they knew the unwritten ways in which the Ministries and the individuals concerned inter-related with each other, and I did not. Worse still from my viewpoint, the intention was that the vital Ministries involved, Health, Education, Finance, Planning, would be represented by their top people, the Principal Secretaries. After only six months in this new country I had to conceal my sense of inadequacy at these sessions. I think I managed to hold my own by the honest tactic of referring each item to John Chipangwi for an authoritative and acceptable summary, and the more disreputable tactic of trying to reduce every issue to a question in arithmetic where I felt much more comfortable.

The early months of the Project did not go at all well. There was the irritating question of Dr. Chipangwi's salary, with the depressing thought that if such a relatively straightforward matter was so difficult for top Civil Servants to resolve, how would they cope with the complexities of the building of the School? Then the senior members of the committee sent their deputies along with the result that the fast decisions needed had to wait for consultations within the Ministries. The early aim was to seek help from the World Bank, either directly or by the influence it could assert over other donors, and the right way to approach the World Bank was to write a project document. The Department of Economic Planning and Development offered to provide this, but the person appointed to undertake the task seemed to be for ever away at courses and conferences, so that for meeting after meeting the project was never there. I took my first initiative by breaking the protocol about such projects and asserting that surely someone at the University was capable of producing the goods if the Ministry could not. So Albert Jeremiah, our young Deputy Finance Officer, with Dr. Silumu from the Economics Department worked over the Christmas holiday and produced a full document indicating clearly the need for the Medical school and calculating the costs. The document they produced so quickly was in my opinion superior in quality to that of the World Bank consultants who were induced to come to Malawi and take us more seriously on the strength of our project. When the opportunity came, I had no hesitation in recommending Albert's promotion to University Finance Officer when still in his early thirties. He is a man with great prospects, and the document he produced was the first morale-booster in the life of the Committee. Other encouragements followed in 1988. We had a most positive visit from the World Health Organisation who were impressed by the determination they observed to bring a Medical School to the country, and their support was most influential to other donors. Then we had our first tangible offer of help with the UNDP promising to fund a Department of Community Medicine at the School.

However, following the World Bank consultants' visit, the debate shifted to questions of Health Economics. Everyone was aware of the magnitude of both the capital and recurrent cost of the School itself, but the impact of the World Bank and others shifted the debate to a further dimension. Suppose we were able to run a Medical School and produced, as were badly needed, between twenty and thirty doctors per year. Would the government be able to pay proper salaries to keep them in the country? Would they all be provided with houses? Would there be proper facilities for them to work especially in the more remote District Hospitals? Would the Nursing and Technical staff be increased to support their work? Since all these components together would add a substantial percentage to the annual health expenditure, what were the Government's plans for spending on Health, quite apart from the major additional funding needed for the University to provide Medical Education? The debates which followed placed more emphasis on the commitment of the Ministry of Finance than that of the Ministry of Health. The question also arose concerning the ways to raise funds to offset this huge burden on the Government. Would private patients be admitted, would there be health insurance schemes, would there be cost recovery in the Health Service, could there be health taxation etc.?

We could not deny that this additional financial dimension had to be taken into account and provided a serious challenge to the national commitment to found a Medical School. The cost of the School itself was almost beyond imagination, and to take into account not only the initial price of building, equipping and staffing, but also the price of the consequences of the School if it proved to be successful, was alarming but could not be ignored. From this point many of the potential donors focused their questions on the consequential costs rather than the initial ones, and it was not easy to find answers. At this time the whole expenditure on all sections of the Public Sector amounted to about a billion kwachas then equivalent to £250M with just over a tenth each to Education and Health, so the demands of a renewed Health Service following the successful production of twenty new doctors per year would place a disproportionately heavy demand on the Health Budget.

At the time when serious doubts arise on whether a project can be completed and that if it can, whether it would not do more harm than good by imposing major burdens on the economy, it was not surprising that we should be assailed by questions more directly concerning the validity of the whole concept. Why was yet another Medical School needed? Could we not send our students to neighbouring countries instead? Could not the vast sum to be spent on this School be much better used to improve other aspects of the Health Service acknowledged to be in great need, such as the General Hospitals, at present quite inadequate to meet the quantity of demand from patients, the delivery of Primary Health Care, and more significantly would it not be a more successful investment to spend on training the Medical Assistants who already carried out quite serious medical responsibilities? If we really wanted additional doctors, then instead of the huge development needed to produce another twenty per year, why not simply send about six per year to train abroad and do their clinical training in Malawian hospitals before returning home? In planning for a new Medical School were we not looking at a status symbol rather than meeting the real health needs of the country?

Faced with questions like these and the reality that some promising donors showed interest for a time and then withdrew, while others never even answered our requests, we had to be very sure that we were embarked on the right course and that we had the commitment not only to answer this diversity of questions and doubts but to see the project right through.

At this stage particularly I felt the personal need for spiritual assurance, and I did not hesitate to put the issues before all the prayer groups we were associated with. It was not necessarily an issue of spiritual warfare but certainly one in which wisdom and guidance were greatly needed. Some of these groups included people who I know to be unenthusiastic about the School but as we took the question into the spiritual dimension I received the reassurance that basically the project was pleasing to God and that we could seek His blessing upon it.

So we argued to ourselves and to our questioners that the acute health problems of the nation could best be tackled first by ensuring an increasing cadre of high quality medical practitioners. By training our doctors in Malawi we could best ensure that they were prepared for the needs of this country and that while we could never ensure that all would stay to work there, a much greater proportion than at present would remain. The existence of a Medical School whose curriculum emphasis had already aroused favourable comment abroad would serve as an attraction to specialists to come to the country and work towards the improvement in quality of the medical services. The argument about neighbouring countries was not really serious as these nations were hard pressed to offer enough places to their own people let alone from a new source, so in fact we turned the issue on its head and made it a policy that we would welcome students from other nearby countries which were too small to be able to build their own Medical Schools. To this end we sent a national delegation to three smaller countries whose Governments expressed support for the concept and were willing to pay for places in Malawi, helping to reduce the running costs.

The year 1988 had started promisingly with Dr. Chipangwi at last properly in office, the University having written the project document, the World Bank consultants having visited and the UNDP having given the first tangible assistance. But at the end of the year, we had to admit that little more real progress had been made, so we had to make the most regrettable decision that we would not be ready to receive students back for Clinical studies in 1989. This had been the hoped for consequence of sending the students out to Britain in 1986, and it was very much a reflection of our initial failure that we were unable to meet this commitment. We had started too late and too slowly in 1987 to follow up the progress of the previous year and it had not been possible to generate the momentum or even the urgency to convince that we could achieve by 1989.

In the event, the British Government came to the immediate rescue by offering to keep the first cohort of students for another two years to do the clinical part of the studies in Britain. This was not an ideal solution since it was an essential part of our philosophy that the training would take place under Malawian conditions. Students would work clinically with mainly young Malawians (half the population is under 20) out in the country rather than helping the relatively elderly in London hospitals. However we had no choice and were most grateful to the British for giving this second chance.

There was however a very major condition attached to this additional help, and that was that while five years of the course would now be done in Britain, the sixth and final year had to be taken in Malawi. There would be no third chance. If we were unable to provide for these students on their return in 1991, no option would be available. The country would lose considerable face internationally and students who had completed five years of a most demanding programme would be left without qualification or any visible means of completing. We had been reprieved but now faced an even greater challenge. We simply had to achieve by 1991. There could be no excuses this time. The task would be more difficult in that whatever we were able to offer, we would be facing students who already had five years of sophisticated theory and practice behind them, and who would expect no diminution of quality in Malawi. We entered 1989 with a daunting task ahead but at least much better organised, mobilised and motivated than had been the case two years earlier.

There were three ways and eventually a fourth which encouraged me that we could still succeed. The first was the support received from the President himself. I twice had audiences to report about the progress of the School, a matter of great interest to the President since Medicine was his own discipline. On the first of these two occasions he assured me of his support for the project, but made it very clear that he wanted only a first class institution, comparable with Edinburgh where he had studied. This was certainly a tall order but it was a most helpful principle to us in that whatever our resourcing problems might be we resolved always never to look for any cheap options and instead to seek the best quality we could.

The second occasion which must have been in 1989 was when we were in our worst difficulties and I told the President how hard it was to obtain help from donors. Without any hesitation he told me to try the EEC. When I returned home almost immediately I received a phone call from the EEC Representative who informed me he had just been invited to the Palace to see the President about the Medical School! I took the opportunity to brief him on the matter and after seeing the President he told me that although this was not in the Country Plan for Malawi, a request from the Head of State had to be taken seriously and he would take it up with Brussels. It would be nice to complete this part of the story by describing the magnitude of the response, but to my knowledge the Commission has not yet given support, but maybe the matter will be included in the next Lomé agreement.

Secondly it was most encouraging to receive support from the people of Malawi for the medical School. It seemed that whenever I had a press interview, the first question was about the progress of the Medical School, and I would find this interest in almost any more casual conversation. The students at the University were especially concerned that there should be a Medical School and most critical when progress seemed unduly delayed.

Thirdly we were encouraged at the darkest times by the interest from abroad. We would receive a steady stream of applicants for lecturing positions from all over the world and many of these were from highly qualified and experienced medical staff. We did not dare to advertise publicly until 1990 but by this time we already had a substantial file of gifted applicants. One of these was Geoff Dahlenburg, and we all thought that this application had to be given special treatment. He was already at the height of his career as Dean of a large Medical School in Australia, and we decided to invite him over for a ten day stay in Malawi to witness the state of the Health Sector at first hand.

Given a comprehensive tour of hospitals and other facilities, Geoff was even more determined to work in Malawi, and after giving him a formal interview, the University Appointments Committee decided that in terms of medical knowledge, appreciation of the health needs of Malawi, his genial personality and experience as a Dean that he should be the first Dean of the Malawian School of Medicine. Since that time Geoff has been able to visit the country on a number of occasions and his experience in working together with John Chipangwi has been invaluable in putting the various staffing and material resources together to build up the essentials of a new Medical School.

From these three major encouragements followed the fourth and most essential of these, the commitment of the Malawian Government. I have referred earlier to the set of questions raised by donors over the financial problems which might follow when doctors would begin to graduate in significant numbers, and have not yet given any answers. Basically what was being asked was what would the Malawian Government do, once the donors had delivered their part and gone home. The best way it seemed to me for this question to be answered was not by writing a paper or convening a conference, but by demonstrating commitment through some immediate action. The Government not only announced that the Medical School was of the highest priority to them, but proceeded to inject a few million kwachas to ensure the project could start on time.

The coordinating Committee had decided that the School would develop in three stages. The first stage would be in 1991 when the first students would return from Britain to do their final year in Malawi. The second stage aimed at 1992 would have the whole three year clinical programme in Malawi, and the third, hopefully to be well before the end of the century would offer the whole intended programme with integration of pre-clinical and clinical studies in Malawi. The main centre would be at the Queen Elizabeth Hospital in Blantyre, and three District Hospitals, one for each Region would be used as placement centres for the Primary Health Care work. The Government has already produced the funding to provide hostel accommodation and to refit the hospitals concerned to be able to provide medical tuition.

This quite substantial injection of Government funds has I believe served to demonstrate to donors the sincerity of the country and by 1990 it was possible to perceive a new attitude among the donor organisations. The British Government decided to support three professorial posts, and also to continue support for their own specialists in the country but moved to Blantyre to contribute to the School. Other countries have indicated similar support in staff, equipment and books, and a momentum has been achieved which will help others to contribute and to meet all the needs.

When the first cohort of students who went to Britain in 1986 returned to Malawi in October 1991 they were able to continue studies through their final year within a new College led by Professor Dahlenburg with three other experienced Professors and about a dozen other staff. The Medical School of Malawi was under way.

Chapter Thirteen
The Theology Degree

The third, and unexpectedly the trickiest ball to juggle, was the degree in Theology. It should have been a straightforward academic issue, but it turned out quite a spiritual battle.

For about ten years, the University had been validating a Diploma course in Theology. Nobody seemed quite sure about when and how this programme began, but certainly in 1987 it existed. I can be sure of that fact because one of the first things I was asked to do was to conduct the diploma awarding ceremony for graduates of this programme. Further, there had not been a graduation of this nature for a number of years so there was quite a backlog of diploma holders to receive. This was how I discovered at first hand that this programme already had a history behind it. The ceremony was a most pleasant one with former students now mostly ordained ministers coming back from as far as Zambia, and with at most thirty graduates present, I was able to talk to each one.

This Diploma I discovered, was unusual in at least two very different ways. First, it appeared to be the only award offered by the University for a programme presented entirely outside itself. Second, the diploma was an unusually oecumenical enterprise.

The same programme of work was presented at the Zomba Theological College which prepared both Presbyterian and Anglican students for ordination, and also at the two Catholic Seminaries. This type of theological harmony was most admirable, and making use of a combined Board of Studies it seemed to work very well. There were some good scholars at the Colleges concerned, who by pooling their learning resources, taught a very respectable course. Care was taken to observe normal University standards. The trainees could only take this course if they had the proper entry requirements; the examinations, the marking and any syllabus changes were scrutinised by University staff from our Religious Studies department, and most of the staff at the Colleges had sound academic backgrounds.

My almost immediate reaction to the discovery of this most desirable programme of work was to raise the question that if a diploma could be presented in this way, why not a degree? One of the unexpected discoveries I made particularly in my first year was that coming new into an ongoing situation, there were many ideas for reform and improvement which seemed almost self-apparent, and that whenever I discussed these with those most concerned, there was hardly any disagreement. All that was needed was an extra resolve to achieve something. This was particularly true about the need for a degree in Theology. All those concerned agreed that this is what they had been wanting for years. Why then did it not happen? Because they had been given the impression that the University might tolerate an outside presented diploma, but not a degree. I looked into this question, found nothing in the Statutes which might be discouraging, and added that we could answer critics by ensuring that the main part of the degree would actually take place in the University.

At this stage I could not imagine any opposition to a proposed degree in this field, and dwelt only on the very strong case for going ahead. The arguments could be rehearsed as follows: Looking at the issue nationally there was a great need for a better educated clergy. Malawi was and remains a very Christian orientated country with a high percentage of the population attending church regularly, and consequently with great responsibilities and opportunities for the clergy. The priest, pastor or minister would invariably become a leader of the community, and with expectations that he would lead in educational, health and physical resource extension as well as spiritual development. These were potentially key positions in national development, and with improved theological education, this vital work in the community could be achieved more effectively. This concept of the minister as community leader concerned to improve the standards of village living we believed to be properly biblical and at the same time provided a dimension to the type of curriculum we envisaged, and this leads to the second advantage of the proposal.

Since Theological Education in Malawi ended at Diploma level, any studies to degree or higher level necessitated going abroad. This meant in most cases that the course of study undertaken tended to have a narrow academic bias, and ministers would return certainly better qualified, but without necessarily having gained much that would help them in the work they would be doing. We believed on the contrary that further study in Malawi could have a better applicational framework to prepare for this most important of vocations and professions.

Thirdly, the concentration of higher theological studies with the prospect of appropriate postgraduate work and interaction with high level related disciplines would provide a strong centre from which the major issues of Christian development in the country and the neighbourhood might be analysed and penetrated.

Fourthly, we wanted Theology to be recognised as a proper University discipline, and to demonstrate that the normal rigours of scholarship applied here, widening the spectrum of academic debate. Finally, it was my hope also that this would set two good examples for the University to follow.

One was my continual concern about Chancellor College. While the other Colleges of the University were beginning to offer well constructed programmes of study suitable as preparation for specific vocational areas, Chancellor College persisted in old fashioned general degrees which lacked both coherence and direction. To operate a degree in Theology with such a clear vocational outlet would I had hoped, set a precedent for the multitude of other subject areas to follow.

Second, the pattern of a degree course offered partly outside the University with the concluding stages inside seemed a good one to follow. It necessarily put us in contact with the world outside,

178

and at a time when it seemed so difficult to physically expand the University, the prospect of numbers of students working outside the campus seemed a good thing to encourage.

Having stated these arguments, and convinced myself that there were both sacred and secular reasons for going ahead with this degree proposal, I return to the story of what actually happened.

The basic plan was to attempt two things at once. There were by now over the ten or so years of operation of the Diploma, a number of graduates who wished to move on to a degree qualification. The Diploma had taken three years of full-time study beyond the normal entry point of 'O' level, but we decided that a further two years would be needed to the degree, and then only for those with a credit or distinction rating on the Diploma. At the some time it was thought that a degree in Theology would be an attractive proposition for the normal school-leaver coming to Chancellor College, and this route within the Faculty of Humanities would take the usual four years.

This meant that the programme designers had to produce something which fitted in with the normal pattern for the school-leavers, implying a common Humanities first year, a specialised year in Theology for the second year and then two years in common with Diploma group. The four year group would have to match the degree of specialisation already attained in the Diploma while the former Diploma students would require something of the broader subject range acquired by the school-leavers. With a judicious selection of options in the latter two years, the job could be done, but it was a most unusual constraint, and certainly not easy to achieve.

In Britain I had worked with the CNAA (Council for National Academic Awards) and become a firm believer in the value of the peer-group review that is normally associated with this type of validation. In Malawi the way of doing things was quite different. We had meetings of Senate to which sometimes up to fifty were present, and this was the body which was responsible among many other things, for the validation of academic programmes. This was done by examining together the series of new or revised modules placed on the agenda. There appeared to be no consideration of the programme as a whole, nor even any thought for the purpose of the individual module within the programme. It was always assumed that if there were enough people in the room, then some-body must be present who knew something about the subject mat-ter in question. Most of the debate, however, was about whether the module was correctly formulated rather than about its content. I wanted to change this dysfunctional system and was most relieved when someone else suggested that surely the new Vice-Chancellor could propose something better than this!

My response was to put before the next meeting, a modified peer-group review system which involved scrutiny of a new or revised programme by a panel of experts from inside and outside the University. One consequence was that I was expected to chair each of these panels. As with much academic documentation, most submissions only just made it before the deadline, and this multi-plied the work in setting up the panels. On one occasion towards the end of the 1988-89 academic year, we had to work through ten programme proposals all in different subject areas in a single week. Mrs. Faustas Msonthi who was secretary to these panels actually succeeded in producing experts and employers from out-side the University in every one of these ten, and between us we supplied full reports for Senate to discuss in the following week.

The purpose of this digression is to explain that this is how we treated the new BA (Theology) proposals. As the validation idea was then new and few members of the University were familiar with the system, it was not surprising that the first proposals we received were not well thought out, and regrettably this certainly applied to the Theology presentation. The proposal appeared as a set of units related to the interests of the members of staff concerned, and without setting a coherent philosophy for the programme. It did not address itself to the structural problem, and left wide gaps in the curriculum one would have expected. We could not recom-mend the proposal to Senate for approval in this state.

Fortunately this was not too difficult a problem to resolve, although it did set the project back for a year. The staff were most capable of producing a good programme if given some direction, and they were joined at this time by Rev. Dr. Ken Ross. Ken had only just been appointed to the staff and he sat through the valida-tion meeting quietly but clearly formulating ideas of what could be done. The Church of Scotland has for many years funded a mem-ber of staff at the University, and Ken came to us in that role. He immediately took a prominent part in the academic and spiritual life of the campus and the town. He even learnt Chichewa to the extent that he was able to take on the pastorate of a village church in addition to his academic duties, and ministered effectively to the local congregation.

With the additional impetus given by Ken, the reinforced Religious Studies department was able a few months later to assemble a very sound degree programme which the most critical peer review group would have found hard to resist. We were now able to approach the approving committees with the confidence that we were offering one of the strongest programmes available in the University.

This was the point at which academic matters no longer became an issue, and to my recollection were never discussed again. The ground for the debate became very different. The programme proposal was put before Senate in July 1988. Prior to this time I had found Senate always open to reason, and I cannot recall opposition to any paper I had presented in my first eighteen months. This had included a variety of measures intended to take a reformed approach to research, consultancy, programme validation, staff allocation, and other programmes approved by the CNAA type method. But the atmosphere for the Theology proposal seemed different. For a start, none of those who had written the programme were present and worse still, there was not a single representative from the Faculty of Humanities which had earlier passed on its own approval at the meeting. I found myself in the strange and unexpected position of being the only person in the room in sympathy with the programme, but bound by the impartiality of the chair.

The discussion consisted only of opposition to the proposal. One prominent argument was whether the diploma was a real diploma or not. Since it was taught outside the university by staff who were not members of the University, could it really be considered equivalent to our own genuine diplomas? I pointed out that earlier at the same meeting we had approved awards at this level for graduates of the Theological Colleges on the same basis as we had for our own students, but the critics were not satisfied, and it needed some delving back into decisions of Senate when first encountering this proposal to settle the issue some time later. Then

181

there were resource arguments. Had the proposers properly calculated the cost of the new programme in terms of staff, books etc.? How would the former Diploma students be catered for? Where would they be housed and fed, and as they were to be taught at Chancellor College, would they take a significant share of food, sports facilities, consumables etc.?

I have no objection at all to critical arguments being presented at a meeting like Senate. In fact this is how academic advance is made and the right sort of objective comment should always be welcomed. On this occasion, however, there seemed to be something quite different present. The arguments presented were non-academic, unconstructive and easily refutable. The atmosphere of the meeting had a sneering, cynicism about it in contrast to what was normally experienced at Senate. For the first time I realised that the opposition was more than carnal and had to be treated in different ways. It also became clearer why this particular degree had been so slow in arriving.

The proposed degree was not going to start in October 1988 as hoped, but the door was kept open by Senate on the chairman's suggestion, agreeing to a referral back to the originators. The points made at Senate were taken seriously and each was refuted without great difficulty. The resource questions could be answered by the Theological Colleges undertaking to look after any former student accepted for the degree, and in fact there would be so relatively few of them that they would make minimal demand on normal consumables; if necessary, these small costs would be covered by a fee. The prestige gained by the operation of this course, the only one of its type in the Region would attract foreign students and donor contributions to enhance rather than diminish resources. The department together with the Dean of Humanities took these answers directly to the Principal of the College, who in the debate had raised some of these objections, and so convinced him that he became a supporter of the degree. The issue was brought back to Senate and cleared without much debate. All that was needed now was to gain the approval of Council at its next meeting in July 1989 and at last a start could be made that October.

In most Universities a positive decision by Senate on an academic matter is sufficient for a new programme to go ahead. In Malawi, however, it has been the custom for the approval of the

University Council to be obtained before anything can happen. My experience up to this point had been that provided the resource issues had been properly worked out, Council would go along with the Senate recommendations. The previous year had seen Council give warm approval to a whole bunch of new programmes. This included a total revision of the Engineering degrees and diplomas, changing the former General Engineering to specialisms in Civil, Electrical and Mechanical Engineering, a Diploma in Laboratory Technology, an M.Sc. in Applied Chemistry, and a B.Sc. in Technical Education open through British funding to all countries in the SADCC Region.

After the difficult passage through Senate, the prospects for approval from Council bearing in mind our good relation with them, and the willingness to support the previous year, looked very good. Already as if in anticipation of the outcome, qualified applicants who had waited years for this opportunity had begun to write to us. But the path was going to be even rougher than with Senate. I should have anticipated this much earlier. In May 1988, I was at the Garden Party in the Sanjika Palace grounds to celebrate Kamuzu Day, the President's official birthday, talking to one of Malawi's leading churchmen about the prospects for the degree. As we talked together, we were joined by John Tembo, and as this was the subject of the conversation, I immediately said that we were hoping for a Malawian degree in Theology quite soon. He said something before moving off which sounded to me like a token of assent, but my friend who knew better disagreed and gave his opinion that Mr. Tembo would not be in favour.

Those familiar with Malawi will appreciate the significance of this remark. Mr. Tembo, the Chairman as I describe him in another chapter, runs the show in the country. If Mr. Tembo does not want something to happen, then it does not happen. As among his many other functions, he is also Chairman of the University Council which he has been for about twenty years, a particular new programme which for any reason he does not desire, has negligible chance of success. The other members of Council with good reason, do not dispute his views, and often make every effort to obtain his favour by thinking additional arguments to support whatever he has said.

It was therefore somewhat naive of me to expect that the

splendidly presented proposals, reinforced by the refinement given by Senate, would win the day at Council. After my presentation, the Chairman went straight into the attack, claiming that the resources had not been adequately calculated and that here was yet another Vice-Chancellor trying to deceive Council into launching a programme whose costs would become unduly expensive in its later years. Further he claimed that Theology was not a developmental subject, and therefore of no concern to the University. As anticipated, I had to face these objections alone. The Chairman's arguments were supported by the other members, one of whom even stated that in view of the supreme importance of the Medical School, we should be saving all our money for that purpose and not launching any other new programmes.

Even the Chairman accepted my counter that we could not hope to run a University if there were to be an embargo on any new ideas other than medical ones, but his two basic arguments required a response from me since nobody else on this occasion would be willing to do so. It was all the more difficult as there was a personal attack implicit in the way he had put his case, and I would suspect this was quite intentional. The objection about resources was hurtful in that I had always taken great care to ensure that any proposal reaching Council had been thoroughly examined for resource implications, and all that they had received in my time were either without additional cost, or if there were a cost then an explanation of where the extra funding was coming from, would be provided. In the case of the Theology proposal there was the additional assurance that Senate in a highly critical mood had asked the same question, the matter had been carefully explored, and the answer accepted without difficulty.

The objection about Development was novel, but equally hurtful. To convince University staff of the major importance of commitment to assisting from our unique position in the task of National Development rather than attempting to become like a third-rate old-fashioned Western ivory tower institution was a priority task for me right from the beginning, and I would claim that no-one made a larger contribution to this than I did. All the new programmes devised in my time had this objective, and our internal validating system ensured that this could not be ignored. Certainly it was our intention that Theology would be both acade-

184

mically sound, and most intimately vocationally and developmentally inclined.

I left this meeting quite dejected. We had done everything possible to present the best programme we could, we had answered all objections, yet still not only had our ideas been rejected but even our motives and integrity had been questioned. Further we had identified as an enemy of the scheme, a most powerful opponent. The only consolation, was that the proposal had not been rejected but referred back for more information. Either my lone arguments carried sufficient merit, or more probably the secretary had made a providential mistake in recording the decision.

My colleagues who came to see me the next day were equally dejected. There would be no start to the degree in 1989, and yet again, our applicants would have to be disappointed. Our major decision, however was that we should not give up. As we had dealt with Senate by patiently looking at the objections and replying to them, the same should be done with respect to Council. A paper on the Developmental nature of Theology, and in particular its interpretation on this degree was prepared for the next meeting of Council, and with respect to the resource issue, a more positive approach was devised.

The degree proposal was becoming known internationally, and in particular we found two strong supporters, the Church of Scotland and the World Council of Churches. The Church of Scotland has always helped the University, and provided a fully funded member of staff, at present Ken Ross who has made such a fundamental contribution to the development of this degree. The Church offered, on hearing of the acceptance of this degree, to send a second member of staff. The Council of Churches offered scholarship funding to help develop Malawian staff to teach on this degree, and also a substantial book allowance. With help like this and the prospect of attracting fully-funded foreign students, we were able to go on the offensive and assert that far from this proposal being a resource waster, it would in fact be a resource gainer.

More important, we recognised much more now the nature of the opposition. There was no rationale for opposing this degree on academic or financial grounds. It was opposition to the objectives of the degree which was now seen as the fundamental one. There was opposition which we had observed manifested in various forms, to the whole intention to provide a better educated clergy with all the benefits that could accrue from it. Powerful forces did not wish this to happen and were using human agencies unknowingly or deliberately to secure this purpose. Therefore we had to recognise the nature of the spiritual battle we were involved in and to resist, using spiritual weapons, and particularly that of prayer.

The issue returned to Council early in 1990, and this time with an even better case, answering the objections made earlier, it was hard for Council to maintain its stand. However, just as I had needed on two previous occasions to take refuge in the device of 'referred back for further discussion', this time the Chairman had to take similar evasive action. He stated that he was still not convinced that the financial question had been answered, and that as Council had its Finance Committee, then the matter should be thoroughly investigated by them with a report back to Council. This was almost as discouraging as an outright rejection since this Committee was unlikely to be friendly to the proposal and met infrequently so that yet another year might be lost.

The way in which the matter was finally resolved was amazing, truly an answer to prayer rather than any human skill. I was away in England about the middle of September that year, and on my return I discovered that Finance Committee was going to meet the next day with the degree in Theology on the agenda. I asked to see the paper prepared for this meeting and as I read it saw to my dismay that the issue had been slanted to make the degree proposal seem enormously expensive. Then as I studied the document I noticed some fallacies in the compilation. The chief one was that the actual cost rather than the additional cost of running this degree had been calculated. For example, the cost of the school-leaving students entering the first year had been included in the total, and this made a substantial contribution. But I pointed out that these represented student places and therefore costs which we would incur whether we ran a Theology degree or not, and therefore should certainly not be included as additional cost. Further I found that having included unit costs for the students concerned, the costs of lecturers' salaries and library books had actually been added to these, and no account taken that two of the lecturing posts would be donor-funded.

Rather to my surprise, but certainly to my pleasure, the Finance Committee completely accepted my arguments, and agreed that the additional cost of the proposal was negligible. This would be recommended to Council who were due to meet in a few days.

When we arrived at the Council meeting, the Chairman informed us that he had much business to do with the President that day, and therefore would miss most of the meeting. However, there were certain items on the agenda that were not to be discussed in his absence; the remainder could be dealt with as Council wished. When he read out the lists of the two categories, he had in fact placed the Theology proposal in the second category. We were free to discuss and decide without him!

When this item was reached, the acting chairman stated that the only remaining issue on the acceptance of the degree was the financial one and that in his opinion the recommendation from Finance Committee looked most straightforward and acceptable.This view was agreed without any further discussion. At last the BA in Theology had been approved, and the first students were able to start in October 1990.

The three examples given in these last two chapters illustrate the difficulty of achieving anything substantially different. Each of the three was a costly project, but finance, though it looked like being the chief obstacle to progress, was never in fact the major problem. The money was there provided it could be released for an effective purpose, and so long as the ideas were strong enough to prevail, resourcing became the secondary issue.

Reference has been made earlier to Stanley Nyirenda's doctoral project on the subject of implementation. His field research concerned the growth of the Secondary School sector over the 1970s. He endeavoured to discover the causes why a well planned and heavily supported programme actually produced hardly any growth over this period, and many examples could be given of how magnificent plans, especially in this part of the world, do not achieve fruition.

From my much more limited experience, as illustrated by what has been described in these chapters, I have become very aware of the spiritual dimension of what I deliberately describe as a conflict. Especially in the Theology degree, but also in the

Medical School and even the Bunda Road, the necessity for prayer, and taking up the weapons of spiritual warfare, became abundantly evident. These were of vital importance in first assuring us that our intentions were right, then in receiving wisdom over the tactics to employ, and finally to overcome the obstacles to achievement.Our struggle was not against flesh and blood, but against principalities and powers who manipulate people for their own purposes.

I have tried to give the reasons why the people of Malawi needed a more effective Agricultural College, a Medical School and a better educated clergy, the latter point being well illustrated by the exceptional influence that the united churches are having upon the country in this transitional period. Naturally I am most satisfied to have played some part in bringing these institutions about, but it is my firm conviction and immediate experience that but for the grace of God, and the combined prayer of my friends, very little would have been achieved.

Chapter Fourteen
The Tracer Study

arly in 1988 I had an idea. It should have worked supremely well and made a substantial contribution not only to the University of Malawi, but also to Higher Education generally. In the event it did succeed to a certain extent but nowhere near as I had hoped. The opportunity is still there for someone else to try, but my initial attempt did not go entirely according to plan. This chapter tells the story of the concept of the Tracer Study, how it was implemented and what it did achieve.

The basic idea was that it would greatly help in our planning and policy making if we could find out what had happened to our former students. Had they obtained employment, and if so had this been with difficulty, how long had they waited, how had they progressed, how many had reached the top of their professions, what were their salaries, and mostly, how had their University education prepared them for what followed? Related to this we wanted to know how this education had helped in their personal development. If in addition to all this we could obtain information from employers on what they thought of our graduates, then we would have abundant information to help us in correcting any mistakes and providing more appropriate programmes of study in future.

It was my intention to do this on a large scale, not just taking a sample, but inviting all our former students to contribute. An exercise of this magnitude would be most costly, and certainly beyond our own means, but when the USAID scheme of Human Resources and Institutional Development (HRID) became available, the funding question could be resolved, and the ambitious intentions, never before attempted, as far as I was able to discover by any University, could go ahead.

I first discussed the proposition with Rudi Klauss, the project director, and he was most helpful. It seemed a natural consequence of the project that as training needs were identified, the University would become the major local institution to meet these requirements, and that anything the University could do to evaluate and improve its own performance would be good for the scheme as a whole. The problem of financial support was solved.

We agreed that the best way to start the study would be to select suitable researchers from each of the Colleges, and then to bring in a consultant to advise on the research methodology and the instruments to be used. It was also my plan that the long vacation from July to September that year should be used to locate our former students. We had some records which could be used, but much more needed to be done using the media to promote the exercise and invite participation. Since Malawi is a well organised country it should not have been too difficult to locate the great majority of our graduates. Then we would employ students during this vacation to send out and receive the questionnaires. In fact, I even had it worked out that the University Football Club, who normally have to camp out in Blantyre over the long vacation to complete their league fixtures, could receive gainful and remunerated occupation for its players in the long periods between matches, through involvement in this survey.

Rudi worked very quickly and within a short time he had secured the consultancy. It turned out to be a double blessing because we received from the University of Massachusetts, a husband and wife team providing sociological and numerate skills respectively. Having met this couple and enjoyed a good briefing session with them, I left them to discuss in more depth with the selected researchers, and set off for my mid-contract leave in

190

England, happy that when I returned in September I might be in time to take part in the final analysis of the results.

It was good to be back home even if it turned out to be a wild and wet British Summer. The most notable feature of this vacation was that at last we moved away from Sidcup. We reasoned that on completing in Malawi we would not necessarily need to return to Sidcup, and that instead we should move to wherever was most useful for us as a family. Rachel by then was a student at the University of East Anglia in Norwich, so we decided to move there, and for the next two years she looked after our new family home with her friends from the University. This turned out to be a timely move as shortly after leaving Sidcup, the rumour emerged that the cross-channel railway link was to come that way with Sidcup as a major terminus. This never actually happened, but it was a good rumour, and property became very difficult to sell as a result.

When we returned in September I was most disappointed to discover that the Study far from being near to completion so that we could start to work on the implications of our findings, had in fact hardly begun. One excuse given was that the printers had been slow in providing the initial letter to the graduates that had been identified, but whatever the reason, the opportunity of the long vacation had been wasted, and work had to start in term-time when the staff concerned would have much less time available, with my footballers back to their normal studies.

Consequently the Study started very slowly, and this immediate loss of momentum was hard to restore. The procedure we adopted was that letters of invitation were sent out to the many graduates who had been identified, most of them replied, a sample was selected, the main questionnaire sent to them and then returned. The numbers involved were still quite manageable. The University had been in existence for twenty-three years at the time of the exercise, had started very small, and grown steadily but slowly to a total population of about 2,500. On studying the records from the Colleges we had to eliminate the double achievements of those who had gained first a diploma and then a degree. This meant on counting the graduates that just 5,557 had passed through the University, and this implied as a thought to note, that less than 0.1% of the population of Malawi had a University qualification.

Using announcements on the radio and the press to augment

our own knowledge, we succeeded in tracing 3,012 of these, a reasonable return of over 60%. A sample of 1,561 was selected, and from the questionnaires sent to them, we received 1,153 replies supplying an abundance of material to be digested. One of the points of interest was to make comparisons between the four different Colleges which made up the University. In order to balance the differing sizes we decided to split Chancellor College since it was the largest, and had been graduating students for the longest time. This was quite an easy vocational split to make since an almost equal division was made between students who had taken Education courses and the rest. This distinction besides modifying the differences in size between the now five groups, also enabled Education to be singled out for more separate treatment than if left in the mass of Chancellor College. We also made the decision that in order to both compare and examine particular vocational and other features from each of the Colleges, the respondents would receive two questionnaires, one of a general nature concerning University education as a whole, and the other designed to ask specific questions about the College they had attended. There was a third questionnaire sent to employers of our graduates.

Quite apart from the loss of vital time at the beginning, it seemed that a number of basic mistakes were made. Each College had its own Computing facilities, and used what they had to store and analyse results. It was extremely time consuming later on to try and transfer all the data on to a single system. The main instrument of the research, consisted of a string of questions in which a simple statement is made and the respondent relies either very satisfied, satisfied, dissatisfied, very dissatisfied or non-applicable. I was always uneasy about our method of analysis in which we gave these responses the values 3,2,1,0, respectively without being confident on how to handle the non-applicable type of reply, and then averaged out the scores. It seemed to me that we were in effect offering only discrete integers as the response, and yet drawing conclusions from rational averages of these. Thirdly we found that the experiment as initially designed allowed little scope for cross-referencing, or considering variations over time.

The questions, however, were both clear and comprehensive. We asked all respondents, for example, how effective the University had been in the provision of basic studies, in major areas of study, quality of instruction, availability of courses, accessibility of staff, assistance in employment and appropriateness of training.

The five constituencies, from different disciplinary areas, offered the opportunity to look for comparisons between them, and this turned out to be a good way to notice significant differences. There was a noticeable, but not unanticipated difference over success in preparing for employment between the College of Nursing who responded with a high average of 2.5, and the essentially non-vocational Chancellor College who averaged a low 1.5 on this issue. It was encouraging to learn that the College of Agriculture which had placed much emphasis on studies in Science, received a score as good as 2.3 for the provision of basic studies from their graduates.

We went on to ask, 'What is the importance of the University in helping you to discover vocational interest, earn a good salary, prepare for a career, be of service to the community, gain general knowledge, develop leadership skills, become a good manager'.

From this set of questions we learnt that the University had done quite well in the eyes of its graduates in fostering a sense of service to the community, which was pleasing to hear, but not so well in most of the others. In particular, there were low scores in helping to provide a good salary, especially for those in teaching or nursing, and in preparing for management in which only the nurses, who had some background in this field, gave even a respectable score.

This bad response was most interesting, as it opened up a debate on the function of the University. As earlier noted, less than a tenth of a single percent of the population were University graduates, and one implication of this was that almost everyone of our graduates would have a managerial role in whatever profession they took up, or at any rate would be expected to do so, and yet the University was providing almost as little preparation for management as it was doing for marriage. Further many reports on the state of the economy and the service sectors stressed the great lack of management ability, and put this as a prior need for national development. What then should the University be doing to help? Certainly we had a small Management department at the Polytechnic, but this served largely to give short courses to professionals already in employment, and there existed virtually no provision for undergraduates. In the discussions that followed, most staff I spoke to accepted that in conformity with the needs of the nation, the University should take responsibility to give some preparation for management, but regrettably no one inside or outside the University seemed to have any clear ideas on how this could be done.

A number of other interesting facts emerged from this study. We discovered for example that while through the agricultural policies of Malawi, only about 10% of the population live in the four cities of Blantyre, Lilongwe, Zomba and Mzuzu, probably over 80% of our graduates can be found there. Again up to as many as half of our graduates have been able to go abroad for further study, nearly one fifth taking Masters' degrees. Then apart from the deficiency in management preparation, the gross lack of cultural education was stressed.

There was inconsistency in the way in which the College aspect of the study was conducted. Grace Machili, then Principal of the College of Nursing went about the task with great energy to discover the effectiveness of every aspect of the Nursing curriculum. While others sent surveys by post, Grace visited all the Hospitals where our graduates were employed, and obtained information of quality which could be reliably used in further planning. In contrast, the Education researchers completely missed this opportunity, so that we obtained very little idea of how effective was the way we prepare teachers for Secondary Schools. In general, the staff from Bunda College, KCN and the Polytechnic performed the work with interest and ingenuity, but both halves of Chancellor College produced defective work in comparison. This also added to the delay as we tried without success to bring all reports up to the same standard, and also to persuade more employers to share their views.

We were most saddened that Grace became seriously ill and died during the course of the study. She had done her work in exemplary fashion, and provided data which became the basis for a whole day's discussion which is described later in this chapter, between the University and senior staff from the nursing profession.

In order to help clarify some of the issues which were emerging from this study, we were joined by Simeon Chiyenda, the Vice-Principal of Bunda College, and an excellent statistician. He began to provide the help we had been lacking in this key area, and should have employed at the beginning, but before he had a chance to make his contribution, he too contracted a sudden illness and died shortly afterwards. There is no doubt that his input would have made a significant difference to the quality of the Study and we all had much cause to lament his tragic death. He had made a start on the application of statistical packages to the data and it was a cause of further regret to me that I could find no one able or willing to continue this work.

The Study which I had hoped for completion at least by early 1989 was still unfinished when I left Malawi at the end of 1990. However I felt so committed to its completion that I gathered up all the papers and took them back to Norwich with me. Much of the first two months of this terminal leave was spent in compiling the Study which I was able to complete and send to Rudi Klauss in Lilongwe. The World Bank also asked for a copy, and so I hope the study will have some influence directly on the present University management, and also on our main donors. A summary of the Study was also accepted for publication in the *Higher Education Quarterly, Volume 45, Number 3,* which appeared towards the end of 1991.

One effect of finishing the Study on my own was that I wrote a concluding chapter based on the findings from the Study and proposing ways in which the University might develop from there. For the benefit of those interested in the growth of the University of Malawi, I offer these recommendations for further consideration.

BUNDA COLLEGE

Bunda College of Agriculture has 1372 graduates and 1067 of these were traced, a very high proportion indicative of the affection which former students have for this College. A sample of these received the questionnaire and 332 of these responded.

The College based questionnaire was well devised and enabled Bunda to learn much about their graduates, also gaining some new information about the nature of the agricultural industry in Malawi. There is no doubt that Agriculture is by far the most important sector of the economy with tobacco, tea, coffee, sugar, cotton, beans and groundnuts as the major exports, and at the same time an expanding population, now over nine million to be fed. As the country's leading College of Agriculture, Bunda has potentially a most vital role to play, and one of the main interests of this Study has been to evaluate the extent to which the College is providing what the nation needs from it. Certainly much has been achieved, but this Study taken with other reports and observations indicates that very much more could be done.

There is a general criticism of Agricultural Colleges in developing countries, that unless there is a firm attachment to both the public and private sectors, there will be the danger of academic drift away from national cooperation towards the type of College in which the specialist interests of staff become the dominant factor. in the case of Bunda there was a quite specific mention in a USAID report of 1986 which indicated that while the best qualified agricultural researchers in the country were there, most of their time was spent at a relatively low level teaching Diploma students, while the Ministry of Agriculture had to engage its own, mostly lesser qualified staff to work at its research stations. The report gave as one reason for this state of affairs, the attachment of the College to the University, in turn related to the Ministry of Education whose interests in supporting agricultural research were clearly not too high.

This was something of a caricature but there were strong elements of truth and coming to the College in 1987 it was possible to detect some clear symptoms. There appeared to be no formal link with the Ministry, as the report had indicated, and little except in a very informal sense with the private sector; the College had a large commercial farm running consistently at a loss which to the newcomer would appear to have a most negative effect on aspiring agricultural students, but even worse, the staff did not appear unduly worried about this. Whenever the opportunity occurred for staff to take short intensive courses to improve their knowledge in specialist areas, always it was the long-term Ph.D. training that was preferred. Even with the great opportunities offered by the HRID scheme which provided an open door for Bunda development, I twice needed to refer back proposals from the College as being far too Ph.D. orientated. On another occasion the Israeli Ambassador brought a visiting Professor of Irrigation from this country which is probably the most successful in this technology of such great need to Malawi, but after a good academic discussion there was no follow up by the College.

Various improvements have been made, and these are implicit in the Study. A liaison committee between the College and the Ministry, chaired by the Principal Secretary of Agriculture had been established with the President's approval so that there is now an official channel of communication; new management has been appointed to the Farm with proper incentives and three successive years of profit have followed; the Research Coordination Unit at the University Office has enabled Bunda to benefit from a number of externally funded research contracts all in areas of vital national need; above all there have been welcome changes of attitude by staff as the eminently outgoing nature of the College questionnaire had indicated.

The survey carried out by the College demonstrated some differences over time. For example, the employment patterns showed that whereas in 1969-72 over 75% of graduates were going into Government service, especially in the Agricultural Development Divisions of the country, by 1985-87 this proportion had reduced to 42%. Whether the emphasis of the curriculum had sufficiently taken into account this movement towards the private sector is not known, but certainly this previously unknown factor should influence further thinking in devising suitable academic programmes.

The College also concentrated on discovering form its graduates, the relative importance of the five departments with respect to employment prospects, and within each department, the relative value of the courses presented. The significance of the approach was that the College had reviewed its undergraduate programme in 1986, changing what was becoming an outmoded general diploma and degree to the provision of specialist paths within these two awards, and clearly feedback from graduates was needed on the acceptability of the specialisms provided.

The response with respect to the departments indicated that Crop Production with a 2.5 rating was by far the most relevant to vocational needs, while Animal Science rated poorly at only 1.5. Rural Development was rated well at 2.3 with the courses offered by this department in Rural Sociology/Extension, Farm Management, and Agricultural Economics being particularly appreciated. While noting the importance of Crop Production, particularly when the leading exports of the country are considered, it was still disappointing to discover the low view being taken of

Animal Science. It is ironic that when the SACCAR organisation offered with German financing, a range of Masters' degree courses to four Southern African countries, Malawi was actually selected to provide the programme in Animal Science. In fact the staff is strong in this area, but confirmatory to the graduates' views on the subject, it has proved most difficult to recruit Malawians for this particular course. It would seem that Bunda has a mission to convey to the nation the need to think again about the great value and potential of Animal Science.

As with the other Colleges, there was a great demand for further training, especially from diplomates wishing to complete their degrees. Out of the 1372 graduates of the College, as many as 951 have passed the diploma but have not had the chance to go on for the degree. At present there are not many opportunities for this type of upgrading since the University policy is to give priority to school-leavers to take up places at the College.

The responses of employers were of a generally critical nature. The performance of graduates engaged in research was considered moderate; those working in tea or coffee were not entirely satisfactory; a lack of management skills, especially in personnel management was observed, and in conjunction with this, a general lack of preparation among those working on large estates was noted.

It is clear that Bunda has potentially a most significant role to play in national development, and if the issues raised by this study can be given serious consideration, then the deficiencies observed can give rise to some radical thinking to transform the effectiveness of this College. As a starter I would suggest the following:

A major effort is needed to follow through in greater depth the criticisms, especially those made by employers in this sector, in order to gain a clearer idea of how the country is progressing agriculturally, to determine what the basic needs for higher level teaching and research might be. Despite some worthy attempts to update the curriculum there still appears to be a mismatch between the type of graduate needed, and the type actually produced. At one level, many of the country's major export crops are not studied at Bunda with the reason sometimes given that the physical location of the College precludes the production and processing of these crops. If this is the case then the suggestion made in the

Study, and supported by employers is that the programmes should include periods of industrial attachment in different parts of the country, where more specialist knowledge of particular crops can be obtained.

At another level there is consistent complaint about the lack of managerial skills, and attempts should be made to rectify this within the curriculum. Experience of attachments would again be helpful, and in addition the department of Rural Development could naturally extend its activities by the inclusion of Agricultural Management and Marketing.

The newly established liaison committee can be made more effective by increasing formal links with the parastatal and private sectors, and by giving some staff specific coordination roles.

A recent report from the organisation SACCAR, estimates that by the year 2000, countries in the SADCC Region will have enough qualified agriculturalists at diploma and certificate level, but there will be a shortage at masters' and doctoral level. The M.Sc. programme which they have initiated for Malawi, Tanzania, Zambia and Zimbabwe is a first attempt to rectify this, and the whole tenor of this report is that Colleges in the Region like Bunda, should seriously consider upgrading their work.

At the same time, taking into account the desire that diploma holders have expressed to train to degree level, and also that while Bunda continues as the only College in the University to perpetuate the three year diploma/five year degree programme with only one third of the diplomates going on to the degree, it will be in danger of losing its share of better students who will look instead to Chancellor College or the Polytechnic for greater chances to obtain a degree. The time is now right to make a radical change in policy over student selection.

The proposal I would offer is that the College should cease to offer the diploma which can no longer provide that amount of specialism to meet present vocational requirements, and replace the main programme by a four year degree course. At the same time the College would be able to offer substantially more opportunities to diploma holders to return and complete more specialised degrees. The College would be able to provide more postgraduate, research and professional development courses, which not only meet the current national and regional need, but also employ the talents of the highly qualified staff.

CHANCELLOR COLLEGE

As has earlier been stated, Chancellor College is the original College of the University, founded by the University Chancellor and Life President in 1965, at first in Blantyre, but then transferred with splendid new buildings to Zomba in 1974. With these advantages, and its five Faculties of Science, Social Science, Humanities, Education and Law, the College should be the figure-head of the University. In some ways it does achieve this and in other ways it lags behind the other Colleges. Regrettably this proved to be the case in the response made to the opportunity provided by the Tracer Study, and while graduates responded well to the general questionnaire, the chance to learn much more through the College based part was not well taken by the staff concerned. There is therefore not a great deal that can be added from the Study, and the comment which follow are based more on my own speculation than on fact.

From both the Educational and non-Educational reports, the demand for further training is as evident as at the other Colleges and the majority would prefer to return to the College for this purpose. As with the other Colleges shortage of space is preventing much additional training from taking place, but in recent years the College has utilised the long vacation to present a number of new programmes to those for whom there would be no room in the normal term time. In particular, an M. Ed. in Educational Planning and University Certificate in Education (Agriculture) have been successfully presented in this sandwich mode, and this would appear to be a useful device to handle requests for in-service training.

The demand to introduce a range of programmes at Masters' level is being met. Besides the one described at Bunda College, there are such programmes started at Chancellor College in Education, Industrial Chemistry, Fisheries Biology, Sociology of Women in Development, and another in Economics is soon to follow. As described elsewhere, three at least of these have been made financially possible through the HRID provision. These desirable courses apart from meeting a national need for specialists in these areas, serve to demonstrate the increasing maturity of the University, and encourage staff to work at a higher level with appropriate research in support. It also lessens the need to study abroad for higher degrees.

While the incursion into the area of higher degrees and the constructive use of the long vacation period are to be commended, the College needs to perform a long overdue revision of its undergraduate programme, and related to this, to consider what to do about its very small departments. Since 1965 the College has attempted in its role as the non-vocational part of the University to provide for the nation as many such disciplines as possible. There are now in the five Faculties no less than twenty-two different departments. This would be a splendid achievement if the College were large enough to admit such diversity. Unfortunately physical and financial constraints have so far prevented growth much beyond one thousand students. The consequence is that there can be a total of only 110 staff who are spread over the 22 departments at an average of just five per department. Under this arrangement, unless there are proper amalgamations, no department is large enough to support its own degree programme. To complicate the issue, there has over recent years been a most pronounced swing to Science in the College. This has been largely caused by the desire to increase the number of Mathematics and Science teachers as described in an earlier chapter. The more numerate approach to the Social Sciences and the popularity of Computing have further added to the load on the Science departments.

These are all desirable trends, but since the single national University philosophy makes it virtually impossible to close a department however unpopulated by students it might become, and each such department must retain an irreducible minimum of staff, then given a fixed maximum total of staff relative to the unchanging number of students, the pressure and ratios borne by the subjects in greater demand becomes increasingly intolerable. The only real answer is to double the size of the College, and let increased staff numbers match those of the students more naturally. This could only be financed by an organisation comparable to the World Bank, but given the successes achieved by students at both undergraduate and postgraduate level, this would be an exceptionally worthwhile investment. For the present, I would advocate some judicious combining of departments, counter to the current tendency to fragment, in order that more specialised degree routes can be established. I have little confidence in the degrees being obtained as a fairly randomised collection of units at present, and would hope that the example demonstrated by the new B.A. in Theology will be followed by others.

KAMUZU COLLEGE OF NURSING

Taking part in the study might have been considered premature for the Kamuza College of Nursing (KCN), the youngest of the four Colleges, founded as recently as 1979. At the time of the study only 110 (all women) had graduated and all but two had been traced, with 71 of these responding to the questionnaire. Some male students have been recruited to KCN but none had yet graduated. Over 99% of the graduates were still under thirty and consequently had not moved far in terms of promotion or salary.

In 1987, the Blantyre School of Nursing became part of the College so that from 1991 there will be a double output of graduates from Lilongwe and Blantyre at the rate of up to sixty per year, but the single output over a short period of time accounted for the very small sample of graduates available at the time of the survey. In the circumstances one would not have expected too much from the report, and would have reasonably deferred judgement for a few years further. Fortunately KCN did not take this attitude, and instead seized upon the opportunity to do a very thorough investigation and evaluation of the whole teaching programme, emphasising both academic relevance and professional preparation, and as will be demonstrated, this has already had important effects upon the College.

Nursing is a matter of great public interest in Malawi. The College came into existence as part of the University because in response to complaints about the national standard of nursing, the Life President decreed in 1979 that training should be upgraded to University Diploma level, and he provided funds for the building of the College in Lilongwe. Consequently students and graduates from KCN have always had a high national profile and criticisms about the profession as a whole often attributed to the performance of the College itself. Such criticism has not always been fair since as will be seen from the figures just quoted, KCN graduates are still a small minority within the profession. However, the College has always been concerned about its public image, and in particular took advantage of the opportunity given by this study to help evaluate its performance.

In reviewing the report from the College two points emerge at once. The first is the standard demanded by the College; when the combined satisfaction scores are used, anything less than 100% is a cause for concern to the staff. It is their desire that each subject and each component will fulfil a meaningful purpose, and in most areas very high satisfaction ratings relative to other Colleges are obtained, but even these are not good enough for KCN. There is always room to improve, and the College is to be commended on the way it seeks to do this. The second is that in the context of vocational preparation, it is not so much the concept of 'satisfaction' which is tested but rather the questions of 'relevance' and 'adequacy'. The College is not out to provide diplomas for school-children but to produce mature professionals for this honourable vocation.

In response to national criticisms about nursing care and standards, the College had boldly embarked on a patient-centred approach emphasising the Nursing Process in which the nurse cares for the whole needs of the individual patient through processes analysed as assessment, planning, documentation and evaluation. This was a brave response to a public who expected its nurses instead to go about the traditional daily routine and who were prepared to criticise if aspects were neglected. It was therefore all the more satisfying for the College to obtain such a positive response from their graduates to the question of the adequacy of the teaching of the Nursing Process. Much less successful was the response concerning Midwifery, and this question is discussed below.

The graduates were asked their views on further training and while it appeared there was a good demand for management courses, requests for Advanced Nursing were even better. The employers made a very helpful response with full replies from 29 out of the 33 approached. It is likely that the high standards required at KCN were shared by the employers so that the general confidence implied by their positive responses is most encouraging. The graduates scored highly on work attitudes, productivity, knowledge, skills, appearance and punctuality. Adverse scores were recorded in understanding of science and quantitative thinking, which regrettably did not come as a surprise.

The College is to be congratulated on the very thorough survey it carried out particularly as it illustrated the continuous interaction between the College and employers designed to improve the national standard of nursing. The report on KCN was the subject of a meeting between senior staff in the nursing profession who included the leading officials in nursing at the Ministry of Health and matrons at the largest hospitals and senior staff of KCN together with the University Registrar and the Vice Chancellor. The meeting was a fruitful one in which the profession underlined the great improvements being made at KCN and the college in turn indicated what they had been doing. The question of job preparation was specifically addressed and one cause agreed was that as the students took a compulsory one year course in Midwifery after obtaining their Diplomas in Nursing, it was unfair to thrust them immediately into positions of responsibility on the wards without the opportunity to review their earlier skills and knowledge. It was therefore agreed that each hospital should provide an induction programme to ease the re-entry into general nursing with a view to preparing the graduates for leadership roles in the service.

The meeting stressed also the paramount importance of human relationships, and the College undertook to make this fundamental issue more prominent both by formal tuition in Counselling and Interpersonal skills, and informally through normal interactions among staff and students. There would also be a short course on Ethics and Etiquette as part of the curriculum.

A basic problem for resolution is the compulsory year in Midwifery, taken between finishing the three year Diploma and starting work. With the population rising by over 3% per annum, and a still high infant mortality rate, it is clear that it is hardly possible to practice Nursing in Malawi without experiencing a heavy load of childbirth, baby and maternal care. However, the emphasis in training on compulsory Midwifery does imply that the other specialist skills in Nursing are neglected, and the immediate year away from more general aspects of Nursing causes the discontinuity noted earlier. It is also likely that only about a quarter of an intake will take up a specialist role in Midwifery, so that the case for a more varied fourth year in which other specialisms can be offered ought to be considered seriously.

POLYTECHNIC

The Polytechnic is located in Blantyre, Malawi's largest city and industrial centre. The opportunities for developing responsively to the needs of the growing economy are most exciting and the Polytechnic has always sought to meet the academic and professional needs of the commercial and industrial community, as well illustrated by the robust, interactive nature of the College questionnaire it produced.

It has been observed that the Polytechnic also enjoys an advantageous position through being an integral part of the University. In other countries where the Polytechnic or its equivalent is a distinct institution, it inevitably becomes downgraded with inferior students, staff and resources, but in Malawi the parity with the other Colleges and the ability to offer University awards, enables it to maintain a more esteemed position. In fact recent experience has shown that the best qualified students at the Malawi Certificate of Education, equivalent to 'O' level, prefer to join the Polytechnic, and the degrees in Engineering and Business Studies consistently attract recruits of high calibre.

It is most commendable that in view of its great potential as a provider of high level training in key areas, the Polytechnic has expanded its student intake from 500 to over 900 in the last three years, and could easily double again if only the accommodation were available. There is certainly an outgoing attitude in the Polytechnic, but by its nature the College must continually be seeking to respond to and even anticipating developmental needs, and it can be argued that the current approach is not radical enough. The prospects will be discussed in the final section, but prior to this there is much to be extracted from the results of the questionnaire, and some of these will now be considered.

Industrial Training

The Polytechnic has for several years encouraged students to take industrial attachments during the long vacations and the majority are able to do so. The four year programme for Technicians presented by Polytechnic staff but not yet recognised as a University course has two formal periods of six months training, and the Diploma in Public Health now has an assessed attachment as an integral part of its programme. The responses given by the graduates on the helpfulness of attachments in the survey, are

205

somewhat indifferent and should cause some reconsideration of the benefits of this largely voluntary exercise. The employers at the same time raise questions about graduates' practical and managerial abilities, and it could be that the larger programmes in Engineering and Business Studies should follow the example of the Technician and Public Health courses in formalising the industrial placement as an integral and even assessed part of the courses. The matter is worth serious debate at the Polytechnic especially bearing in mind the successful use of sandwich courses in Britain and other countries, but ultimately it is industry and even the Government who will need to be convinced. There will need to be a dialogue with industry to ascertain if in order to improve professional preparation of graduates in these subjects, periods of attachment for as much as a whole year can be financed, and this is one of many pointers that the Polytechnic needs to establish closer relations with Malawian industrialists. The Government in turn which through the Ministry of Labour already gives direct support to the Technician programmes, will need to be convinced of the merit of attachments for degree students and to agree financial measures with industry to enable it to happen.

Short Courses

Coupled with the desire for further training is the support expressed to take specialist short courses at the Polytechnic. The College is in a strong position to offer a much wider range of short courses than it does at present, having the facilities and without rivals. It is therefore hoped that the authorities will take note of this strong demand from potential high-level customers.

The Polytechnic being in the centre of Malawi's largest conurbation is also very well placed to offer alternative modes of study by part-time day release, evenings and use of vacations. For several years over two thousand students per year have attended lower level evening classes at the Polytechnic, and now the opportunity ought to be taken to transfer these elsewhere and offer more professional level courses in their place.

Computers

The report from the Polytechnic is the only one which has drawn attention to the needs of Computing, and the analysis indicates the present lack of facilities at the college which therefore has to provide a poorer preparation for the modern world of business and industry. It is encouraging that some help in this respect has been negotiated with international donors, but the Polytechnic will now need to integrate computing processes more fully into all programmes and continually seek to extend and upgrade the hardware and software available.

Employers

Apart form the observations about lack of management and practical skills the views of Employers are most supportive, and on the scale of satisfaction, a warmer response is given than that received in any other College. The basic components of appearance, punctuality and clear writing are most highly commended, indication that these professional qualities are well presented by teaching and example at the Polytechnic.

The College questionnaire and the responses given, have supplied the Polytechnic with much cause for open-ended discussion and the onus must now be upon the College management to ensure that the issues raised are fully debated and bold changes made where these are seen to be necessary.

There are many issues besides those which emerge from the study here, but all relate to the fundamental question of the closeness of Polytechnic interaction with industry, commerce and society, particularly in the Blantyre setting. Decisions must be made, for example, on the need for a Management Centre with sufficient autonomy to function effectively, on how to provide more places for students when the demand for graduates in these areas is still wide open, whether to meet this need by a division of the year into two six month periods with much greater emphasis on attachment for the remaining time. and whether to modularise all programmes to the extent that there can be direct industrial sponsorship for some. The Polytechnic can afford to be bold in its thinking and action. There is much to be gained and little to be lost.

This chapter has concentrated on the results of the Tracer Study as it effects each College in turn, but at the same time there is much for the University as a whole to consider. General problems common to all Colleges have emerged, such as the need for more cultural education, the lack of preparation for leadership and the necessity to draw ever closer to the professions which the University serves. There is the continuing need to expand, to provide many more opportunities for young Malawians as well as in-service and professional development training for the more established, and in doing this to maintain and raise the quality of educational provision. There are gross shortages of student accommodation, staff housing, classrooms, laboratories, computers, books, journals, scientific equipment, library space, sporting, aesthetic and medical facilities even for the size of community we already have, let alone the greatly expanded University which the country needs and deserves.

It is hoped that this report will not only help the University to improve itself, but will also demonstrate to those outside the University, something of the achievements, the potential and the prospects for the University to fulfil its noble purpose in service of the whole Malawian community.

Chapter Fifteen
Final Broadcast

During my time as Vice-Chancellor, we had great support from the Malawi Broadcasting Corporation. With their co-operation and advice, we had a regular Saturday evening spot in a programme known as University Magazine. The MBC allowed us to use their valuable time on the simple agreement that we could actually provide a programme each week. Thanks to our energetic Publicity Committee, we managed to fulfil our part of the deal, and the Corporation never had to fill this time with light music or any other substitute through lack of material from us. We provided round up reports from each of the Colleges, discussions of Curriculum innovations, Research ideas, Music, Sports and Student matters of interest. As the University is such a reflection of Society, we were never short of ideas, but there were some tense times as we struggled to put the material together in time for the Saturday evening broadcast.

In my last week the Corporation broadcast an interview with me, and this chapter is a transcript of that programme. Some most interesting questions were put by the interviewer, Mr. Sam Gundwe.

SG: Vice-Chancellor, you are shortly to leave the country after four years. What do you feel have been the highlights of your time in Malawi?

JD: In a sense the whole of the four years has been a highlight for me because certainly this time in Malawi has been the best part of my career without any doubt at all. I had never worked outside London before coming here, and I wondered how I would adapt to Malawi. But this has been no problem at all. The people of Malawi have been most friendly, the staff at the University have been very co-operative, and the Life President has made us most welcome. I feel that I have been able to enjoy the work immensely and at the same time to have achieved something.

Now you asked for particular highlights? Well the work of a Vice-Chancellor is a continuing one, with many quite different things happening at the same time. It is difficult to say at any one time, that some goal has been achieved. Take the Medical School for example. This has been discussed years before my time, and it will go on being discussed for years to come. It so happened that in my time here the decisive steps had to be taken. I think I would describe the time we spent planning as alternating between despair and hope. Just when we thought something significant was going to happen, it didn't happen. There was always this uncertainty. Anyway I can now assert that there will be a Medical School here and starting in October 1991. This to me is a very major highlight. I won't be here to see it start but it has been very satisfying to be involved in the preliminaries, certainly something to remember.

Then there has been the construction of other new programmes. Again, all these have long drawn out procedures of negotiation, communication, dialogue, validation, and then the programme begins, the first students arrive, and it's all very satisfying.

Then there are more mundane things like the Bunda Road to give one example. Almost from my first week here the question was put to me, when did I propose to do something about the construction of this road? I suppose my contribution has been to write and nag at the authorities until the money was provided by USAID and it has been another highlight to see this work commence. This road should really put Bunda on the map and help it become an international centre for Agriculture.

These are a few highlights which come to mind, but as I said, it's hard to pinpoint them when so many interesting things are happening all the time, and all at different stages of progress.

SG: The University of Malawi is a relatively young Institution if we compare it with Universities in Europe or elsewhere. What developments, expansions or innovations as far as the academic work at the University of Malawi would you like to see?

JD: It is quite right that the University is still new, and it is I believe in a healthy position with some very good work having been done over twenty-five years. About seven new Universities were started in Britain at the same time in 1964. Recently I read a report about a conference these new Universities had held to assess the progress over these years. It seemed that they could not find much to celebrate and had very few ideas on what their future might be. This is not the case with the University of Malawi. We have many ideas, and look forward to the advance of the Medical School, we can anticipate the benefits of Distance Learning to reach more of the population, and we are a national University. Essentially our aim is to meet the specific educational needs of Malawi as they can be identified. The basic point is that if anyone can demonstrate a national need that we are not meeting then we have an immediate motive for becoming involved in that very area.

For example, one very major feature of Malawi is our huge Lake. This present all kinds of challenges for research and teaching, in Fisheries, in Tourism, in Geology, yet with a very few exceptions, hardly any work was being done in this area. Now we have introduced at Masters' level, a programme in Fisheries Biology, leading to many research opportunities in this important field.

Then we look in other directions, In Engineering, and this counts as another highlight for me, we were first able to reduce the unnecessarily long and general six year programme to specific five year degrees in Civil, Electrical and Mechanical Engineering with a remarkable number of distinctions by students in these courses, but even this move leaves us in far too general an area. The country needs more specialised areas in Mining, Chemical, Processing and Textile Engineering.

Then we should be developing areas like Architecture, Surveying and Building. The University is just beginning to enter these important areas. It was a surprise and delight for me to visit the Polytechnic at its Open Day during the 25th Anniversary week,

211

and to meet a new lecturer in Surveying just arrived from UK, and then to see the first steps in the teaching of Architecture. Again, the country has great potential for Tourism, and the University should be supportive by providing programmes here, not sending people abroad for training. There are many other vocational areas which we would be expanding into.

The general academic coverage provided is good, apart from these areas of need which I have specified. However, as I keep on saying, the major need of the University is to grow, to expand, to give many more opportunities for students to come here. I am most pleased that when I arrived there were only 2,000 students at the University, and now there are nearly 3,000. This rate of growth must be kept up and even exceeded.

SG: No doubt while you were in Malawi you made many links with academic staff and also with the public. What word do you have for them now on leaving the country?

JD: The academic staff have been very helpful. I would just wish to impress on them, the importance of intellectual independence. I had the feeling when talking to staff early on that as the great majority of Malawian staff had obtained their higher degrees in Britain, America, or other places abroad, that they looked to these countries for their source of inspiration. I would hope instead that staff would have more confidence in themselves, and that the University will stand on its own feet and develop its own thinking.

The second thing I have always tried to impress on staff, is to think more about what they are doing. There is a tendency, experienced the world over among academics, to study their own field, acquire expertise and then just give out lectures on that theme. Very few are able to think around their subject, understand how it is developing, and work out the implications for the curriculum, for teaching and learning and the progression of students.

This University is very good at helping students to pass examinations, and because we have achieved such success in doing this, I have advocated that we should extend the challenge to our students. Not just to pass more and harder examinations, but to look at the material in a more open-ended way, to solve problems which may not have a determinate solution, to do more research projects as we have been introducing into most subject areas, to develop professional attitudes where appropriate, and to mature as people. One thing which our own research into our graduates has shown is that there is a feeling we have not prepared them in any way to take on positions of management or leadership, and that as there are still very few graduates relative to the size of population, they are likely to find themselves in these positions often much sooner than they think. The University staff should be thinking out how to respond to this clear need.

As far as the public is concerned, I think that certainly they give the University much more support and esteem than Universities receive in Britain, and this is a source of great encouragement to us. In turn I think we need to interact much more with sections of the outside world, especially the Government and the private sector. We need to win the confidence of Government officials that we are able to provide the help that the country needs. We need to show that when the need for a major Consultancy arises, it isn't necessary to bring in someone from abroad. We have local expertise and when this is combined with local experience which does not need to spend several weeks trying to understand the nature of the problem, then we can offer a much better service than the excessively paid invitees from abroad.

In turn I hope the Government will recognise that we have in the University probably the strongest and most diverse range of expertise to be found in the country, and that in recognition of our potential for research, consultancy and the provision of highly educated workforce, they will give higher priority to our development budget so that the buildings and equipment we need to extend these activities may be forthcoming.

I would hope also that we could arouse more interest among the Business community, and during this silver jubilee year we have raised an appeal for funds specifically directed at the private sector. The rationale for this is that we provide graduates for both the public and private sectors, rather more for the latter if anything, and it would seem appropriate for this sector which freely receives these trained graduates to contribute towards their continuing provision. It is particularly in subject areas like Accountancy, Marketing, Computer Science and Engineering, of special interest to the private sector that we are in the greatest need of help if we are to continue to produce graduates of the right quality. It is hard to attract and retain good staff in these areas as salaries in the private sector are much higher. However, if the sector wants us to continue producing the people it needs, then we must receive more help from them.

Looking at our relations with the public more widely, I would mention the press who have always been most encouraging to us, and who have reported our activities with accuracy and understanding. I must, of course, pay tribute also to the MBC who have strongly supported us, especially through the weekly programme University Magazine which we have had the honour to present with you. The Radio has greatly helped in making the national University known to the public.

SG: What will you be doing when you return to Britain?

JD: Well certainly retirement is not on my agenda! I enjoy working hard and expect to continue to do so. One thing I will say is that I have now been working continuously in Higher Education for 33 years, and unlike many of my colleagues at the University I have never taken a sabbatical, not even for a single term. So my reasoning is that 33 years makes 99 terms in succession, and therefore my 100th term will actually be a sabbatical.

We will first go back to England and stay for about three months in our home at Norwich. One of our daughters is being married there in February, so we will certainly be there as well. After that I expect to be working again. I cannot say too definitely at this moment but there are one or two good probabilities but not yet confirmed, and I do expect to be working in a similar type of job sometime early in 1991. It is even quite probable that it will not be too far away from here, so I am looking forward to re-appearing in Malawi from time to time.

SG: You must have set out from Britain four years ago with some set objectives of what you wanted to achieve in Malawi. Are you going back home satisfied that you have been able to accomplish these objectives?

At this point the programme stopped abruptly and the News started. We had over-run our time by a minute. I do remember that at the recording session I came up with some very profound answers to this question, but as the discussion was spontaneous and unscripted I had no record, and unfortunately could not remember what these last minute profundities were. That must be a matter for re-construction in the final chapter.

Chapter Sixteen
The Last Minute

Sam Gundwe's question did not get an answer, as our recording had over-run by a minute, and the listeners received the headline news instead. So in this closing chapter the aim is to reconstruct with more time available, and the retrospect of almost two years, what I might have said in that last minute, with some latitude to extend the time interval.

Sam had asked about my initial aims on leaving Britain for Malawi, and the extent to which felt these had been accomplished. I will therefore try to recapitulate what my thinking had been in 1986, based on years of experience in Higher Education as outlined in chapter four, my two visits to Malawi in May 1986 for interview, and November 1986 for an exploratory week, and the many contacts I had tried to make in preparation for starting in January 1987.

I would say that I set out fundamentally with a vision, out of which particular aims could be derived. In personal terms I regarded the remarkable opportunity to lead a University in an African country as the culmination of the life experiences I had been given. To be precise I always looked on this opportunity as a calling, a mission for which I could look back on my times in the London Polytechnics, the fellowships particularly at Sidcup, South Chard and Giggs Hill, and with my own family as a very specific training for the work I was now privileged to attempt. To feel called in this way gives a continual confidence and an inner strength to perform a complex task, but at the same time provides an additional responsibility. Not only is there the need to evaluate the progress of the University, but also to be deeply concerned about how faithfully the calling is being followed.

However the accountability implied by such a vocation, worked out in my experience to be no continual guilt-trip, forever looking back on personal failures (of which there were quite a few), but rather in a joy and peace of exploration, conflict and sometimes accomplishment. I simply praised God for placing me in this position where uniquely in my experience I had both the opportunity to achieve something significant, and the personal resources through my earlier preparation exactly suited to perform this task. At no time in my life have I been more fulfilled.

The vision I had was to see Malawi as a nation in need of the right kind of development, and the University as a major vehicle to bring this about. As the University could be made to progress, so the nation would progress. As the University with far and away the greatest concentration of multi-disciplinary talent to be found anywhere in the country, could take on its natural leadership role, so national problems of Agriculture, Business, Economics, Education, Health and Technology would be met by the appropriate provision of research, consultancy, advisory services and professionally prepared graduates. Even the giants of poverty, ignorance and disease could be encountered.

It is apparent that the type of vision just described, is not fulfilled quickly or easily. It was better to regard it as a process rather than a completion, and in this light it formed an essential background to all the existing and new activities that we attempted. From the vision it is possible to formulate aims and objectives at every level of operation. But if the vision is lacking, I do not know how the problems of running a University in a country like Malawi might be tackled.

In terms of achievements, those which seemed to be successful, those which laid a foundation for others to build on, and those which were downright failures, are all documented in the earlier chapters. It will be quite clear which of these were my own favourites, and which gave the greatest satisfaction. However, to achieve an objective with respect to a complex institution like a University is seldom easy to demonstrate.

I have continually been challenged by some words of John Beishon, the most innovative higher educational leader in my experience. After nearly six years at South Bank, where he had challenged the whole system and injected so many new ideas, he remarked to me that he still felt that 90% of the College remained exactly as it was when he arrived. Institutional inertia is hard to overcome. In fact he was showing a rather uncharacteristic modesty. He had made enormous differences to the improvement of the Polytechnic. With this example to follow, and in very different circumstances, I would like to feel that I achieved a comparable degree of anti-inertia.

The rate of change and development is however, not directly related to the ideas and energy of the Vice-Chancellor, but rather to the extent to which he is able to influence colleagues to go along with these, and if this can be done to any noticeable degree, the extent to which he is able to receive ideas in return, and work towards mutual implementation. Only when there is such agreement of purpose is there a valid development and any reasonable chance of successful continuation after leaving the scene.

It was always my intention to encourage this sort of debate. I announced early on that I held to the Popperian philosophy that an argument became stronger not through attempted verification, but by falsification. We cannot prove; we can only improve. Therefore I advised colleagues that the best way to help me in my own learning process was to refute my arguments. I did not always enjoy it when they actually did so, but at least the opportunity for constructive dialogue was there.

How this dialogue worked out can be best illustrated by looking at a few of these initial objectives, and seeing what became of them over the four years. Here are seven very basic ideas and the outcomes:

(i) Following immediately from the vision, to develop a University suitable to meet the needs of the people of Malawi.

(ii) One such need being for greater opportunities to pursue Higher Education, to increase the size of the University.

(iii) To increase the range of specialist programmes available.

(iv) To be responsive to identified needs for new programmes or other activities.

(v) To be continually raising academic standards, and improving the value of the programmes being offered.

(vi) To devise new educational methods suitable for the professional preparation of graduates.

(vii) To initiate postgraduate courses and research work.

After the vision and the consequent aims, comes the practical outworking, and the realisation that in the realm of the possible, not everything desirable will be achievable. The aims were, however, a constant reminder of what needed to be done. The seven as defined constitute a reasonable framework to evaluate performance, and I will now try to indicate how effectively or otherwise, each was achieved.

(i) To develop a University suitable to meet the needs of the people of Malawi is a very general aim, and I have described in chapter five my own philosophical approach to the question. Also in chapter two when challenged by the World Bank about the necessity for the expense of a University in a developing country, especially in relation to the needs of the primary sector, I gave as justifications the role of the University in teaching, research, cultural leadership, and national morale.

In terms of the programmes we offered, I have earlier stated the need for a vocational approach, and indicated that the great majority of our students were on courses that led to specific careers in areas of national importance. Further the efficiency which ensured that almost all of these achieved graduation in the minimum time without any disruption of study, meant that a most valuable service to the community was being given. At the same time it is necessary for a national University to offer as diverse a range of subjects as possible, and there was always the opportunity for more academic areas as well. However, as I pointed out to staff, while Malawi needed its poets and philosophers as well as its engineers and agriculturalists, it actually wanted many more of the latter than the former, and this should guide our selection over the Faculties. In practice this was never a problem, since the students themselves were well aware of this relativity, and not unnaturally chose the areas where the jobs were likely to be found.

I was reasonably content that our academic profile at undergraduate programme level met the needs of the country. We were producing a constant supply of hard-working and well prepared graduates in the right proportions of need. Whether we were producing enough is a matter for the second question.

The research as will also be described was beginning to provide a valuable service, but my major concern in this section concerned the questions of cultural development and leadership. In the Tracer Study described in chapter fourteen, the main causes for concern raised by the graduates were the lack of cultural facilities and the neglect of preparation for managerial roles.

The first of these should not have been a problem at Chancellor College since it had the marvellous facilities of the Great Hall and the Fine and Performing Arts Department provided by the Chancellor. Some very good work was done by this department and I have already given the examples of the annual Choral Workshop and the Travelling Theatre. However, despite exhortations from the Vice-Chancellor, there seemed little response to making these facilities generally available to the students outside the department, or to take responsibility as potential custodians of Malawi's cultural heritage. The situation was worse in the other Colleges which lacked the facilities enjoyed by Chancellor College, exceptions being the Orchestra founded at the Polytechnic, and the annual College drama festival. The potential is there since when we celebrated the 25th Anniversary of the University at Kamuzu Stadium in December 1990, the students made some magnificent contributions to indigenous dance and drama.

The Management issue is an important one since bearing in mind the still acutely small numbers of graduates relative to the size of the population, almost everyone will step into a leadership role within a short time of graduation. The normal full-time student receives virtually no management preparation, except in the Nursing Faculty where the implications of vocationalism are taken seriously. Further it is a common complaint among the leaders of industry in a developing country that it is lack of management rather than lack of technical skills which hinders effective progress. In Malawi we have recognised the problem but have not solved it.

One further area in which the University relates to the country as a whole, is in the provision of workshops, symposia and seminars of a specialist nature. These are the places in which different sections of the community can meet with appropriate staff from the University, problems are identified. and sometimes a way ahead can be worked out together. We certainly had an abundance of such conferences, most of them initiated by the University, and in this way the University was able to fulfil its essential role in national leadership.

(ii) It was always my ambition to increase the size of the University. This was achieved to the extent that when I arrived there were just over two thousand students, and when I left four years later there were nearly three thousand.

I would immediately give the credit for this achievement to my colleagues who worked with great diligence to find additional accommodation, make it fit for students to live in, and establish a means for some students to live outside the Colleges. All this was achieved without help from the Government, apart from some small additional finance, which was quite inadequate to do the job effectively. Other countries in the Region had grasped the importance of Higher Education, and in several cases a University expansion was the consequence of a Government directive. Sometimes these increases were too large and not well prepared, but at any rate the purpose was there. In contrast the Government of Malawi appeared to have very little ambition for Higher Education, and planned only for a small increase to be taken up by the Medical School and what was described as extra-mural education. The initiative for the expansion at Malawi came entirely from the University itself, and the outcome was even in contradiction to the Government Plan. By providing more opportunities for students, the standards did not decline, despite the lack of supporting resources, and the graduation rate, and hence the productivity of the University increased significantly. It is one of my greatest satisfactions to have been associated with this achievement.

However, relating this expansion to my reasons for wishing to expand, it was not nearly enough. There are three basic reasons to desire expansion. The first is to meet a social need. Despite the lack of opportunities at secondary level, the numbers of students passing the Malawian equivalent of 'O' level, and thereby qualifying for Higher Education was increasing by 10% per year, and with input from the Malawi College of Distance Education as well as the secondary schools, had reached over four thousand. The University could only offer seven hundred places, and the rest of the higher educational sector together with scholarships overseas, could barely raise this figure to a single thousand. Not all of these 'O' level passers were suited for University education, but I was confident that from this highly motivated group, we could double our intake figure without danger to our standards.

The second reason was economical, and based on the fact that almost everyone of our graduates was in a vocational field such as Nursing, Education, Law, Engineering, Science, Agriculture, Business, Technology, Accountancy. These are all areas of great national need where the demand is for many more qualified graduates to help expand the economy.

The third reason relates to both in that if the University could be expanded it would operate more efficiently, and could offer a wider range of subject areas and vocational specialisms in accordance with both individual abilities and professional requirements.

These arguments were presented continuously during my term of office, and the success achieved relative rather than absolute.

(iii) The need to increase the range of specialist programmes arose form the recognition that the country now required specialists in technical fields rather than the rapidly trained generally educated civil servants needed immediately after Independence. This was not an original concept; clearly some of the Faculties had already seen this and were acting upon it. My function was more to give general recognition to this movement, and to encourage it on its way. Not only was there the motivation to prepare students more effectively for the professional world, but also I remembered Hermann Bondi's inaugural address when a student of his at Kings College. He actually chose the need for specialists as the title of his talk, and he made the point that only by specialising in a subject does it become interesting.

In contrast, the general situation I found at the University was that it was normal for students to study for three years in a number of subjects to qualify for a diploma, and then only the top third were permitted to do a further two years to take a degree.

This seemed to me to offer the worst of both worlds. The majority of students were compelled to give up before they had really grappled with a subject much beyond the equivalent of 'A' level, and whatever their chosen profession, they would have little to offer at this stage. The consequences of major reform in this area would impinge on the number of places available for others, but reform still seemed very necessary.

One exception was Engineering in which the lucky third were subjected to not two, but three further years to a degree. I asked the question on my first day of office, why was it that students with the same 'O' level qualifications could go to Chancellor College and obtain a degree in four years, to Bunda and graduate in five years, but if they chose Engineering it would take six years? Because nobody seemed to know the answer, I determined at any rate to reduce it to five.

The reason the course as presented took so long, was that it was a General Engineering degree, incorporating Civil, Electrical and Mechanical Engineering, and the reason it was General was that visiting British consultants ten years previously had declared that it should be so. It proved to be possible virtually at a stroke, to change at once to three specialist degrees in these different disciplines, reducing to five years, specialising the diploma in a similar way, and with the resources saved by this reduction to allow many more diploma holders on to the degree routes. The staff and students responded very well, and the first group of students through this new scheme secured more distinctions in the final examination than the rest of the University put together.

The diploma became abandoned first by the Education Faculty in favour of a four year degree, and then by the Faculty of Commerce with new four year degrees in Accountancy and Business Administration. My one disappointment in this area was Agriculture which before my time had introduced more specialism into the curriculum, but still continued to retain the three year diploma with only the best third progressing. I hope they will have changed by now.

(iv) Always there was the quest to look out for new programmes as required, and to seek other ways to fulfil the objectives of the University. This was an area in which I experienced both success and failure, in retrospect mostly the latter.

These failures occurred mostly in areas which were supposed to generate funds, and I suppose this is a field in which the academic should tread very warily. In principle I supported the idea of income generation. If it could raise much needed funds for the University, provide additional income for members of staff so that they would want to stay rather than seek greener pastures, and at the same time bring the staff more immediately into current professional practices to help make teaching more relevant, there seemed everything to gain.

One of the first causes I took up was the policy on Consultancy. I discovered that the University did permit Consultancy by members of staff provided that the project was approved and registered, and the person concerned was allowed to keep 20% of the fee. I asked how many Consultancies had been registered under these circumstances, and was not surprised to learn that the number was zero! We set up a new Consultancy working-group which among other recommendations, put the personal share at 75%. This idea seemed smart at the time but received very few takers from among the known Consulting fraternity who preferred to collect their normal 100% and not tell anyone. However, I was able to use the device on a few occasions when Consultancies were addressed to my office and I was able to pass them on to the appropriate expertise. This was particularly gratifying as I had been arguing that the international organisations in particular, should instead of bringing in expensive Consultants from abroad, look to the talent we had at the University whose additional local knowledge would enable a project to be completed more quickly and effectively.

My efforts to put these interactions on a more business like basis following the advice given by Professor Ashworth, and the reasons why it didn't happen are described elsewhere, as well as the most successful introduction of CISNA (Computing In Southern Africa) by my colleague, Omar Selim.

One idea which did materialise almost as anticipated thanks to funding from the HRID scheme, was the postgraduate conversion course. I noted early on that although we had some very good staff in the Faculty, comparatively few students were registering for Humanities, and those who did, tried to slip into the Social Science Faculty, one assumed because of the better job prospects. I wanted students who were able, to take degrees in Humanities and complete the final year without the worry of looming unemployment to follow. I remember receiving a visit from a graduate who reminded me that he was the former Chairman of the Students Union, voted by his colleagues as the student most likely to go the furthest – but, his degree was in Classics, and after several months he was still seeking work.

This seemed a blatant contradiction of what the President had always affirmed as the value of a classical education, and I tried the Civil Service for this young man, regrettably without success. In the end we gave him a job as a University Administrator, where he is doing very well!

However to avoid using this device too often, I formulated the idea of trying to initiate graduates of Humanities into professions which were known to be seriously short of personnel. This was achieved by offering a range of one year conversion courses, initially in Marketing and Accountancy which would at least give a starter into a new profession. The potential employers were enthusiastic about this proposal since they would receive graduates whose learning experiences were much wider than those normally received into these professions. As indicated at the beginning, this idea worked partially in that while it was meant for Humanities graduates, it was in practice taken up by a much wider range of disciplines who also liked the idea of moving without too much pain into Accountancy or Marketing.

Possibly my greatest disappointment in this section, although it could still be rectified, was my attempt to bring Distance Learning into the University. It seemed to me that every year we were through our limited size, turning away at least two thousand potential students who would most probably never have another chance for Higher Education. While physical growth of any magnitude seemed out of the question, the only alternative it seemed was to parallel the Malawi College of Distance Education by offering this mode of study beyond 'O' level and even up to degree level.

After several months obtaining Ministry of Education approval, we secured the services of a Consultant from the Commonwealth of Learning in Vancouver, Dr. Prebble who operated the Distance learning scheme at Massey University, New

Zealand. He visited us in May 1990, and was most encouraging. Under certain conditions Distance Learning would be possible, and the cost would not be as prohibitive as we might have thought. There might even be substantial cost recovery as the scheme developed.

After putting the proposals through the required committees, and placing the matter largely in the hands of the Faculty of Humanities who would initially be the major users, I had to leave the scene, and it is a matter of regret partly to me, but mostly to the many Malawians who would have welcomed this opportunity, that the idea appears to have progressed no further.

(v) Standards are what everyone believes in but few can define or even recognise when they see them. It was my intention to raise academic standards and improve the value of the programmes being offered. This is most important for a University because first and foremost we should be concerned about the quality of our products. I have to admit to being totally output orientated. I am not so much interested in the calibre of students when starting a programme, nor other input indicators like research funding gained, but rather in the value of the research done, and the achievement of those who graduate. It is much more difficult to assess output performance, let alone what value has been added by our tuition, but the attempt must still be made. This was the motivation in presenting the Tracer Study. The intention was to probe into the immediate and subsequent graduate performance, and from this to determine how best to improve the undergraduate curriculum.

There were other ways to determine if the quality reached international standards, without which our work would have been valueless. All our subject areas had carefully selected External Examiners, and as most of these had to be flown in from all parts of Africa, this was a considerable expense for the University but one which we struggled to maintain. These examiners chosen for their academic ability and international experience were often critical, and we always discussed these criticisms extensively, but at the same time their reports frequently included some most complimentary and unsolicited statements about the overall quality of the work in comparison to international norms. It was most gratifying, to give one example, that when we first changed the Engineering programmes as described above, obtaining a large number of distinctions, we had two British Professors of Engineering present as examiners, who endorsed the calibre of the work produced.

Another useful indicator was that a number of those successful at degree level were awarded scholarships to take Master's programmes at British Universities, and most of these were able to succeed in the normal period of a single year.

An argument less easy to sustain, but one which I believed in, was the success rate achieved by students in end of year examinations. I had no previous statistics to work on, but when reviewing end of year performance in July of my first year, it immediately struck me that the results were surprisingly good. In fact when performance at the September supplementary exams were taken into account, I calculated that about 95% of the whole student body had passed their respective years. I made a point of referring to this remarkable achievement in my first Graduation Day speech that November, and unashamedly called for an improvement the next year which proved to be forthcoming, and the rate went up to over 98% by my fourth year.

These results were most gratifying since I have always taken the view that given reasonable standards, in our case endorsed by external examiners, students who are properly selected, work consistently and are well taught in an efficient learning environment, should pass. If students drop out for other than personal reasons, fail to take their examinations or fail them in significant numbers, then something is wrong with the Institution. The high pass rate, on the other hand, is an indicator that the University is healthy, that students are well motivated, and that staff are caring and diligent.

Not everyone would agree with this argument, and I found some who would interpret a pass rate of this magnitude as an indicator that standards had in fact declined! It is, of course, very possible that despite the vigilance of external moderators, courses can be made easier to pass and any such laxity is hard to detect. I preferred to take the stance that standards should always be maintained and wherever possible, improved. To this end I initiated debates in all the Faculties on this issue. Since students were able to succeed in such high proportions, I contended, it should then be reasonable to increase the demand made on them, and I invited Faculties to propose ways in which more could be expected of their proteges. Unfortunately nothing very positive came from this challenge, apart from a few rebuttals from Faculties who claimed that already their standards were so high that it was not possible to improve them! At least this partially refuted those who claimed that a high level of passing necessarily implied a decline in standards. In any case to have persuaded all members of staff to take part in a debate on the intangible question of standards, drew sufficient attention to the issue to have resulted in much potential improvement.

My major contribution towards the raising of standards was the system described earlier for scrutinising new programme proposals by means of peer review with relevant professional advice. We had some excellent discussions on these ideas, and in most cases succeeded in launching new programmes in the right direction.

(vi) It was always my hope to encourage new educational methods, to look for appropriate alternatives to the chalk and talk lecture, and the conventional examination as the major means of assessment. After four years it is probably true that there was as much chalk in the air, and as many three hour unseen exams as ever. It is hard work to introduce and sustain any significant change. However, a few attempts were made.

I had always been inspired by John Beishon's concept of the Technopark as the equivalent for Engineering and Business students of the teaching hospital for Medicals, and tried to encourage Faculties and Departments to work out their own parallel simulations. It is not surprising that the Nursing Faculty with the admitted advantage of a large hospital next door, went the furthest in the integration of theory with practice. Most of the more academically restricted subjects made use of the research project as a significant part of the assessment, and in all areas, course-work provided a good proportion of the overall performance.

As indicated in chapter five, there were active Committees for Teaching and Learning in all the Colleges, and some interesting ideas were proposed. Certainly there was a good nucleus of staff who desired to see change and improvement in this respect, but not too many radical ideas were visible.

This was one area in which the lack of facilities through the frugal funding we had to endure was quite evident. One clear example, but by no means the only one, was the scarcity of Computer provision. When I travelled abroad, and saw the extent to which Computers were being used in all aspects of the curriculum in more fortunate countries, I could only lament our own deficiency with the consequent lack of opportunity for our students.

In 1987, Chancellor College and the Polytechnic had minimal facilities and the other two Colleges, effectively none at all. Eventually, the British provided staff, hardware and software for Chancellor College, the Chinese donated Computer Aided Design assistance for the Engineers, several of the HRID projects included Computers, and a large donation from the World Bank will enable the faculty of Commerce to have some good facilities.

While taking some comfort from these exceptions, this area of educational innovation is one in which I would have liked to have seen much more progress over the four years.

(vii) A University must be committed to Research and Postgraduate work, not because this is the conventional thing that Universities do, and rather like doing as a pleasanter task than teaching undergraduates, but as an essential basis for the proper support of the teaching programmes, the development of expertise and the solving of problems of national importance.

One of my first thoughts as I settled into this new work, was that objectives like these were not being seriously addressed at the University. Curiously, it appeared that when it came to staff promotion time, success in research heavily outweighed most other considerations, and one might have expected that this would have served as a major source of motivation. However, when examining the research which was actually being done, it could be characterised as individualistic, often following directly from isolated Ph.D. experiences abroad, seldom related to development, and grossly under-funded. There were also, I discovered, whole departments in which no research was being done at all.

In fairness it must be added that it is not easy to do research in Malawi. Research can be a challenge to a one-party state, and as a consequence all projects, especially those which involved interviewing people, had to be cleared for security purposes, and this could sometimes take so long that the initial enthusiasm had disappeared before clearance was given. There was a National Research Council which sometimes was helpful, and at other times provided a further barrier of bureaucracy to progress. As an indicator of the difficulties encountered by researchers, I recall in my early days, a request from this Council for research projects from all national bodies with research capability, in order presumably that they might be assessed and funded. Within a very few days I was able to collect over eighty such proposals from all parts of the University, and hand them in to the office in Lilongwe. Despite the urgency generated by the Council, nothing more was ever heard of these research ideas.

One exception to the generally unsatisfactory nature of research from the University was the Social Research Centre which had for many years devoted itself to pursuing research of national interest. The Centre, most ably led by Lewis Msukwa, was continually attracting funds from international donors to the extent that it was not possible to respond to all the requests made. It was Lewis who indicated to me that the funding available to his specialist area was also potentially available to other disciplines in the University.

It seemed that we had all the ingredients at hand; there were many ideas as indicated by the first unsuccessful attempt to gather them together, several able staff to work these effectively, and potentially large sums available to enable large projects of national importance in all disciplines to take place. What was lacking was co-ordination, the means to link effective researchers with appropriate donors, and to enthuse those who had relied previously on the peanut funding which we were able to hand out, to raise their ambitions to the much larger projects, often with international collaboration, that could be achieved.

We therefore established a Research Co-ordination Office and appointed by internal secondment Dr. David Munthali, then the Head of Biology as full-time co-ordinator. David's enthusiasm for research, combined with his genial personality succeeded in both encouraging many more staff to take an active part in research and persuading the international donors to support our projects. In a very short time the research output of the University greatly increased, and virtually without exception in areas of considerable national interest.

The corresponding build up of postgraduate courses was also a matter for much satisfaction. For any University this is a most desirable development, and for Malawi it seemed to me that every new Masters' programme which we could design and implement, was a significant step in he path towards self-reliance and intellectual independence. There were a number of staff capable of operating at this level, but one major problem which had to be overcome each time was the funding needed. Postgraduate courses are by nature more expensive than at undergraduate level since the work is highly specialised, and classes are relatively small. The type of student to be recruited would normally be more mature with a number of family commitments, and there were no specific Government grants to support either the individual or the course. As a result, it became necessary that every such programme should be externally sponsored.

It has been described in the chapter on donors how various provisions were made to enable these programmes to take place, and here they will simply be put together. The Education Faculty had already instituted the first such Masters' courses in Science Education and Mathematics Education, intended mainly to reinforce Primary School teaching in these two subjects, and later on offered programmes at this level in Educational Management and Media Resources. These were presented at Chancellor College in the long vacation, with students continuing in their normal work for the rest of the year with some supervised assignments. The programmes were supported by the United States Information Services who sent over American specialist professors in the vacations.

The German organisation GTZ supported Agriculture in the Region, and designated colleges in Malawi, Zambia, Zimbabwe, and Tanzania to provide individual specialist courses. As mentioned elsewhere, Malawi presented the Animal Science programme at Masters' level. Another international organisation, ICLARM, enabled us to work in Fisheries Biology through Masters' degrees by research.

The help given by USAID through its HRID scheme has been lauded many times already, but among the fruits of this enterprise were the support to new Masters' degrees in areas as wide apart as Industrial Chemistry and Sociology of Women in Development. In the former case, the very enterprising Chemistry department searched around for a number of donors to sponsor students, and eventually achieved security to function when HRID provided scholarships for women students recruited. In the other case the part of the scheme to support women in non-traditional subject

230

areas was used to bring an American professor to help design the programme and see to its start, while training two of our staff in USA to continue when she departed.

In addition to these courses which led to Masters' qualifications, we had an increasing number of people from outside the University who registered with us for higher degrees by part-time study.

Our last month in Malawi was a marvellous experience, particularly as our own departure coincided with the twenty fifth anniversary celebrations of the University. This coincidence was achieved with a few anxieties on the way. We were set to leave the country on 20 December 1990, and relating this to the potential celebrations, the University, it had been agreed, actually started when the first students arrived in 1965. We assumed that the silver jubilee had to take place sometime in 1990, and preferably towards the end of the year.

However such an important event requires the approval of both the Chairman and the Chancellor, especially if it is hoped that the latter will be in attendance. We waited so many weeks for a decision from these two about a date, that we began to wonder if 1990 was still a possibility. However, with fairly short notice for the elaborate preparations to be organised, the word at last came through that the main event which the President would attend, could take place at the National Stadium in Blantyre, on Saturday, 1 December. From our point of view, this meant that the whole of our last month would be a continuous round of celebrations, parties, farewells, and quite a considerable number of speeches.

The Anniversary had a magnificent start in Kamuzu Stadium. The radio and press had given a great build-up, and many thousands of people filled the Stadium for what was designated through the presence of Dr. Banda to be a State event. Through the uncertainty of the date it had not been possible to receive many guests from abroad, but there were numerous greetings from Universities around the world to read out, and in compensation fro the lack of overseas visitors, the entire Cabinet, Ambassadors, and heads of international organisations came for the occasion.

The students built a display of floats depicting the entire work of the University, and they filled the afternoon with dances,

231

displays, dramas, tableaux, speeches and songs. It was a most happy commemoration for all concerned, and a splendid example of the very high profile which Malawi gives to its University. Few British Universities can ever have experienced the fanfare of esteem and approval.

The next day was Sunday, and we used the Great Hall at Chancellor College for a Thanksgiving Service conducted by Stewart Lane in which all four Colleges and former students were able to take part. In the afternoon the University Football Club played a celebration match against the national superleague champions, the Limbe Leaf Wanderers. The University had not had one of their better seasons, and only escaped relegation from a lower division by drawing their last match, but actually won the game 2-1. Sceptics might have thought that this was the Wanderers own unique contribution to the celebrations, but I am assured by those who saw the whole match that it was good football and a genuine result. I had to leave before the end in order to attend our first personal farewell provided by Zomba Baptist, about which more later.

For the next four days, each of the Colleges in turn put on an Open Day for the public, and I travelled around the country attending all of these, learning much about the work of the University that I wish I had known four years earlier rather than in my last month, but observing both the wide range of the efforts put into these displays, and the interest of the public and the press in what they saw.

On the Thursday our chief guests arrived. Ian Michael had been the first Vice-Chancellor and he had stayed for the first nine years of the University. We were most honoured that Ian and Mollie had been able to join us for this occasion, and now in their mid seventies, to see the great esteem in which they were held by the Malawians. It is our hope that the University will remember to invite us when it holds the golden jubilee in 2015.

Their first function was to attend the anniversary dinner held at Mount Soche Hotel, Blantyre, that evening. The Chairman had again invited the diplomatic corps for this occasion, and in the midst of a most memorable evening, I recall him actually leading the applause for a point I made in my speech! Ironically the cause of this most unexpected enthusiasm was my remark about the University as a whole never having lost a day through student action in its twenty-five years. At any rate I had just managed to preserve this record during my term of office, but the recent demonstrations for democracy have now rightly blown this record away with a number of closures especially of chancellor College. Student contentment may no longer be taken for granted until there are fundamental changes in the running of the nation.

On this Friday we presented a garden party at our house. We had been blessed with several acres of garden and had always intended to hold an outdoor party, but until the incentive of the silver jubilee, had restricted our gatherings to indoor evening affairs. Now with Ian and Mollie who had moved into our guest-house for the remainder of their stay in Malawi as chief guests we were able to launch this venture intended not only for the University but also for the Zomba community who came in good numbers and were entertained by Mitch Strumph, Black Pweseli and a group of student troubadours that Black had trained.

On the Saturday, to close the week of celebrations, we had our annual graduation in the Great Hall. This was my last public speech and I chose as the theme, 'The Future of the University' with emphasis on the five points of Diversity, Growth, Research, Recurrent Education and New Technologies.

Quite apart from the considerable uplift given to the University as a whole, this glorious week served as a wonderful finish for our four years. Over the next twelve days as we continued to prepare for our departure, there were official farewells at the Colleges, the University Office and Council, at MANEB with several private parties, our last visit to the Lake and our final audience with the President.

I try to make it a principle to give a different speech on each occasion, and there was so much to be thankful for, that this was not difficult to achieve. What is more difficult is to listen to speeches of appreciation. The time I remember best was the one at Zomba Baptist. This was supposed to be a farewell service, but instead of anything at all formal, Rendall Day invited anyone in the congregation to stand up and say anything they wished about us!

No less that eighteen people responded to this invitation, and I regret to say that while it was a moving and humbling experience, I have with one exception forgotten what was said. The exception was a young lecturer from England who with his wife had done a great job at Chancellor College, in teaching Mathematics and Physics respectively. He said that what I had done to help him, was to encourage him to pray big, to expect to be able to influence events through prayer, and to anticipate real tangible answers.

I was absolutely delighted to hear this because to me this is a most important issue, and one which I hope had characterised my whole approach to the work in Malawi. To have this recognised and to have been able to convey this to others was the most rewarding of all that I heard during this last month. I believe most strongly and sincerely in the power of prayer, and that we should expand our prayer experience, taking authority in prayer and exposing this power of God to the major issues of the day. This had been my own experience throughout the four years. It had been necessary to pray for wisdom, for assurance, for direction, and even for seemingly adverse conditions to be changed, for mountains to be removed, and many illustrations of the answers received, have already been given.

This is all part of Resurrection living which I had learned from my earlier experiences, and which is so profoundly expressed by Paul in the opening verses of Colossians chapter three. 'Since, then, you have been raised with Christ, set your hearts on things above, where Christ is seated at the right hand of God. Set your minds on things above, not on earthly things. For you have died, and your life is now hidden with Christ in God.'

The Resurrection of Christ is not a theory but a reality, and it follows from this that prayer will be real and vital. It follows also that Christians should be very positive and optimistic about the future. Even though present circumstances may not look promising, and in a developing country like Malawi there is often every reason to despair, yet faith in the Resurrection demonstrates that God is able to achieve far beyond anything that we can ask or comprehend.

Therefore I made it a point in all my public utterances to be very positive about the University and its place in Malawian society. My work at the University was the way in which I expressed my faith. When I set out for Malawi it was my basic intention to release my faith mediated through my experience and ability to achieve whatever God desired to achieve through this. I still marvel at what I was so privileged to see God doing.

We left the country on 20 December 1990. There were innumerable memories, some of which I have tried to recall in this book, but there were few tears. Rather we journeyed back first to Amsterdam and then to Norwich with a sense of completion. There was and remains still much to be accomplished in Malawi, but we had finished for the time, the part which we were intended to play. Our hope was now for the future, but whatever this future had for us, our lives would always be conditioned by these four glorious years in Malawi.

We had our four months as a kind of sabbatical in Norwich, and then set out in April 1991, for our next work in Botswana. Malawi and Botswana are both land-locked countries in Southern Africa, but this is where the comparison almost finishes, because as we were to find, the two are quite different in almost every other respect. Any suggestion of continuity in my work was quickly dispelled, but challenges of a very different nature emerged, and this can only be material for a sequel!

Since our departure from Malawi, we have not gone back, but hope the time will come when we are emotionally and spiritually ready for this return. However, events in Malawi have not stood still, and we have been astonished to learn of things happening which could scarcely have been imagined in 1990.

It was at this time that old and discredited regimes in Eastern Europe started to crumble, and the domino effect began to move even through Africa, but came to a determined halt at Malawi. As the problems of transfer to democratisation became more apparent, diverting attention away from the need for further liberation, it seemed that the fate of countries like Malawi, still under corrupt rule, were of little interest to the rest of the world. Dr. Banda and the Family, apart from donor pressure leading to the release of some political prisoners in 1991, seemed to be exempt from this world movement.

But then to everyone's total surprise came the opposition from within, and from one of the most unlikely sources, the previously quiescent Catholic church. The extremely polite, loyal but factual letter from the Bishops, read out in the churches, demonstrated clearly the poverty, oppression and misrule which the country was suffering. Such clear opposition had never before been expressed, and the remarkable courage shown by these clergy gave new hope to the nation. The Malawi Congress Party had no qualms about the spiritual status of these men, and resolved that all should be summarily executed and only the immediate intervention of diplomats prevented this from happening.

The stand taken by the Catholics was followed by the other churches, the students and the workers, and by the dramatic return of Chafukwa Chihana. What has followed has been the referendum on multi-party democracy which proved to be free, fair and without violence, and the promise of a general election in May 1994. With the President seriously ill, the country was temporarily run by a triumvirate from the Malawi Congress Party which includes John Tembo, and some formerly repressive laws are being relaxed. The opposition to the Government gained 64% of the referendum vote, but there is division between the democratic parties which may give the Congress Party the chance to do better than might have been expected.

The pace of change is now so rapid, that this book will not be able to keep up, but it is the hope of the author that the forces of change and democracy will prevail, and that the country may be blessed with effective new leadership. This will only be the start of the problems which need to be tackled, several of which I have tried to indicate in the earlier chapter on Malawi. However, the hope I expressed at the end of that chapter remains my hope, and I have every confidence that the Malawian people will be able to overcome these immense problems in exemplary fashion.